Indigo
Awakening

A Doctor's Memoir of Forging an Authentic Life
in a Turbulent World

by
Dr. Janine Talty

Elite Books
Santa Rosa, CA 95404
www.elitebooksonline.com

Library of Congress Cataloging-in-Publication Data

Talty, Janine.
  Indigo awakening: a doctor's memoir of forging an authentic life in a turbulent world /
Janine Talty — 1st ed.
     p. cm.
  ISBN: 978-1-60070-063-7
  1. Talty, Janine. 2. Osteopathic physicians—Biography. I. Title.
  RZ332.T35A3 2009
  610'.92—dc22

2009009661
© 2009 Janine Talty

Cover design by Victoria Valentine
Editing by Carolyn Bond
Typesetting by Karin Kinsey
Typeset in Perpetua and Calligraphic
Author Photo by Kenneth Esterson
Printed in USA by Bang Printing
First Edition

10 9 8 7 6 5 4 3 2 1

Bill and Janine, 1986.

To my dad—

We always threatened to
write a book together one day.

I think we just did...

CONTENTS

Christine Page and Janine.

Foreword

The term "Indigo Children" was first coined by a gifted psychic named Nancy Ann Tappe. In her 1982 book, *Understanding Your Life Through Color,* she wrote that the color indigo was increasingly prevalent in the auras of those born in the late 1970s, though Indigo Children (like Janine Talty) had been incarnating before this. The husband and wife team Lee Carroll and Jan Tober expanded on her findings in their 1998 book. *The Indigo Children: The New Kids Have Arrived* explored the characteristics commonly found in these children that distinguish them from previous generations.

Such characteristics include well-developed psychic powers, empathy, an altruistic sense of purpose, desire for fair play, and the ability to connect almost telepathically with others. These traits commonly put them at odds with authority, especially when the authority figure is not walking his or her talk. At other times, their sensitivity to the suffering of others and their poor personal boundaries can cause them to be overwhelmed by responsibility for others or feel a strong desire to isolate themselves from large groups of people.

Another frequent finding, as Janine describes so clearly in *Indigo Awakening,* is a learning disorder known as dyslexia. In my experience, these young people are whole-brain thinkers who perceive concepts as if they are three-dimensional pictures. In other words, they "see" the whole rather than just the parts, much as one looks at the picture on the cover of a jigsaw puzzle box. Through appreciation of this gift, it is easy to understand how difficult it is for Indigo Children to describe one piece of the puzzle in isolation from the rest. Yet this is exactly what is expected of them when their schooling demands that they break words into individual letters and math solutions into numbers.

I first came upon this particular challenge for Indigo Children in the mid-1990s when I met a teacher who was herself dyslexic and the mother of two Indigo Children. I can still remember her saying: "These children do not have learning difficulties but learning differences. It is time for schools to realize that they have an epidemic on their hands which is going to change the face of education." It was clear to me then that these children were heralding a shift in consciousness in which unity, authenticity, and compassion would be key words.

My teacher friend explained to me that many of the most gifted, intelligent, and creative people in history had experienced problems with conventional learning. They received information not only from books but as insights that appeared to arise directly from the Source. These insights are not limited to present-day reality but, as Janine explains, often emerge from other realms of existence such as past lives, nature kingdoms, the world of spirit, and even from extraterrestrial sources. Ultimately, they are all concepts found within the phrase "collective consciousness."

One story I remember clearly. There was a little boy who had difficulty reading aloud in class because he couldn't "see" the words. His teacher suggested that instead of believing that his eyes were in their normal position, he should imagine they were located in an orange suspended above his head. With ease and trust, he shifted his awareness into the orange and immediately could read the words, as he was no longer focusing on the letters but on the concept or bigger picture. Pleased by his efforts, he realized that he could move his "orange eyes" anywhere, and saw the orange enter the classroom next door. Immediately, he started to read the words written on the blackboard there, because in his mind there were no boundaries.

This concept is highlighted in Janine's story as, time after time, she reaches beyond her limiting beliefs to prove that anything is possible once you free the mind. This is a message that we are all receiving at this amazing time in the history of humanity. For the first time in 26,000 years, we are the most closely aligned to the Galactic Center, the access portal to the eternal and abundant Source of all our dreams and aspirations. In order for us to enter this portal, we are all being asked to release our hold on the old baggage that surrounds our stories, to complete karma, and to remember that, first and foremost, we are light beings.

Janine is a master healer clearing her own path of the past while using her extraordinary gifts to bring healing to those who are not invested with her clear focus, compassion, and determination.

Christine Page, MD
Author of *Frontiers of Health; Spiritual Alchemy; 2012 and the Galactic Center;* and *The Return of the Great Mother*
www.christinepage.com

Prologue

If you have been drawn to this book, a part of you likely resonates with the concept of the Indigo Children. Or you may be curious because you have identified many of the traits in your child, grandchild, student, niece, or nephew—or even yourself. Yes, an adult can be an Indigo, too. The unique characteristics that have been labeled "Indigo" are not the sole domain of children. In fact, half of the kids born in 1970 were of this persuasion. That means that many of us Indigos came in much earlier than the primary wave that arrived in the mid-1980s, and that wave is also in adulthood now.

Indigo Awakening is the story of one Indigo Child's journey of growing up with these fantastic abilities and perceptions and coming to understand who I actually am and why I am here. It need not take Indigo Children half a lifetime to understand their deeper purpose in being here. It is my hope that reading this book will enable you to find the answer much sooner than I did. My story is a lesson in trusting your intuition, which is there to guide you to the people and the information you need to move into your next phase of development.

This book is unique among those written thus far on the Indigo phenomenon because it is an insider's perspective on what it feels like to grow up Indigo. My story brings you behind the eyes of a child trying to comprehend the world with a brain and a nervous system wired differently from those of the people around her. It takes you through the struggles and pain of always feeling different. On my journey, nonordinary perception allows me to communicate telepathically and gives me direct access to past-life knowledge, from which I intuit that I am being groomed for some grand scheme, though I will not understand it until the foretold age of forty-two. *Indigo Awakening* tells of my grooming process and my relentless quest to answer my deepest haunting question, "For what purpose was I born?"

Mine is just one of thousands of stories currently being lived out by Indigo Children of today and some of the adults who have come before them. Many of the themes in my story apply broadly to the Indigos, while others are unique to my journey. Not every Indigo will discover what makes them tick by becoming a triathlete or a physician, but every Indigo will read something of him or herself in these pages.

Everything in this story is factual (though I've changed some of the names of people and places to protect privacy and a reputation or two). I took great care to stick to the facts, knowing as I do that some of the circumstances and events are difficult enough to believe as they are. If I had not personally lived through them, I would likely question their authenticity. But I have kept a journal since the age of seven, and these records helped me confirm specific facts and recreate some of the events that time had diminished in my memory. The level of imagination it would take for me to make these things up is well beyond my artistic flair. I am a scientist who just happened to grow up in the arts—I no longer live there.

Reporting the data in their purest form is what makes these realizations so powerful. And as with good science, I am fully prepared to produce all documents, photographs, original journal entries, book passages, and dates and times of certain occurrences to support the statements I make herein. As for the information that came to me directly from Source, I have no material proof. In those cases, you will simply have to take my word for it.

Indigo Awakening can be described as a metaphysical coming-of-age tale that mixes the wonders, magic, and misunderstandings of childhood with the experiences and realizations that eventually led the adult me to the knowledge I share here. As you will read, the Universal Forces had to knock themselves out to get my attention and lead me to share with you what I learned. If this book resonates with you, thank them, however you experience them. During a recent parapsychologic session, the ones who bring you this story identified themselves to me as the members of "The Council of the Blue-Violet Ray." I am simply their dutiful messenger getting the word out.

As I am guided to sit down and write this, I am filled with a deep sense of completion—my age-old question regarding my purpose has been answered. It is my sincere hope that my tale will ignite a spark of wonder and remembrance in those of you who have felt isolated on your journey of preparing for a deeper purpose that has not yet been revealed to you. If you have always known that you came into this life to participate in the awakening that is currently upon us, perhaps my story will inspire you. My tale begins where all good stories do—at the beginning.

PART I

Exploring Perimeters

Mom and Dad's Wedding. From left to right: Kathryn Talty, William Talty, Carol Caputo-Talty, Nicholas and Jenny Caputo, 1958.

Childhood's "Old Memories"

Y*ou came in with a keen sense of your surroundings. With "eyes wide open," you have a broadened awareness of what is around you and give the adults who care for you the uneasy feeling of being watched. The adults get the sense from the first time they see you that this defenseless little being in their care is hiding the secrets of the Universe (because you are). You are not disconnected from your soul's wealth of knowledge and physical skills accumulated throughout the centuries. You have access to and use past-life knowledge in your everyday interactions, though you may not have a context in which to understand what these old memories are. You are difficult children to raise and test to the core those who try. Due to your differences and difficulties in trying to fit in, you tend to be shunned by the larger group. Besides, children of your type seem so much happier when left alone to ponder life's great mysteries. This is part of your unique collective journey. Adult suspicions are soon confirmed as you begin to show uncanny traits and talents that other children your age don't display. There is, however, usually someone—a parent, grandparent, aunt / uncle, or teacher—in the sphere of these special children who recognizes these differences as gifts, fosters their development with fierce conviction, and acts as the child's protector throughout the early years.*

The first time I remember being seen as different was during art period in kindergarten. I was painting at an easel, wearing one of my father's old dress shirts as a smock, its length covering my rubber-toed

Keds. An unfamiliar lady came into the classroom and, with our teacher, looked at all the children's paintings under way. When they got to me, the lady whispered to my teacher and started asking me questions, interrupting my process of remembering what it looked and felt like to be in the scene I was painting. It was a detailed underwater scene of brightly colored fish swimming through a kelp bed with the sun's rays filtering through the multi-shaded water, viewed from the ocean floor looking up at the hull of an old wooden sailing ship. I felt simultaneously in my brain and chest all the sensations of color, shading, shadows, movement, pressure, and wetness of the scene.

The lady wanted to know where I had seen what I was painting. Knowing that I had never physically been to the bottom of the ocean with the ability to look up toward the surface in my six short years, I remember realizing in that moment that I saw such pictures in vivid detail all the time and they came from somewhere else besides my experience in this life. I tried to explain this and watched her face actually crinkle up in her attempt to understand. Finally, I asked, "Doesn't everybody see things like that?" She looked uncomfortable, and I felt uncomfortable then, too. I decided I better keep my perceptions to myself from then on.

Increasingly after that, I felt like a different species from everyone else. I began to feel very alone and subsided into virtual mutism. I would often escape from my uncomfortable life into a familiar reality of vivid images and full sensations. The scenes I lived there included riding wildly into battle, wearing a feather headdress and slathered with war paint; sensing the terror and camaraderie of my brethren hunkered down in a muddy bunker with gunfire and shells exploding all around us; feeling a deep sense of connection as I peered out at the Himalayas from a monastery window; and living as a gutsy American frontier woman, a young pharaoh riding a camel past the great pyramids at Giza, a swaggering pirate, a dignified knight in full armor, a debonair British doctor in Africa, and a castaway Polynesian islander swimming with dolphins and whales. Such remembrances were so much a part of my inner world that I never questioned their origin and had difficulty distinguishing them from experiences I was having in what I later came to know as "this lifetime." I assumed that everybody had similar internal experiences. Later, I termed them my "old memories."

I went home from kindergarten that day with a note for my parents stuffed into my lunch pail. It was from the teacher, asking my parents' permission for the lady to borrow my painting when it was finished. Years later I learned she was a child development expert who had featured the painting in a book she was writing. My kindergarten teacher had alerted her that my visual and creative abilities were seven to ten years ahead of my age group. As a result of all the attention, my art-teacher mother had visions of her daughter becoming the next Rembrandt or Picasso.

At recess I would become absorbed in the most intricate particulars of the natural world. I recall sitting in the dirt on the kindergarten playground and marveling at the wavelike motion of a centipedes' legs as it walked. I would gaze at the colors and patterns of a butterfly's wings and want to draw them to capture their beauty on paper. I would ask friends of my parents questions like "Whatever possessed those clouds to do that?" or "What is the ocean trying to remind us of by sending us its waves over and over again?" I remember them looking at me with uncomfortable expressions.

While our teacher read to us in class, I would imagine the scenes from the book in three dimensions. I thought not in words but in pictures that often included graphs and force diagrams, elements I later learned were higher order physics diagrams. I loved to be read to and looked forward to one day reading on my own.

My interactions with people were strange and confusing to me. I didn't feel like one of them; I felt like a foreigner in a body that only looked human. At first, the differences were less obvious, since my father seemed to understand me and our family was unconventional, though not in the same way I was.

My father, William Talty, grew up the bastard son of an Irish immigrant who worked for the mafia in Omaha, Nebraska, during Prohibition. The Irishman abandoned his young family when my father was six months old. My father's mother, a spunky Sicilian named Katie Marcuzzo, had, as a teenager, helped her widowed mother provide for their family of nine by producing bootleg whiskey and running it in the middle of the night in a beat-up, rusted-out truck to the speakeasies in Omaha and Council Bluffs, Iowa, across the Missouri River.

Great-grandmother Marcuzzo's operation was well known to the authorities, and she was often arrested. During her arraignments, this four-foot-ten-inch woman would stand before the bench, barely able to see over it, and explain to the judge in broken English, "What is a single woman raising nine children to do, your honor?" He always took pity and sentenced her to a few months of "house arrest." Since she was famous for her Sicilian cooking, this meant showing up at the judge's house at 10 a.m. to prepare his lunch and dinner. She was allowed to return to her own house by 3 p.m. when her children got home from school.

Grandmother Katie, a free spirit, took herself on a joy ride to California in the family truck one spring and ended up staying. Later, after her Irish husband disappeared, she was known to run off with men, leaving my father and his two siblings in the care of her mother. Or so my uncles said when they came from Nebraska for her funeral. I had only known the woman who worked three waitress jobs to make ends meet or was busy in her kitchen, apron on, cooking us family dinners on Sundays.

Her wild streak had ended at forty-three when she was diagnosed with malignant breast cancer and faced the only lifesaving procedure known at the time, a radical mastectomy. My father was by then a second-year student at Bellarmine College Preparatory, a private high school for boys. He was paying his own tuition by working at the local supermarket. Somehow this fifteen-year-old kid convinced the doctors that he would take responsibility for the bills. He took on more hours at the market. He challenged classmates to pool matches before school to make his lunch money. If he lost, he did not eat. On the street corner in the early mornings, he sold doughnuts, which my grandmother had made at 4 a.m. The medical bills were paid off in three years.

At Bellarmine, he was studying side by side with boys from influential families who lived in dignified University Avenue estates. As he made friends, he would be invited to their homes. An amicable and polite kid from the other side of town, several of his friends' fathers took him under their wing like one of their own sons. He developed relationships with these families that lasted his lifetime.

The upbringing of my mother, Carol Caputo, contrasted sharply with my father's. Her mother, the child of first-generation immigrants from Naples, Italy, was a college-educated real estate broker and accountant. Her family eventually moved from New York to California, where my grandmother met my grandfather, Nicholas Caputo, an Italian immigrant who had earned his passage to America by fulfilling a commission to sculpt the bust of a prominent New Yorker while en route to Ellis Island. In California, he made a living as a machinist while gradually purchasing land and planting orchards in California's fertile Santa Clara Valley. Eventually, he farmed hundreds of acres of fruit and nut trees while he and my grandmother raised three children. Later, as the valley's economy shifted from orchards to silicon, he moved from farming into property development and management, and the family's wealth increased exponentially. For Mom, life was always a party, and she was always the star squeezing as much fun out of it as possible. She did, however, study art history and earn a teaching credential. Though she dated many suitors, she ended her wild ways the day she met my father. There was one problem. He was Sicilian, or at least half, and in the late-1950s no right-minded upscale Italian father would let his daughter marry a Sig (Italian slang for a Sicilian), his Irish surname notwithstanding.

My father was self-conscious about his heritage and also the fact that he had no money, so he was very nervous about asking my mother's father for permission to marry her. He did not even own a car; my mother had to pick him up in her two-door sports coupe to bring him to the house. When my grandfather opened the door, my father held out his hands and said, "Sir, I am in love with your daughter, and I ask for her hand in marriage. I have nothing to offer except my hands and my heart. I promise to work hard to make you proud of both of us." Sicilian or not, he had spoken words that resonated with my grandfather. And he made good on his promise.

Three years later, on March 16, 1962, I was born. The pregnancy was uneventful, although Mom admits to fashionable smoking and enjoying a social cocktail on the weekends. The delivery was another matter. Mom's belly churned, thumped, and quaked. I was actively changing positions, the doctor said, flipping around as if to avoid the inevitable squeeze through the birth canal. Eventually, out I came, looking very different from her firstborn, who had presented as a light-skinned, towheaded Gerber baby. I had bright red skin and not only black hair on my head, but black fur extending from my eyebrows up my forehead, down the back of my neck, torso, and legs. Mom thought she had given birth to an ape.

In those days, breast-feeding was not fashionable, and I proved to be highly allergic to baby formulas, projectile vomiting across the room. My mother would pick me up and try to comfort me. I would shake wildly and throw up all over her. Anticipating how difficult our home-coming would be with a two-and-a-half-year-old at home as well, my father hired a nurse for the first week. I am convinced she was a spirit guardian placed in my path to help ease the transition back into this world. The moment she would pick me up, I would stop crying. She suggested feeding me goat's milk instead of formula, and the vomiting stopped. At the end of the seventh day, however, when the door shut behind her, all hell broke loose again. For the first year of my life, I was a colicky, unpleasant baby who screamed and squirmed when anyone picked me up and cradled me in their arms. Family friends and relatives would look in on me in my bassinet and, seeing my eyes fixed on theirs, make comments like, "That stare! What is she looking at?"

My earliest memory is from eighteen months of age. I remember waking up from a nap one afternoon to the sound of movement and rustling in my room. I peeked out through the bars of my crib to see my father setting up a real bed for me. A surge of excitement ran through my body as I realized I was finally going to be released from this "cage." Even then, I remembered the ancient viscerally sickening feeling of being restrained. Because I was such a challenging child, my mother sought the advice of a psychiatrist, who recommended that she return to teaching to get out of the house for a while. By the time I turned two, she was leaving me home weekdays with a baby-sitter. I vividly remember standing in my jammies and bare feet on the front porch in the cold morning air as her car pulled out of the driveway, screaming through the tears running down my face, "Don't leave me, Mommy, don't leave!" She would always leave anyway. This and similar experiences endemic to a busy two-income family throughout my early years seeded me with a fierce sense of self-reliance, another trait that would dictate many later choices. I learned that ultimately it was up to me to take care of me. Because I saw my mother's leaving as abandonment rather than helping with the young family's finances, I often felt as if she didn't care and she was often too busy to help if I had a question. That was not the case with my father, however.

From the beginning, he and I had a way of understanding each other's thoughts and intentions without having to speak them, as if we knew each other beyond the confines of this current experience of playing the roles of father and daughter. He was my greatest teacher. I relentlessly asked him why, about everything. Why are leaves shaped like they are? Why do dogs have fur? Why do we always need to breathe? Why are we warm? Where does the rain come from? How is snow made? How do cuts heal? Why do animals eat each other? Why, why, why, why. It must have driven him mad, but he patiently tried his best to satisfy my burning curiosity about the world and how I fit into it.

Defying Disabilities

You, the Indigo Child, possess a brain that is wired differently from the brains of others. You and the other Indigo Children are, in fact, the next evolution of the human species. You possess a natural ability to communicate telepathically with each other, some adults, and animals. You see in three dimensions, process whole pieces of information at one time (spherical thinkers), and become extremely frustrated with our school systems, which teach in the old linear fashion. Learning to read is sometimes very difficult. Because you didn't "get it," you were identified early in your scholastic career as being "different." Testing often leads to the labels of ADD, ADHD, and dyslexia, despite your overall intelligence, ability to grasp higher concepts easily, and profound common sense, which place you far ahead of your age group.

You are the warriors who have come here to blaze new trails through the old Piscean (split-brained) consciousness. Your warrior spirit shows itself early on. It is your nature. It is this tenacity that you will rely on when you begin to move into positions of leadership and find yourselves in direct conflict with the way government, politics, banking, and the media have been controlling public perception of reality. This same trait gets many of you into trouble with the very systems you have come here to tear down.

You might not think the rest of your life could be impacted by a single comment. Yet this is possible if the comment comes from a person you are supposed to respect and have learned to fear. At the ripe age of six, my world collided with a force that took me from feeling pretty special in kindergarten to feeling completely worthless in first grade. Mrs. Wilson, the first grade teacher, was an old and bitter woman. She wore dowdy dresses and those black, square-toed, low-heeled, old-lady shoes. She gave the impression that she hadn't had a bit of fun in decades. She was known to call her students names and to knock them down psychologically. I was one of her targets.

It was during reading period that I first suspected that my brain worked differently from the brains of the other kids. They were able to sound out letters to form syllables and words, and then string words together to make sentences. I had difficulty matching the letters with the right sounds. Part of my brain saw the shapes correctly, but when I went to say the letters out loud, something happened, and what came out of my mouth was all wrong. There seemed to be a disconnection between one part of my brain and another. When I tried to correct how I pronounced a word, the written word would simply disappear off the page. When I looked again, a different word would be there and I would say something that sounded close but meant something completely different. I thought at first my eyes were playing tricks on me. When I tried to read a sentence, I would skip over some words as if I did not see them and inadvertently insert words that were not there.

I tried to keep up with the other kids, but fell further and further behind. It seemed the harder I tried, the worse it got. When Mrs. Wilson found me struggling, she would come over to my desk and repeat the directions, only louder, as if I had not heard her the first time. She offered no further help, and I quickly learned not to ask.

One day during reading period, she had each student stand up next to his or her desk and read one paragraph aloud from our Dick and Jane readers. As the hot lava of humiliation moving through the room slowly oozed its way toward me, I began to shake and my heart raced. I knew I could not take whole words from the page and speak them correctly. I wanted to run away out of sight to avoid being swallowed up by the molten tide.

When it was finally my turn, I stood trembling as I held my book. I tried to say the very first word of the sentence, "the." I knew it began with a "te" sound, but the next letter was an *h,* as in my favorite word, "horse," and the last letter was an *e,* usually pronounced like "ee." As all of this was going on in my mind, my voice remained silent and my heart felt as if it were coming out of my chest. I knew the class was waiting and Mrs. Wilson's temper was getting short. Still, nothing came out of my mouth. Finally, making my best attempt, I took a deep breath and something sounding like "taahee" came forth. The whole class began to laugh.

Mrs. Wilson bellowed from where she was sitting behind her desk at the front of the classroom, "Sit down, Janine. You are stupid. You cannot read."

Her words cut through me like a saber and sliced my heart in two. I had never in my short lifetime experienced such raw emotion. The year before, I had received positive encouragement by being different in art; I now got to experience being different in quite the opposite way.

The wound Mrs. Wilson inflicted on me that day traveled with me for decades, to the point that in graduate school I found myself unable to read aloud during study sessions with other students or any other time for that matter. My mind would still lock up and my tongue would tie. I would still speak words that did not exist and be blind to ones that did. Reading aloud fluently eludes me even to this day.

That moment in first grade also marked my entry into a personal living hell that lasted for seven years. School became my nemesis. It wasn't only letters I couldn't make sense of; I couldn't keep the meanings of numbers straight either. At first, I couldn't even count, so to ask me to subtract or multiply—impossible! I could see the numbers, but sometimes they appeared backward or upside down. One second they were straight and made sense, and the next time I looked they had changed, just like letters did. I remember thinking someone was playing tricks on me. I soon hated math, reading, and spelling. I flatly failed at all of them.

I lived for recess and art period. But when I tried to play with other kids on the playground, many of them would shout comments like "There goes the stupid girl. She can't read. Dummy!" Their words caused a pain so deep that I was forced to dissociate from my feelings and isolate from my peers. I resorted to sitting alone under the redwood tree in a far-off corner of the playground or playing with my brother, Mike, and his friends, who were three years older than I. I competed as an equal on their soccer, touch football, and softball teams and felt protected by my brother's presence. At least they had no idea they were playing with a worthless mentally retarded girl.

They were not in my classroom when I was escorted out during math and reading periods with two other students who had low-set ears and thick necks and were known to drool occasionally. We were taken to special education where I would sit next to a girl who would often quietly throw up on her desk after lunch and then gather the fluid and stomach contents and sweep them back into her mouth, pretending like nothing was happening. To my "normal" classmates, "special education" translated into "class for the mentally retarded."

I had nothing in common with kids in general, never mind the mentally slow. I did not understand kids my age. I was not interested in anything they had to say. They were mean and unfeeling. No one ever showed up to protect me from their daily barrage of heart-wrenching, gut-tearing humiliations. I was completely alone in these experiences and never shared with my parents what was happening to me at school; I didn't want to bother them with my problems.

Sensing even then that my suffering had a higher purpose, a reason I could not yet see, I wondered frequently, "For what purpose was I born?" From the perspective of that pondering, I found myself forgiving the name-calling kids; after all, they were just kids. I remember thinking on many occasions: "If they only knew who I really was, they wouldn't treat me this way. Someday they will understand and regret their actions." I sensed that my being here at this time was to help *them*.

At my elementary school, the fifth and sixth graders used the "big playground," leaving the first through fourth graders to divvy up the territory of the "little playground." If you were caught in the wrong area of the little playground, the reigning kid gang would challenge you to a fight, which usually took place behind the big green backstop after school.

Occasionally, these kids would track me down and try to upset me by spitting on me as I walked past them or by calling me names. I learned to take a lot of abuse and my sensitive spirit retreated behind an increasingly crusty exterior. At times I would lose my composure, especially when they called me "girly." That term meant weak, delicate, and prissy—all the aspects about being a girl that I hated. So to prove that

I was not like any other girl they had ever met, one Friday I challenged their ringleader, Dennis, to a fight behind the big green backstop when school let out.

I arrived first and hid behind a garbage can to see who would show up. As expected, Dennis and his boys headed my way. I had no fear. A rage came over me, arising from a place inside I hadn't known existed, yet at the same time it felt familiar. As they approached, a volcano of raw emotion was building within me, about to blow. As they rounded the curve of the wooden backstop, I jumped out into the open in a stance that meant combat. Dennis approached, taunting me with "girly, girly, girly." This only fed my rage, which suddenly linked with all my pent-up anger at every kid and adult who had ever made fun of me as well as a deep pain that felt older than my eight years. I somehow knew what to do in hand-to-hand combat: quickly take the first shot, the one he would not be expecting. I walked right up to Dennis and punched him squarely in the face. He fell to the ground, and it was over before it even began.

I could not believe how much my hand hurt. His friends stared in utter amazement. There he was, the playground bully, lying on the ground with a bloodied nose delivered by a girl a year younger than he. I readied myself for his comrades to come at me. I was fully prepared and committed to die in that moment, but all they did was stare. Then they picked him up and led him away. Not another word was spoken. I came away wondering where those tactics and cunning had come from. The episode changed the way I was treated, at least by that gang, for the rest of that school year.

The academic aspect of school changed for me that year as well. I was in Mrs. Neal's third grade class, and she was my favorite teacher so far. Mrs. Neal was the first to truly try to get through to me. Even though I still had to leave the classroom and go to special ed, she asked the teacher to read to me rather than make me try to read. That year I fell deeply in love with stories like *James and the Giant Peach*, *Black Beauty*, and *Jack and the Beanstalk*. As the words left the teacher's mouth, the story unfolded in my mind as if I were watching a movie. I would often draw those scenes during art period and at home. Mrs. Neal encouraged me to work with blocks, clay, and Legos. I sculpted and built massive structures with ease. She saw that I learned when I could plug a concept into a three-dimensional context. Using my hands somehow made my brain focus differently. The information made sense if I could feel its texture, temperature, and consistency first. On weekends, Mike and I would put together model cars, planes, and ships. I never needed the instruction sheet. I could look at the picture on the box and immediately figure it out.

Janine on pony for the first time.

Experimental Education
for a Nonlinear Mind

Y ou, have always been deeply connected to the environment and all of the beings who live on Earth. From early on, you demonstrated a concern over global issues such as pollution, animal rights, and deforestation. With your broader perspective, you can see how local or national environmental policies can affect the entire planet. Part of your mission for being here is to correct the imbalances that the humans have created from greed and lack of concern beyond their own individual needs. You communicate with animals and each other through telepathy. This type of communication is no different for you than speaking to your parents or siblings using your voice. In fact, you prefer the wordless communication. You have a natural aptitude for music, the arts, sciences, engineering, and healing.

Those around you often interpret your persistent challenges as simple examples of "bad luck." You constantly face obstacles that seem insurmountable. Breathe deeply, parents reading this, as "tempering of the metal" experiences are part of the warrior training of Indigo Children. Think back, Indigo adults, and you will see the greater purpose of your early struggles; they are the reason you now know who you are. You new beings could not become fully who you are and reach your highest potential without these seemingly unfair and horrendous challenges. You needed to learn the ways of the Universe before you obtained the right to wield its powers with discretion later on. Many Indigos are not native to this planet; for some, it is your first time here. You are beings who have come here from *other solar systems at this time to assist humankind in ushering in a new way of thinking and being on this planet. These challenges come in many forms that are unique to each individual. No two personal stories are ever the same. All that is consistent among you is how different you are / were from the rest of the kids and how you feel / felt like an outsider looking in.*

My mother, father, and brother felt like my only human friends at the time. Our home often flowed with fun and laughter. My parents would host huge parties where bus loads of people would come through the front door to be immediately escorted into the backyard, often straight into the pool, clothes and all. My parents knew how to play. People of all ages, races, and sexual orientations were welcome, and many ended up staying for extended periods. Mom and Dad showed Mike and me how to love and accept others for who they are, not for what they have to offer.

I remember feeling awkward when trying to interact with people, though. Because I had no friends of my own and felt self-conscious about my apparent intellectual deficiencies, being around people was stressful. No matter how hard I tried to relate to them, they would always talk about what I perceived as the meaningless details of life, never heart-based subjects that made my body tingle with truth.

I spent most of my time alone, in silence, my awareness tuned into different eras of old memories stored in that place between the brain and the heart. In my imaginary life, I was respected—as a hero, villain, or saint. I would simply pull up a visual pictogram and enter the scene, like an actor on a movie set reports for the take. I spent so much time in this interdimensional state that I was often unclear in what century my "real life" was occurring. Looking at myself in the mirror, I often wondered who was staring back at me. I continued to ask: Who am I and what am I doing here?

I am not sure at what age my fascination with animals began, but I do remember how comfortable and easy wordless communication was with them. When I was too little to know how to care for them, they surrounded me in stuffed form. My bed was a mass of colorful, furry creatures with big soft eyes and striking spots, stripes, and fins. As I grew, I learned that animals felt comfortable around me.

When I was four years old, our dog Pixie got pregnant. Her belly kept getting bigger, and my dad explained that it was because she was carrying babies. I sensed when her time grew near; her behavior changed and she looked into my eyes differently. This was her first litter, and her eyes spoke of fear and anxiety. To comfort her, I put my favorite Teddy Bear in her doghouse. Two nights later, I woke from sleep, having just dreamed it was Pixie's time. Without thinking, I headed for the garage with my comforting pink blankie. On opening the garage door, I heard Pixie whimpering. I turned on the light and crouched down near the doghouse to witness the birth of her first pup. When she saw my face in the doorway, she tried to crawl toward me. I gently pushed her back and stroked her reassuringly. I spent the rest of that night on the cold garage floor as she delivered each breathtaking new being into the world.

I loved all animals but took a special liking to horses and dolphins. It was the joy and playfulness of dolphins that stirred me so. Nothing ever seemed to make them sad. I cherished their happiness, something I lacked and was so desperate to have. I waited for the moment during bath time that my mother would step out of the bathroom, so I could transform my washcloth into Flipper coursing through the sudsy water, leaping over my outstretched legs and reentering the water nose first with a big splash. When I swam in the pool in our backyard, I felt like I was a dolphin.

I collected every kind of horse statuary, poster, toy, magazine, and picture book available. I dreamed horses, drew horses, sculpted horses, and painted horses doing all sorts of things—grazing in pastures, pulling coal carts, charging in front of Roman chariots, carrying cowboys into skirmishes. I loved to draw Pegasus, the winged horse with the windswept mane and tail, and daydreamed of flying away on his back, far from my troubles at school, to a place where we could live out our days in peace and freedom.

My first real horse experience occurred one afternoon when I was five. I was playing in the front yard of our house when down the street strolled a man with a camera slung over his shoulder, leading a paint-colored Shetland pony. I could not contain my excitement. I ran up to pet the pony. As my fingers swept through the thick horsehair and mane, I pressed my nose against the neck and breathed in deeply. Ah, I thought, the sweet familiar musky smell of horse. The scent echoed a resonance of finally being home, a different kind of "home" from what I had experienced so far. I felt strong, whole, and expert in what this animal and I were capable of. The man handed me some papers and said that if I got my mother's permission, I could ride the pony and have my picture taken for a fee. I could barely believe what I was hearing. After so much pretending, here was a real horse standing on my front lawn.

Mom was on the couch with one arm slung over her eyes when I burst in, unable to speak in full sentences. "Horse...outside" was all she could understand. I would not take no for an answer. I still have the pictures of a little girl in a big-brimmed cowboy hat, scarf, and boots, with a smile the size of Texas.

The summer between second and third grades, Geri, my neighbor across the street, invited me to join her and her friends who were headed to Tulley Road Riding Stable where horses could be rented by the hour. I had ridden in my head ever since I could remember but had sat on a real horse only that one time for the picture. My heart raced again as I went inside to ask permission.

At the stable, we had to fill out a sheet that asked about our level of experience. I checked the box marked "advanced," which prompted a wide-eyed stare from Geri. I was given Roman, the biggest horse in the lineup, and jumped into the saddle as if I had been doing it my whole life. I wanted to kick him as hard as I could so he would explode with speed. Instead, our little group of horses and riders plodded lazily down a hill toward a dry creek bed. We came upon a large downed tree. I was longing to ride the way I did in my old memories of being a Native American. I jumped onto the horizontal tree trunk, uncinched the saddle, pulled it onto the tree, and then jumped back on Roman—bareback! He seemed to sense what was coming next. A swift kick and scoot with my hips, and we were off at a full gallop down the trail, with dust billowing behind us. I had never in my life thus far experienced such exhilaration. The horse's back and my body flowed together as if we were one, forward and back, up and down, the wind in my hair. I felt absolutely no fear and showed innate balance and strength on a horse—skills I had not learned in this lifetime.

This was the first verification that my old memories were not purely imaginary. I seemed to be tapping into previous experiences and accessing abilities beyond my present-day know-how. Where, then, was this knowledge coming from? Where was this experience stored? I began to wonder if there were other levels of reality about a person besides what we know in this present life. I tried to ask adults if they had similar experiences or recognitions. All I was met with were strange looks and postures of obvious discomfort. These were the only topics of conversation that even remotely interested me and I soon learned not to mention them. No one at the time seemed to have a clue what I was talking about. The message I got was more of the same: I was weird; no one could relate. So I retreated deeper into the sanctity of silence.

My gentle sensitivity found an outlet interacting with the natural world. I watched how animals communicated with each other through eyes and postures and became sensitive to their nonverbal messages. I knew when they were comfortable and when they were weary. I found that even wild animals were unafraid of me. It was uncanny the way many of them came to me sick or injured. Perhaps they sensed that I knew what it was like to be in pain. Out in nature, I would invariably come upon birds that had been shot with a BB gun, attacked by a cat, or had a broken wing; baby birds that had fallen out of their nests; rabbits with skin abscesses; abandoned baby bunnies; squirrels with cancerous tails; or frogs with broken legs. I would bring them all home and make enclosures for their convalescence. My room looked like a pet store.

Thank God, one of my parents shared my fascination; my father was always there to help with the latest emergency project. When he and I were together, we did not talk much. Like the animals, we could communicate with our minds, which I would later learn is called telepathy. When caring for our hospitalized friends after school, I would often find that we had run out of food or supplies. All I would have to do is think about what was needed and Dad would magically show up with the exact items, having stopped at the feed store on his way home from the office. We never needed the telephone to send our messages back and forth. When I was with my dad, I could sense he understood me and I didn't have to hide who I really was.

He would always make sure we had the proper feed—crickets, worms, berries and fruit, honey, and cat, dog, or bunny food—for whatever we were rehabbing at the time, along with loads of medicine droppers. I came up with all kinds of concoctions to squirt down the throats of these magnificent beings. I once found a ring-necked dove with a hole in its neck, probably from a cat attack. When I infused the nutritious solution past its beak into the back of its throat, the solution came out the wound in the neck, so I surmised I could introduce the solution through the wound, making sure it went down the correct tube. I did not know what the esophagus and the bronchus were then, but information that seemed to come from my old memories told me one could be lifesaving and the other fatal. I also created splints and casts for broken legs, and herbal poultices to apply to wounds. I wasn't sure how I knew what to do in each situation; the information seemed to come from a source above my head, dropping into my brain and creating absolute knowing.

My father and I did our best, and many of our early patients survived. When the day would come to set them free, I always had mixed emotions. They were the only friends I had, aside from my family. They gave me a sense of direction, and I basked in their natural unconditional love. Yet no beauty so profoundly touched me to tears as the sight of a wild creature flying or hopping away. It was the ultimate act of love to release them. I could feel the animal's exhilaration at being free again, back in the environment where it would flourish. My own heart felt such a passion for freedom that it would often prompt flashbacks of scenes from my old memories of being captured and caged for eternity. To lose your freedom is to lose your dignity. I understood inherently that no creature, human or otherwise, deserved such treatment.

Dad was genuinely interested in whatever Mike and I took a fancy to. In fact, he would usually get more excited about it than we would. My father could not wait to have children, Mom used to tell Mike and me. He longed to share with them the opportunities he had missed while growing up. He had an amazing capacity to play with us on our level—and we did play. In summer, he took us camping, water-skiing, bike riding, canoeing, and, his favorite, deep-sea salmon fishing. In winter, he was hell-bent on making us champion snow skiers. Having packed the car the night before, he would get us up at 4 a.m. and with my Uncle Dick and cousins head to the Sierras for a day of skiing. At first, as a six-year-old, I was petrified of the hills, the speed, the cold, and especially the rope tow. My hands were so small and so chilled that I could barely hold on long enough to get to the top of the bunny slope.

Dad started with us on the beginner slopes and seemed to be having way more fun than us kids. Eventually, we graduated to more advanced hills and to the chair lift.

One afternoon when I was eight, we took a new lift up to a run that was marked intermediate. Dad had asked if I thought I could do it. What was I going to say—no? That would sound like such a girl. So up the mountain we went. Mike and my cousins set off down the hill with my uncle. When I got to the edge of the bowl, however, I took one look at the very big moguls and suddenly lost my nerve to do my usual snowplow down the slope. My body froze, and I refused to go down. No matter what encouragement and coaching Dad offered, I simply could not budge. After what felt like all afternoon, Dad turned to me one last time and said, "I cannot do it for you. I will see you at the bottom." Then he faced his shoulders downhill, leaned forward, and disappeared over the crest of the mountain.

I was stunned. He had left me standing on the top of what felt like Mount Everest, with the wind whipping through my hair and my fingers numb with cold—alone. I could not believe it. I had no other choice but to tuck my head, transfer my weight to the front of my skis, and move down the hill toward what felt like intentional suicide. As my skis picked up speed, I found it easier to deal with the moguls by keeping the skis parallel rather than in the wedge position. One mogul after another, I pointed my skis over the top and then down the side as my knees and hips worked like shock absorbers. I slipped into an amazing groove and was suddenly skiing the bumps like a pro.

As I neared the bottom, I scanned the crowd for Dad. He was getting back in line. I could tell by his body posture that he wasn't sure it was me he was watching. As I skidded to a side stop in front of him, spraying him with snow, his facial expression told the story. "Where did you learn to ski like that?" he asked.

Still amazed at myself, I quipped, "Maybe you should leave me to rot at the top of mountains more often." As with the previous summer's ride on Roman, another innate skill had showed itself. There was a bigger lesson, however: I could overcome huge obstacles all by myself, if I believed I could do it. I was responsible for what I got in life, and the only one who could get in my way was me. Sure, I had learning problems, but look what they were teaching me. If my life had been easy, I wouldn't know the depth of emotion that makes one ponder life's biggest questions.

The main question continued to haunt me: For what purpose was I born? Somehow I knew, even at the age of eight, that the answer, now held in my subconscious, would be revealed to me when I reached the age of forty-two. Not only did I have to wait that long, but this process of becoming would continue until then.

On the weekends, Dad loved to take us to drive-in movies. Mom hated these and rarely came along. Dad, Mike, and I would choose long, gory war movies or, my favorites, King Arthur and Crusades-type flicks. We would munch on handfuls of popcorn as the characters on the screen shot, stabbed, and pelted each other with the airborne missiles of the day. Dad and I both felt a connection to the warriors of those eras and on the way home would talk about the camaraderie among them. Mike was usually sound asleep by then. I would ask about the cowboy and Indian times, the Middle Ages when knights did battle on horses, and other ancient cultures and their wars. We would get lost in conversation about these times and places. It was all about standing up and being willing to die for what you believed in.

Our discussions often turned to what happens to a person after death. I had not heard about past lives then, though the idea was implicit in my old memories and in the skills I was manifesting. The more we spoke about such things—partly serious, partly in play—the more they made sense to me. They offered an explanation for my deep connection with my father. Had we shared other lifetimes before this one? Our ability to communicate without words, the way we simply *knew* what the other was thinking, was grounded in a profound familiarity, as if we had spent many lives together. There was an unnamed connection that extended beyond the bond of father and daughter and touched me at a deep level.

As I grew up, I was convinced that he was the only person in the world who really knew me. He was the magical firefly hidden in my back pocket when the kids at school teased and humiliated me. I knew there was no other person on the planet whose love was worth having more than his. It seemed that everyone in the world loved my father—

and every night when he would come home, he made me feel as though he loved me more than anyone else.

I don't remember the exact conversation because there were so many, but one day I asked him how he wanted to be buried. He said that he wanted to be cremated, even though it was not our family's custom. I vowed that if I were ever presented with that situation, I would see that his wishes were carried out. And I told him my desire was the same. I did not want to be in a coffin in the ground taking up space. I wanted my body's elements to be returned to the earth from where they came.

We also talked about how when one of us died, the one remaining should not be sad because we would meet again in some other time and dimension. If it were true that we had lived many lifetimes together before, surely there would be more in the future. It was fun to consider the possibilities. We made a pact that the one who crossed over first would come back and give the remaining one a sign that only he or I would recognize. The sign would be proof that life is eternal, that we had lived together before, and we would meet up again in the future.

Janine — fifth grade.

Affirmation through Art

Y ou, *demonstrated early on that you have uncanny leadership abilities. It is natural for you to take on monumental projects and see them through to the end. You naturally stood out in the crowd when you found your resonance subjects. Wary teachers often tried to talk you out of the complicated tasks you chose for yourselves. Indigo Children hold fast to their visions and refuse to compromise, knowing that they have what it takes to accomplish tremendous mental and physical feats of spirit and will. You lead by example and compassion rather than through heavy-handed rule. You are sensitive to people's feelings and empathically consider what you ask of others. This unique style sets you apart from the way leadership has been practiced on this planet thus far. You seem to understand democracy in the way it was originally intended. Finding the limelight is an unintended outcome for you.*

In contrast to all the magic and practical learning I was experiencing at home, I still had to return to the agony of the classroom each school day. In fourth grade, I began gaining weight, growing out of my school clothes almost as fast as my mother could buy them. Soon I was out of girls' 6X and we were shopping in the teen sections. The pant legs were always too long and needed hemming.

At school, the kids had so much more of me to make fun of. I would watch them play dodgeball, jump rope, and swing from the monkey bars and rings. Every time I tried to join them, their eyebrows would raise and they would scowl, as if I smelled foul. Their looks were bad enough, but what came out of their mouths was even more devastating—words like "stupid," "fatty," "butt ugliness," "dumbo," "retard." What was left of my self-worth shut down. Feeling nothing seemed better than feeling this.

It was as if I were living in two worlds: one where I was a wizard of healing sick and wounded animals and a creator of magical works of art; and the other where people saw me as ugly and strange, too weird to have around. I only saw my dad, my touchstone, briefly at night and on the weekends. The rest of the time I was among strangers. My parents' style was to allow Mike and me to grow in our own unique ways. They did not interfere unless asked, and I never did. Not wanting to contaminate the one place I found refuge, I chose never to discuss the issues I was facing at school with my parents at home. Shouldering this massive burden felt familiar and seemed to hold purpose. I felt as if I had done this before and it was a required component in the grooming process that was afoot.

But being alone without a true reference point to guide me, I began to believe the cruel words directed at me. When I looked in the mirror, I did not like what I saw. When I brought my report cards home, my parents did not like what they saw either. Though I tried, I was mostly making Ds, with the occasional C. My teacher tried to put a positive spin on it with comments like "tries hard," "high verbal abilities," and "polite and quiet in class," but the letter grades were the final tally.

In parent-teacher conferences, they discussed my problems. The teacher had thought I must be lazy, but my parents reported how I would come home directly from school and do homework until dinner, then spend another two hours studying before bed. They always laid the solution on my shoulders: I should work harder in special education class. It seemed the learning problems were my fault. The message was clear: work harder and study longer. But it felt like I was trying to learn a different language from the one for which my brain was wired. They wanted me to learn English and math, but my mind only spoke pictures and wordless communication. This internal war raged, while my self-image was eroding from the sulfuric acid of my classmates' comments.

The next year, however, my luck turned. Mrs. Neal was teaching fifth grade rather than third again, and thanks to my mother's intervention, I was assigned to her class. I could hardly believe it. Mom, who was teaching arts and crafts at Willow Glen High School, introduced Mrs. Neal to the art possibilities at the elementary school level. In fifth grade, this proved to be a ray of sunlight in a scholastic experience that had been a pit of despair.

On the first day of class, Mrs. Neal laid out the schedule for our classes in reading, spelling, cursive writing, math, history, civics, and health. Just as I was thinking it was going to be another long year, she added that we were also going to do a very special project, something no other class at our school had done before. We all perked up in our chairs. We were going to create a class art project and enter it in the school district art contest in early spring. My dread began shifting to hope. She continued, "We are fortunate to have a gifted artist in our class this year to lead this project and to organize you students in accomplishing this lofty goal," and she looked squarely at me. My stomach dropped into my feet; I knew the price of being seen as "special." But the momentary fear of being made fun of again gave way to the joy of being praised. I hadn't experienced this since kindergarten. I loved this lady!

She and I met after school that day, and she described my duties. I was to conduct a class brainstorming session to choose the project and then divide the students into three groups to work on the project during three class periods each day. I would be overseeing all three groups. With a big smile, she added, "Those three hours will be during reading, writing, and math periods." The fact that she was effectively excusing me from special ed slowly dropped into my conscious awareness. I would not be pulled from the room and shuffled off with the mental retards anymore. I could stay in the classroom with the other kids and not be seen by them as stupid. I was thrilled. Yet the level of excitement that day could not match what I felt when this project was finished.

We collectively decided to do a massive stitchery, and after we viewed the many anonymously submitted designs, there was a democratic vote. I knew this project called for complexity, so I had redrawn and submitted the underwater scene I had painted five years earlier in kindergarten. My drawing won—perhaps not a surprise, since as the chosen "art director," I could probably muster the level of detail such a project required.

Mrs. Neal obtained a huge piece of burlap and secured it to a sturdy five-by-eight-foot frame that took up one whole corner of the classroom. She asked my mom to teach me how to transfer the drawing to the burlap. I chose all the colors of yarn. We then split the class into three shifts and went to work. Part of my task was to make sure the stitches stayed within the lines and were even and smooth. I constantly had to cut out sections of stitching and redo them after class. It turned out that not everybody could do this sort of work easily. Moreover, the kids having the most trouble were the class stars at math, reading, and spelling. Even then, I found that correlation, which I would later understand as left-brain versus right-brain dominance, curious. I tried to gently guide and encourage the manually challenged students. I knew all too well what it felt like to be made fun of after trying your best.

We worked consistently for three months. My confidence grew, and so did the other kids' respect for me. They were now talking to me on the playground and inviting me to join in their games. I was still wary, like a beaten dog, always on guard against the next lashing. And I still got lots of "fat pig" comments. My weight was continuing to climb, though I had no idea why. I was not eating a lot. I was now five feet tall, wore size eight-and-a-half shoes, and weighed 150 pounds. My hair was thin, oily, and stringy. I never had to worry about boys making eyes at me, since I preferred to dress like they did. I would often be called "sonny." In my jeans, Keds sneakers with the rubber toe stop, and oversized sweatshirts, I told myself that that suited me just fine.

I tried to join the Girl Scouts, but my growing girth was far beyond even the largest sized uniform. It seemed that I would never develop friendships with people—I was too fat, too strange, and too dumb. I was obviously different from other kids. I could not do basic things they found easy, yet I could do things they could not, and I knew things they did not. *I was being groomed for something,* came the recurring thought. Then again, I would wonder: How could this be? Why me? More important, would I survive it? Age forty-two sounded a very long way off.

We finally finished the stitchery in February 1972. It was displayed downtown at the civic center along with the other entries. We took a class field trip to see the display and be present for the award presentations at the conclusion of the showing. Our stitchery won first place! And that was just the beginning—more honors to come.

After school, Mrs. Neal sat me down and thanked me for a job well done. I had displayed maturity, kindness, and compassion with the other kids and she could see leadership qualities in me. She knew how hard school was for me, and wanted to say that she respected my courage to keep showing up. *As if I have a choice,* I thought. She then proposed another art project, this time for me only.

She asked if I would be interested in painting the classroom windows. I looked up. There were four panels of windows facing onto the playground and a small window above the door. A smile spread across my face. I looked back at her with one burning question, unspoken. She answered, "Yes, of course you can paint during math, reading, and spelling periods." Elation struck again—I could get used to this.

One morning Mrs. Neal encouraged us to take our seats as fast as possible—she had an announcement to make. She pulled a piece of stenographic paper from her book case, held it up in front of her, and peered over the top of those narrow reading glasses that always appeared to be coming off the end of her nose. *This is big,* I thought. She never acted this way. When everyone was settled and the chatter had died, she began reading. "It is with my great honor and pleasure to announce the winner of this year's California State Art Contest at the elementary level, Dover Elementary School, Mrs. Neal's fifth grade class, 'Underwater Adventure.'" The roar that exploded prompted the teachers in adjacent classrooms to send a runner to make sure we were all right.

From that day, things started to change for me socially. Kids began sharing with me how excited they were about meeting the governor of California, Ronald Reagan. As kids, we knew him best for his cheesy Western movies, and the news flashes on TV. The 120-mile journey to Sacramento was our longest field trip ever, and on the bus I sat next to one of the most popular girls not only in our class, but in the whole school as well.

Trisha was what the boys called a babe. She was thin with long, flowing brown hair, dressed well, was from a wealthy family, and had an air of maturity and self-assurance. We chatted the entire way and discovered that we had many similarities. She actually had pondered some of the greatest questions in life: Who are we, where did we come from, and why are we here? I liked her. We ended up spending the rest of the day together. I was amazed that she was hanging out with me.

As we walked down the long hall in the State House to the governor's office, I began to notice the paintings on the walls: scenes of cowboys and Indians in battle on horseback. Something more caught my attention. In every picture, the Indians were winning. I was amazed. I had long suffered the historical fact that the white man had taken this land and brutalized the natives who were its stewards. I was not sure where this information came from, but I had always felt the pain of it personally.

The hallway ended at a door with a plaque that read "Governor's Office." As we filed in, Governor Reagan stood up from his desk and greeted us with his distinctive, pasted-on smile. I could not believe my eyes—there was our beloved stitchery hanging on the wall behind him, where it would stay for the next six months. The drawing from my old memories was now part of another history, alongside the others we had just passed in the hallway.

After presenting Mrs. Neal with a plaque, Mr. Reagan took us on a tour of his art collection, starting with the cowboy and Indian paintings in the hall. When he asked if anyone noticed something different about them, I raised my hand and answered, "The Indians are winning."

His eyes widened. "Yes, that's right. Not many people notice."

Mrs. Neal, forever my guardian, then introduced me as the student who had drawn the scene on the stitchery and overseen the project. He invited me to the front of the line and, putting his hand on my shoulder, ushered me around, discussing what he liked about each picture. I had never thought of him as sympathetic to Indian suffering and gained a new respect for him that day.

The Diagnosis

Y ou, *possess cunning and tenacity with which, if you are left to your own devices during times of hardship, you will create new systems that have never been seen before. You have the ability to recapitulate information that scientists have been collecting throughout the centuries and have handed down from one genera- tion to the next, and take it to the next level of thought. You special beings see in wholes simultaneously and instantly. You have a deeply mysterious connection to all that has ever been as if the wealth of the collective consciousness is avail- able to you at every moment. Tapping into direct understandings of past cultures, earth history, and universal knowledge may explain your familiarity with highly advanced civilizations that have long since disappeared from this plane. Have you noticed that in the past few years you have been collecting healing and com- munication tools that were well known in Atlantean times?*

Art remained my strong suit. In math we were solving long strings of numbers in addition, subtraction, or division. I was almost tracking in these concepts, then we got to algebra equations and word problems and they threw in letters. My answers never matched the ones at the back of the book. I would spend hours at home trying to understand this foreign language. My left brain was still closed for business, and no one was sure when it might decide to start firing.

One day in class, I decided to approach math as I did a drawing, looking at the numbers and the concepts behind them as pictures and wholes rather than a string of separate entities. Suddenly, I started coming up with the correct answers, but not by using the formulas in the book. I would just look at the numbers, squint my eyes, visualize looking at the answers in the back of the book, and suddenly the correct answer would appear in my mind. I found this amazing. Me, coming up with the correct numbers every time? My homework papers started coming back with As and Bs instead of Ds.

The teacher became suspicious. Calling me over to her desk during math homework period, she handed me a sheet of math problems and asked if she could watch me complete the assignment. So I went to work, looking at the problem, squinting my eyes, and writing down the first numbers that came into my head. No longhand writing or showing my work, just the answer. When I was finished, she compared the answers to the teacher's textbook and looked at me in amazement.

"How did you come up with these?" she asked.

I took a deep breath and said I really had no idea, they just popped into my mind, and I wrote them down. There was not much else to say. What really happened was that out of sheer desperation I had somehow accessed a previously familiar mental skill that was held in that place of perception between my brain and chest. It would be decades before I heard the term "remote viewing."

One night I was helping Mom fix dinner while the TV in the family room was broadcasting a network evening news show. We were not paying much attention until I heard the commentator introduce an "up close" piece on learning disabilities. I immediately left the kitchen and sat on the floor just inches from the screen. The reporter started off with the prevalence of learning disabilities and how they are affecting public education. She broke to a family interview, discussing the impact on the children and their home life. Then the report did something remarkable. It shifted to a "through the eyes of" perspective on dyslexia, how a kid with dyslexia sees the world, particularly numbers and letters, math and reading. Tears filled my eyes. My daily internal experience was being broadcast nationally on the evening news. To this day, when I am presented with a truth, my body responds with tingling or tearing. At that stage in my energetic development, I only had the capacity to produce the tears.

The program was over all too soon, but it was enough to hand me the answer to my scholastic frustrations. I practically kissed the TV screen. I shouted to my mother, who was only a few yards away, "I want to be tested! I have dyslexia!"

After the three days of intense testing, provided by the public school system at my parents' request, my folks and I met with the school speech pathologist. As we took our seats around a table, I remember realizing that the information we were about to hear could determine the direction of my entire future. There I was, with a sense of this huge destiny before me, yet robbed of the simple menial skills required to access it. My parents, on the other hand, appeared somewhat disinterested. They thought they were raising an artist, but brewing in the core of my being were inklings of a lifework of grander scale.

The pathologist told us that I had an above-average IQ, and fairly profound dyslexia. Mine was more like aphasia, meaning I could see individual digits and characters correctly but could not store or process them in the normal neural tracks in my brain. In essence, when I tried to retrieve information, I was not able to find where it was stored and so could not speak or write it correctly. When I read, I perceived words that were not there and was selectively blind to words that were. I also flipped letters upside down or backward and/or reversed the sequence of letters in a word, which made it impossible for me to see my own spelling mistakes. I was not even able to remember what the correctly spelled word looked like. Thus I could easily spell the same word six different ways on a single sheet of paper and not even realize it.

As the diagnosis proceeded, I felt as if I were being seen for the first time. There was a word, "dyslexia," that represented a condition whose ravages until that point had left me naked and bleeding on the floor. It lived in a mysterious place within me, causing unexplainable suffering. As the man laid out for us the etiology of dyslexia, a surprising sense of peace washed over me. All of a sudden, so much of my history made sense. It was no longer my fault. I was not lazy, as everybody seemed to have been implying. Nor was I stupid. I had a high IQ and a "problem" with my brain that made me different from the other kids.

I looked at Mom and Dad. They were just sitting there nodding as if this were just one more parent-teacher conference during which all my deficiencies were reported. The psychologist started rattling off some of the characteristics of dyslexics: mispronounced words; difficulty remembering names of letters, even in the dyslexic's own name; inability to associate letters with sounds; inability to read or sound out common one-syllable words; use of imprecise language, such as vague references to "stuff"; mixing up words, like "tornado" for "volcano"; slow to respond orally when questioned; difficulty remembering isolated pieces of verbal information such as dates, names, and telephone numbers; and because of all these difficulties, lowered self-esteem and an internal suffering not always visible to others. On the other hand, dyslexics had certain strengths: curiosity and a great imagination, the ability to get the gist of things quickly, a surprising maturity, talent at three-dimensional and higher-level thinking, and a surprisingly sophisticated listening vocabulary. A dyslexic could excel in areas not dependent on reading, such as math (that did not fit me), computers, visual arts, philosophy, biology, social studies, neuroscience, and creative writing.

He seemed to be describing my life in all its aspects. The diagnosis was a fit. Now that it was decided what I had, I was eager to hear him describe how to fix it. Instead, he proceeded to tell my parents, without even giving me a glance, not to expect me to get into college. I should set my sights on a career in the trades. I would make a great baker, artist, housecleaner, or stay-at-home mom.

I felt like I was hearing my life pass right by me. I had no interest in any of those pursuits. Through my experiences with sick animals, I had been sensing a calling toward a career in medicine. I had never breathed a word about this outrageous idea to anyone, not even to my dad, as it obviously meant being smart and getting through a whole lot of school. But now that I had a real diagnosis, I was seeing a glimmer of possibility, and that whispered notion was becoming a shout inside. I blurted out, "Do any dyslexics go to college? Have there ever been any that actually succeeded in life?"

For the first time in our all-afternoon meeting, the speech pathologist looked at me. With an expression of annoyance on his face, he condescended to list a number of known dyslexic successes, including Leonardo da Vinci, Albert Einstein, Thomas Edison, John F. Kennedy,

Hans Christian Andersen, George Washington, Nelson Rockefeller, Walt Disney, John Lennon, and Henry Ford, to name but a few.

The list included some of my greatest heroes, all creative thinkers who had made an impact on the world. I liked that.

He added, probably hoping to be encouraging, that if I wanted to pursue a college education, the public university system was obliged to offer most classes and textbooks on tape recordings.

My heart sank. That sounded like the college level version of special ed. My mind did not work like normal people's, that I knew. But I had heard the list. The diagnosis did not have to be a condemnation. It was, in fact, permission to explore the unique capacities lying within my thick cranium. It was dawning on me: Perhaps my mind was special in a way that could make a difference in the world.

At that instant, the warrior that had faced off with Dennis the bully reawoke within me. I was going to work hard and show the world I could overcome this, and anything else it might throw my way. Dyslexia did not hold power over my destiny. As the counselor was spewing out all the things I would not be able to do, my mind dropped into an awake imagery. I observed my inner self peel off a limp black replica of my body, stand it up, and punch it repeatedly until it was no more. I could now fight this inner demon from outside myself. I was not lazy or dumb. I just had to build the bridge that would carry me over the abyss of self-doubt to the other side. The bridge was the schooling my goal required. The other side was the physician I knew I already was. I was going to be a doctor. I kept this secret to myself, concealed in my eternally optimistic core.

PART II

Initiations

Janine at first Wharf to Wharf race in 1976.

6

Learning How to Learn

*C*reating a safe and nurturing environment is crucial for Indigo Children developing into their full potential. When you were little, it frustrated you no end to be treated like a kid. You are highly advanced spiritual beings who have taken human form, some for the first time and others who are so savvy in the ways of this world and society that nothing seems remotely new to you. As you pass through your various childhood developmental stages, however, you need a committed, intimate advocate to foster your distinctive growth process. The relationships you enjoy with these advocates are not coincidental. Often they are profoundly soulful and familiar and demonstrate a quality of immediate recognition on the deepest levels.

The Indigo Child comes in knowing the truth and armed with a soul tendency to challenge the dogma of spiritual teachings, regardless of the brand. You have a natural curiosity when it comes to what people believe, when it comes to spiritual matters, often seeking out the knowledge offered by different religions as a means of confirming what you already know. Organized religion of any kind is a means of systematically taking away individuals' free will to think on their own, thus develop and respond to their personal inner voice. That voice is the source of your uncanny strength. From your very first memories, you interacted constantly with this inner wisdom, which never steered you wrong.

The organized dogmatic discourse that purports to follow ancient texts written thousands of years ago, in a time very different from today, and edited *throughout the centuries for ulterior motives no longer applies. The Indigo is a spiritual warrior who has come here to do battle with all that is regurgitated by rote. Expect that in the years to come you will be ripping the roof off the Vatican and other Christian sanctums, Jewish temples, and Muslim mosques, exposing the truth of what lies within. None will be spared the wrath of your truth seeking.*

The mental challenges over the next several years tested me. I chose not to have my classes on tape. The world would not make such accommodations for me when I was finished with school, so I had no intention of relying on a crutch. I would have to learn how to learn my own way, teaching myself what worked and what didn't. I simply trusted that the process of how to do that would magically appear.

Every seventh grader had to take typing class. The eighth graders warned us that no one got higher than a C in typing, mainly because there was no way to cheat. I was sure I would fail miserably. Instead, I found it easy to learn where each letter was on the keyboard when my hands were resting in the typing position. And when I pulled the typing paper from the carriage and compared my work to the published text, it was almost an exact match. Sure, I had dropped some strokes and missed some keys, but somehow my brain could do this easily. I earned an A in typing—my first A as a final grade. Even more important than my stellar grade was the discovery that if I incorporated my hands while processing words, my mind could track the letters as well as their meaning.

I applied this insight to reading. When I read silently, I would move my fingers as if they were hitting keys on a typewriter. My brain could perceive the words as whole objects through my eyes and then break them down into letters with the help of my hands. Once my mind had captured the letters, it could attach appropriate sounds to them. Eventually, I figured out how to track sequences of words as sentences. Finally, in seventh grade, I was actually reading! It was as if a massive veil of darkness in my brain had been lifted.

Another of my early As in seventh grade was in geography. I won the geography bee competition and took the highest grade in the class. In eighth grade, however, I ran into a brick wall. My guidance counselor suggested taking a conversational Spanish class to prepare me for

Spanish in high school. My brother had done fairly well in this class at my age. I agreed to what ended up a catastrophe. I got stressed trying to sound out Spanish words and grapple with Spanish grammar when I was only just getting comfortable with letters in my own language and was still figuring out nouns, verbs, and predicates in English class. My mental and emotional stability began to collapse under the weight of realizing how much I still didn't know. I was so far behind scholastically—could I ever catch up?

I would worry at night. My mind would race as the digital clock on the bed stand counted off the minutes and hours, which made me even more anxious. Every night it was the same. My mind would spin and my stomach would turn with anxiety as the hours crept by. Not long after finally getting to sleep, I would wake up from a deep REM cycle and begin projectile vomiting all over my bedroom just as I did as an infant. Still disoriented, I would go into my parents' bedroom and wake my father. This was the early seventies, when shag carpet was vogue, and Mom made sure our house reflected the latest interior design concepts. Dad would spend hours picking the small chunks of partially digested food particles from the long green fibers. I helped him the best I could. This went on for weeks until I felt so guilty about taking advantage of this kind man's generosity that I decided to sleep outside. If I vomited, it wouldn't matter; I could hose down the pool decking in the morning.

Setting up a chaise lounge by the gazebo on the far side of the pool allowed me to feel as far away from civilization as possible. Drawing from my old memories, I was reminded of being alone out on the prairie, camping under the stars next to a lake. During those nights out-of-doors, a recurring event would transpire. In the middle of the night, my eyes would open just as a large white owl flew directly over me. It was uncanny. There was no sound, nothing to explain my awakening. I was used to feeling that animals were protecting me when I ventured out into the wilds, but this was San Jose, a city of 750,000 people at that time, where owls were a rarity.

Curious, I looked up what the owl symbolized in Native American culture. I wrote in my journal: "Mystery of magic—silent wisdom and vision in the night—silent and swift movement—seeing behind masks—keen sight—messenger of secrets and omens—shape-shifting—link between the dark, unseen world and the world of light—

knowledge of approaching death—freedom." As my understanding of the world and my eventual place in it grew, the meaning of these words became clearer. I carried the traits of the owl. During those midnight awakenings, I intuited the owl was appearing to show me to myself, like a mirror. Reassurance that the forces of nature were protecting me validated for me that my strangeness would one day prove a gift to the world and that society had just not seen one of me before.

My parents petitioned the school to let me drop Spanish class, and with my owl friend watching over me, I slept well and the vomiting ended. I slept outside for one year, in all weather conditions, and absolutely loved it. A part of me felt wild and untamed, as if I did not belong to the circle of people and society. I often wondered how I was ever going to fit in. Now it seemed I did not even belong indoors. The feeling of being a square peg in a round hole with the intention of never fitting in kept coming to mind. I just wasn't built like they were. This was in sharp contrast to how I felt when I was out in nature.

During my later grammar school years, when our family would visit my parents' best friends, the Simonis, at their home in the Santa Cruz Mountains, I used to jump out of the station wagon and disappear into the woods. I would run for hours, taking in the sounds of the birds and the smells of the California coastal redwoods and the moist earth. Looking down at my feet charging over the forest duff, I would envision them in moccasins, just like in my old memories. A multitude of greens, browns, rusts, and golds filled my vision. The iridescent green moss set against the dark redwood bark and the bright orange and yellow lichen growing on downed deadwood electrified me. The different birdcalls announced my arrival, their tone communicating whether I was accepted into their domain or was considered a threat. I knew their calls, and I felt they knew me.

I knew instinctively how to read the signs of the forest. Moss always grew on a tree's north side; the sun and length of the shadows told the time of day. Growing up in the city could not explain this knowledge of the woods. I was innately comfortable out there. These places were woven into the very fabric of who I was. I remember thinking, This is my church; here is where I find God. The profound sense of interconnectedness with the nature spirits resonated in that space between my heart and my head. My chest would grow warm and expansive and my mind would flash with scenes of old memories of similar experiences. This elicited sensations that seemed to open a portal back to different times and places.

Both my parents were raised Roman Catholic and, as is custom, passed on the dogma to my brother and me. Listening to the sermons in church, I was appalled. They were all about giving up free will and living in fear of and paying penance to a God created by people who wrote a book called the Bible. I found this confusing. From my old memories, I knew I was a part of what is called God. I was not mean, loathsome, or a sinner. All I wanted to do was help sick and injured animals, and someday perhaps people.

My discomfort spilled over into catechism class. From the pit of my being, I hated being told how to think and what to believe. And when it came to what we were taught, I had my hand up and a puzzled look on my face most of the time. I simply could not accept that Eve was created from Adam's rib. This defied physiological law. The other story I could not wrap my mind around was the creation of the universe in seven days. In school we had learned about our planet and its moon and the structure of the solar system. These were three-dimensional concepts involving vast times and distances that I could visualize and absorb fully. So I would challenge the catechism instructor on scientific grounds. Some of the other kids knew me from school and were surprised to hear me handling concepts like these, yet I had grown accustomed to having such conversations at home with my parents and their friends. The other kids would be playing down the hall, and I would be in the kitchen or dining room with the adults. There were often comments like "old soul" or "adult in a child's body."

Because my questions disrupted the catechism class, I was frequently sent home early. Sitting outside on the porch while the instructor's wife called my parents, I would again think, I just never seem to fit in. Either I cannot learn what they are trying to teach me, or I know too much already. I don't belong here; someone must have made a mistake. Yet here I am, on this planet at this time. There must be some bigger reason. Did I choose this?

My thoughts would turn until they eventually settled on the knowing that this was all part of a grooming process. I was a wizard warrior. I had to be to get through this part of my life. The wounded child was giving way to a being endowed with the skills of a warrior who had direct access to knowledge far beyond her understanding at the time. I could stand on my own and defend who I was. I could fight in hand-to-hand combat and was at home on horseback. I could challenge my seniors to an intellectual duel. Or I could run away to the forest and be safe, in communion with the wild creatures.

In spite of all of these realizations, I could not seem to master my own body. My weight was still a problem. Suspecting that I had a glandular condition, I insisted that my parents take me to the doctor for examination and testing regarding my weight. All the lab results were within normal limits. For the first time, "normal" was not what I wanted to hear, since it meant the glandular condition I was sure was at the root of my weight problem didn't exist. The doctor took pity on me and offered to prescribe a diet pill—in those days, an amphetamine, which only worked for two weeks—but only if I followed a strict diet with my mother's help and began a regular exercise program.

I took the diet pills for two weeks in the winter of 1974 at the age of eleven. That was also the time I began to run. This was the early seventies, when the self-help movement was in its infancy and Jim Fixx was writing about the highs of running. How fitting it was that my way out of the weight problem would be to take up the activity that looked to be the most strenuous. At first, I could only jog the length of four houses before returning to a walk to catch my breath. Learning the art of breathing, I began extending my course over several blocks. Losing myself in the goal setting and goal accomplishing, the pounds fell off. When I started, the scale read 150 pounds. By the second week, I had lost fourteen pounds. Learning for the first time how to control my body was intoxicating.

One mile soon became two, then three, then six. As the weight came off, I could run longer distances. On July 28 of that year, I entered and completed my first 10K—the Wharf to Wharf Race that starts in Santa Cruz and ends in Capitola, snaking its way along the coast—finishing in one hour, five minutes. My family stayed the weekend with the Simonis at their beach house, which was along the route. They were all there at the finish cheering me on. I felt like the winner of a marathon. My confidence took another great leap forward. I was learning that if I put forth the necessary Herculean effort, I just might be able to attain any goal I chose.

Trisha introduced me to Presentation High School, a private Catholic college preparatory school for girls. Presentation offered smaller classes and teachers who took a personal interest in each student. I knew I needed this alongside my own efforts to teach my brain to learn. Presentation was the girl's equivalent to the all-boys Bellarmine College Preparatory, where my brother was currently a student and where my father had attended in his day. Trisha got me an application, and I presented the idea to my parents. They were a bit surprised that their thirteen-year-old daughter was so interested in her academic future, given the diagnosis of two years earlier.

Two weeks after the entrance exam, my parents and I were invited for an interview. Presentation's principal, Sister Mary Margaret, politely reviewed my scores. I had earned a 90 percent grade in science, 70 percent in history, and 1 percent in math. In English, my scores were 75 percent in writing and content, and 5 percent in spelling and grammar. She looked up from the papers with a quizzical expression on her face. She felt I had potential and wondered what could explain such a performance.

Before the interview I had made my parents swear that, no matter what, they would not mention my dyslexia. I spoke up and said I had gotten a late start in elementary school and had some difficulties with math and reading. Putting a positive spin on it, I offered, "But in the past few years I have really improved in certain subjects; I even scored As in typing and geography." I told her I would work really hard, if I could only be given the opportunity. She seemed impressed with my plea and smiled. A letter of acceptance arrived the following week. I was admitted on academic probation. I had to maintain at least a C average in math and English all four years. If my grade point average dipped below 2.0, I would be expelled.

7

Earth School

*C*hallenges never seem to cease for you the Indigo, nor do the Universal Lessons that come from your life experience. For it is through this avenue of apparent struggle, that you find and strengthen your wings of freedom. The individual experiences of struggle are like spokes of a wheel. The rim holds them together, just as your greater purpose is what unites these seemingly unrelated experiences. Each spoke, just like each experience, provides both tension and compression to the system as a whole, helping to shape it. Both the struggles and the purpose define the Indigo's experience here on this planet.

Relax, parents, and let your child pursue everything that she or he is interested in. Indigo adults can tell you that their lives seem to be a patchwork of experiences and events that, together, create their unique and interesting tapestry. We now recognize that this very uniqueness is transforming our species.

High school marked the beginning of the twenty-two-year period I came to think of as Earth School—my years of formal education but also of learning how to be on the planet. Until then, I had always felt so disconnected, sometime even fantasizing that being here was a mistake. Now the sense that I was here for a purpose began to gain the upper hand. In daydreams (or were they old memories?—I was never sure), I would see myself as a comet, with a long tail of shimmering stardust and sparks, hurtling through the universe on my way to other galaxies and at the last minute diverted to Earth for some call of duty.

Sometimes I would visit a scene in which twelve tall androgynous beings of light wearing red robes were seated around a large round wooden table communicating telepathically. They were guiding the events that would determine the Earth's future. As each one spoke, the others listened in silence. A decision was reached, and all heads turned toward me. I was the member most worthy for the assignment. I didn't want to return to this planet. I thought I was finished with the business of incarnation. Nevertheless, I agreed. As I thanked them and bowed my head, my seat suddenly transformed into a trapdoor portal through which I fell into space, a comet now hurtling toward planet Earth.

In other daydreams, I would see what I had endured as a child as only the beginning. Earth School would challenge me further. I would be honed into a superhero able to endure pain and manifest miracles. I would be given an intellect able creatively to solve the most complex problems, a heart capable of love and compassion, and a spirit of infectious optimism. Teachers would be sent to mentor me. I would instantly recognize them because they would have the same wisdom and kindness I knew in my father. My father, in fact, was the eldest master of the council. We had worked together in many other incarnations. As I collected wisdom, skill, grace, and courage, I would be seen as a natural leader to help guide people through some kind of time portal— shift on Earth.

Information like this always came in ethereal form (that is, misty and limitless), mostly when I was awake and my mind was relaxed. It often included my father playing a significant role, which convinced me that the information held truth, given the profound relationship he and I shared. Sometimes in those states, I would recall actual memories of my interactions with him in other lifetimes, which made distinguishing between the real and the ethereal difficult.

In these states remembering back, I must have been five or six, small enough to sit on his shin as he crossed one leg over the other. We were watching a nature show on television, and a lioness was bringing down a gazelle on the Serengeti Plain. It was difficult to watch. I could feel the gazelle's terror and pain. The camera zoomed in to show the eye of the gazelle just as it was dying. I could hear what it was thinking in that moment and screamed out loud, "Daddy, Daddy, it has a baby hiding in the grass. What is the baby going to do now?"

He was immediately curious how I knew that. At that age, I assumed everybody could understand the unspoken thoughts of animals, even on television. I turned and looked him squarely in the eyes as mine began to tear up. He thought I was sad for the gazelle and tried to comfort me. I maintained the stare, and he grew more uncomfortable. I then said, "You are going to die, aren't you?"

In that instant, I knew my time with him would be limited. He had signed on for a relatively short stay in this realm—perhaps, I mused as I recalled the moment, just long enough to mentor me, then send me out prepared to complete the task the council had ordered.

Both Trisha and I went to Presentation, though we drifted apart. Even then, I saw that her presence in my life had served its purpose: I was now at a school that offered the academic attention I needed, and my ability to learn was gradually improving. Studying came first, before all other activities. Yet I was also, for the first time, making friends with people who accepted me for who I was.

My cousin Paul was attending Bellarmine. He introduced me to Mary Zarka, a hellion and now a classmate of mine he had known in elementary and middle school. Mary Strutner and Shannon Hare had a natural affinity toward each other and with Mary Zarka and me. We all came from similar backgrounds and our families even blended well.

The social highlights in those years were the Bellarmine/Presentation ski trips. We had a blast showing off and racing each other down the steepest runs in full tuck position, just like the Olympic downhillers. If there was a major wipeout, we would gather around the human wreckage encased in snow and hold up imaginary scorecards. Never did anyone suffer a "career-ending" injury—that is, until my crash sophomore year.

It was early March in the High Sierras, one week before my fifteenth birthday. We were skiing Heavenly Valley in gorgeous spring conditions—perfect snow, clear skies, and a light breeze. We were dressed to suit the conditions. After skiing all morning, we broke for lunch in the upper lodge. As we swapped ski tragedy stories, clouds gathered and the wind started picking up. A storm was approaching over Lake Tahoe. We thought we could get one more run in, then Paul and I reconsidered, deciding to take the chair lift down; we were simply not dressed for the thirty-mph winds and freezing rain. The line for the chair lift looked like at least an hour's wait, however. Glancing at each other, we announced simultaneously, "Gun Barrel!"

Gun Barrel is the double black diamond ski run that goes down the face of the mountain directly underneath the chair lift, a 1,500-foot vertical drop over a mile and a half. The moguls that day were as tall as a man, which meant that, as we ascended them, we could not see terra firma below, only more white sky, with snow and freezing rain blowing horizontally into our faces like a thousand tiny daggers slashing our cheeks. After a while, Paul yelled over the wind, "Let's tuck. I'll race you to the bottom." At the time, it seemed like the fastest way to end our suffering. Besides, I could not turn down a direct challenge. With my ski poles tucked under my armpits, knees and hips flexed, I leaned into the tips of my skis and went for it. Flying over bump after bump, feeling like a human shock absorber, I lost sight and sound of Paul in the snow and wind. The blowing ice crystals continued to bite at my face, and after what seemed like fifteen minutes of torture, I could stand it no longer. I pulled to a stop and turned my face away from the oncoming ice and wind. Covering my exposed cheeks with my gloves, I could not even sense pressure on the skin.

All of a sudden, something crashed into me and I found myself hurtling through the air down the mountain. I had no idea who or what had hit me. All I knew was that I was airborne and scheduled to land any second. My arms and legs flailing, trying to regain balance in the air, I crashed hard into the icy snow, butt first, and lost consciousness.

The next thing I remember was warmth throughout my body and the sensation of being in a canoe on a fast-moving river. I was taken into a shed once we reached the bottom of the slope, and someone released some straps that were around me. My legs did not work, nor could I feel the paramedic's fingers lightly touch my shins and calves during the medical exam. The adult chaperones were called. Eventually, two guys carried me from the "med shed" and placed me in my seat on our bus. That was when I realized how much my lower back hurt, even though my legs were still not working right. The only comfortable sitting position was with my knees pulled up to rest on the seat in front of me, which is how the guys left me.

On the way home, I learned what had happened. I had been several yards in front of Paul on the slope. Because he, too, could not stand the wind and ice, he decided to tuck his chin and ski blind, unaware that he was headed straight at me. Traveling at about twenty miles an hour, he hit me squarely in the lower back with the crown of his head. Once I landed, I slid, unconscious, for another hundred yards. People on the chair lift saw the whole incident, and someone called the ski patrol. It took them almost thirty minutes to reach us and another thirty minutes to get me down in the yellow gondola. Paul was not hurt.

After the five-hour bus trip home, I was unable to move from the fetal position. My father and Uncle Dick, Paul's dad, had to carry me, still curled up, and lay me in the back of our station wagon on my side. The pain was unimaginable.

My dad and brother carried me into the house and laid me on the floor of my room. There I would spend the next two weeks, unable to move save for crawling in excruciating pain to the toilet and bathtub. Once I could make it on all fours down the hall and into the car, Dad took me to see his chiropractor, Dr. Meusich. Almost miraculously, after he worked with the joints in my spine and neck, I was able to walk upright for the first time since the accident.

I became a regular patient of Dr. Meusich's for the next four years. I lived with chronic and at times disabling pain for ten. Sitting was the most painful position, so at school I would often stand up in the back of the classroom or kneel next to my desk. At home, my bed became my desk. I would study on my knees, leaning my body weight forward on my elbows while poring over my textbooks. This incident left me with a lot of time to study; there was not much else I could do.

The only exercise I could tolerate was swimming, and I did a lot of that, twice a day. I learned to count laps with a modified abacus system using rocks. In the beginning there were three rocks stacked on the edge, then six, and eventually I had to gather twenty rocks before entering the water. By the end of the summer, I had become a long-distance swimmer.

Swimming allowed me to access deep meditative states. Lulled by the sound of the water lapping against my ears, the rhythmic motion of my arms entering and leaving the water, and the sensation of being completely supported and buoyant, my consciousness would expand.

I learned simply to let go and access an awareness that was free of the limitations of gravity and a human body. The feeling was one of flying through the water, the same that I had tried to imagine as a child when I turned my washcloth into a dolphin in the bathtub. Now, however, I was accessing an awareness of having been a dolphin. I was tapping into a different layer of old memories. I became aware of incarnations as horses, cats, dogs, sheep, badgers, snakes, elephants, hawks, and many other species. I could communicate with animals because I had been them. I understood the wild places because they had been my habitat both when I was in human form and when I was in animal form. In this expanded awareness, I began to perceive that each of us is part of all that is. There is no separation between our physical form and the immenseness of consciousness, which is "the One." The world as we know it, with its separations and differences, is simply our brains' current interpretation. Discussing such ideas with my own age group was difficult. I would spend time with adults who could track on these levels, but even they were hard to find.

Though my capacity to learn was increasing, school remained a tremendous struggle. I would spend hours on homework and writing assignments. My father would spend hours correcting my spelling mistakes. He could not believe that on a single page I could spell the same word four different ways, all of them wrong. I did well on papers he corrected. On exams that involved writing, my weakness shone like a beacon of idiocy. Tests came back marked with low grades and bathed in red ink: "Great content. Poor spelling." No matter how hard I tried, I could not see my mistakes. My eyes tricked my brain into thinking the word my hand had just written was the one I had intended. Math was no better. I could grasp complicated mathematical concepts, but when I applied them to numerical equations, the numbers seemed to dart all over my brain like a thousand Superballs in a carnival game. I simply could not control where or how the information was stored. No one seemed to understand and I continued to feel very much alone, stuck with a brain that had a very large short circuit.

Partly to soothe my self-image, I sometimes retreated back to art, where I felt confident. I drew, sculpted, and wove baskets from pine needles that had fallen in the backyard, the unique designs of which turned out to be exact replicas of Lakota Sioux baskets. I wondered how my innate talents would ever be useful in reaching my goal of becoming a physician.

Forced to discover tenacity, discipline, and patience, I continued to teach myself to learn in ways unique to my own mind. I took notes in pictures and diagrams. I read the assignment, outlined it in the book, rewrote it in my own picture-note form before class, then took a new set of notes in class, and finally synthesized what I had heard with what I had written by rewriting everything again. I did this for every class, every day.

My friends thought I was nuts. "No one should have to work that hard," they would say. I never shared that my very survival in school depended on it. While they spent their free time developing an active social life, I was home studying. At that point, I didn't really miss the dances, parties, hanging out, sleepovers, and mingling with boys. I seemed to have signed up for other lessons on my way to personal growth and maturity. Besides, it was perfectly relaxing to stay home and spend time with my animal family, which by then had expanded beyond the usual domesticated species.

I had chickens, pheasants, doves, chipmunks, squirrels, and a raccoon. Snakes, especially large snakes, particularly fascinated me. Clarisse, my Burmese python, and Billy Bob, a boa constrictor, were youngsters when they came to live with me but eventually grew to about six feet in length and three inches in diameter. As the snakes got bigger, they became masters of escape. On one memorable morning, while I was getting my cereal in the kitchen, the house was filled with a screech of near terror: "JANINE!" I found Mike in his room, holding his pillow over his chest, standing as far as he could get from his waterbed. There was Clarisse, rolled up like a big circular sausage, warm and cozy on the heated waterbed right where the pillow had been. Intuiting that Billy Bob would not have missed such a delicious opportunity, I grabbed the blankets and threw them back to expose the bottom of the bed. There he was, nicely coiled in the corner, away from where my brother's feet would have reached.

After six months of trying to stabilize my back through abdominal strengthening exercises and swimming, I was able to begin jogging again. I had to start all over. In the first two weeks, I was short of breath, my calves screamed in pain, and I developed shin splints. Each day I pushed myself a little farther, transcending the pain that now involved my entire body from the waist down. I learned to hold my belly button in toward my spine, which seemed to help. This elongated my torso and supported my back.

I experimented with distracting my attention from the pain by concentrating on my breathing. With my conscious mind thus occupied, my subconscious was free to expand, just as it did with swimming. I was developing a certain capacity to tap into my old memories volitionally by creating the internal condition that let them flow. As I ran, I would remember more details of the lives from which those memories came. They arrived in fragments and over time, like bubbles percolating through a thick liquid, releasing their contents one by one into my conscious mind.

I would learn much later in exercise physiology about endorphins and encephalins, the neurotransmitters released during heavy cardiovascular exercise. These chemicals are our built-in opiates. Each time I ran or swam, my body was bathing my brain in its own opium—the "runner's high" that was just entering the public vocabulary at the time.

Running became my addiction. I looked forward to lacing up my running shoes each day and hitting the streets, thankful to check out mentally and let my hardworking brain be flooded with well-being and bliss. Physical training like this felt as familiar to me as breathing, as if I had done it for centuries. Dad began running with me on weekends and after work. Jogging together in the dark had a profound familiarity, too, as if we had done this together in other lifetimes in preparation for battle.

We began entering 10K road races on the weekends. I was never fast enough to come in first, but I had endurance. Soon 10Ks were no longer a challenge. I set my sights on half marathons as a stepping-stone to the ultimate mind-and-body transcendence test, the 26.2-mile marathon. This required that I run for longer and longer periods, which meant going into deeper and deeper states of consciousness. Random yet specific thoughts would suddenly occur, usually about people or places I did not know. One day my friend Mary Strutner popped into my awareness. We had talked about going to a movie over the weekend but hadn't made definite plans. Just as I was thinking I should call her when I got home, I glanced up at the next car driving by. It was Mary and her mother. They honked, jarring me back into ordinary awareness as I waved spontaneously. What had just happened? The fact that she showed up just as I was thinking about her blew my mind and occupied my thoughts for the rest of the run.

This phenomenon began to happen with some regularity. I started to pay attention to the wispy, tangential thoughts quietly streaming through my mind while I was running and at other times and then notice their connections with events that occurred within a few days' time. The phone would ring and a certain person would flash through my awareness. My mom would answer the phone and say that person's name aloud in her greeting. Soon the person would pop into my head even before the phone rang. I was not 100 percent accurate at first, except when it came to my father. I always knew when he was calling well before the ring sounded.

Eventually, I was consistently running three to five miles per day. I often ran late at night, sometimes after my parents had gone to sleep. One morning, after a particularly long fast run the night before, my first steps toward the bathroom brought severe stabbing pain to the inside of both ankles. I immediately plopped back onto the bed. What had happened? The previous night's run had felt great. Reaching for my ankles, I found the area just behind both medial anklebones warm and tender to the touch. As I tried to walk again, the pain eased slightly. I hobbled down the hallway to the kitchen, placed ice cubes in two plastic bags, and tied them to my ankles with dish towels.

Mom, who loved her exercise to have a social aspect, was involved in one of the aerobic dance programs that were popping up everywhere. She made an appointment for me with Dr. Martin Trieb, an orthopedic surgeon specializing in sports medicine who had lectured to the aerobic dance ladies on repetitive use injuries.

Dr. Trieb was a tall, elegantly dressed, slightly balding wizard of the art of diagnosis. He took one look at my legs, pressed on the flexor tendons that run deep behind the inside anklebone, noticed my slight wincing and involuntary retraction away from his painful pressure, and said, "Flexor compartment tendonitis. You need orthotics. I will send Bob in to cast your feet, and we will have you back in two weeks for a fitting. Any questions?"

How could I have registered a question? I was still back at the diagnosis. I said nothing. Mom tried to strike up a conversation about people they knew in common, but he cordially avoided it and slipped out the door to see the next patient. We waited for Bob, the physician's assistant.

The first day I used the orthotics, the pain disappeared. This was my first lesson in sports medicine, and I was more than intrigued. Observation was my strength. And it was what had enabled Dr. Trieb to diagnose and treat my legs. He knew the anatomy, understood each structure's function, and, being told I was a runner, came to a diagnosis. The idea that I, too, might one day have this skill was thrilling. Then I woke up to reality. I was a C+ student with a profound learning disability, not likely to get into a university prestigious enough to impress a future medical school admissions committee. Besides, to even get through college I would have to learn higher math. The abyss was still too big to see across. I chose not to think about it and focused on my classes.

Junior year, I eagerly signed up for a class in human anatomy, figuring this was a first opportunity to test-drive my learning abilities in what amounted to basic training for future doctors. To my delight, my learning in this class came with ease. Anatomy is a three-dimensional subject matter, and my mind had no problem thinking in 3-D, which was why model-building and sculpture had been easy for me. Moreover, I could manually handle the bones, muscles, and tendons during lab sessions, using both the right and left sides of my brain to learn. For once, I felt intelligent. Yet I also felt a familiarity with this subject, as if I already knew it, and it was in my experience at this time as a review—a not-so-subtle reminder of the physician I had once been.

When summer rolled around, it was time for our annual beach tradition. When my parents were in high school in San Jose, many of their friends' parents owned beach houses in Santa Cruz. All the families reserved the last two weeks in August every year to descend on Santa Cruz and wallow in the sun and sand, watching their children enjoy the same pleasures they had as kids.

The tradition continued now that my parents and their friends had children. Rich Simoni had been my father's best friend since they were in the fourth grade. He and his wife, Mary, always invited my family to spend as much time as possible at their beach house with them over the summer. They were like second parents to Mike and me. When everybody showed up at the beach, our group totaled about forty. We would convene at noon just to the right of the main lifeguard stand. My father and Rich would go down early with folding beach chairs, towels, and coolers packed with salami, cheese, baguettes, fruit, drinks, and chips. They always brought along a giant Italian flag to stake in the sand so the others in the tribe could easily find them. As the day progressed, friends and family would show up. I will always remember staggering out of the water after getting pummeled by sand blasters, trying to clear my eyes enough to spot the red, green, and white flag waving in the breeze. The beach chairs accumulated through the afternoon and would end up in a giant crescent shape facing out to sea. These were good times filled with fun and laughter.

Rich and Mary, Bill and Carol at the beach.

There were several jokesters in the group, but no one could top Rich. Together, he and my dad were incorrigible. When they found a woman sunbathing topless or a couple making out down the beach, they would come back to the group, make an announcement, grab their chairs and anyone else's who wanted to join in, and set up a viewing station a few feet from the action. Rich simply had no shame. He would watch these people intensely until they finally noticed and then politely taunt them with questions like, "Are you cold?" or "Are you sure you can still breathe?" I would die of embarrassment while the two men exploded in laughter.

Every day was a treasure, and every night a party. My parents loved this lifestyle and tradition so much that they decided to buy their own beach house when they could afford it. When I first stepped over the threshold of the house they found, I felt hugged by a dazzling fuchsia-colored bougainvillea that grew on the back deck and could be seen through the window. The house was perfect, with ample room to host the crowds of people who often ended up there at sunset. The night before the Wharf to Wharf Race every July, at least twenty people would be packed in, sleeping everywhere. This was after a dinner of pasta, garlic bread, and wine, followed by a party that would rage until late, making it tough to get up the next morning, let alone feel like running.

Three decades later, the dazzling fuchsia bougainvillea out back is still there, bigger than ever. The house is in my name now. Those good times at the beach are all but gone, however. When the two main energies dissipated, their flames extinguished not more than six years apart, the tradition faded away. There was no one big enough in personality and character to fill the void.

Michael, Janine, Carol and Bill at Janine's
high school graduation in 1980.

8

People Medicine

As you the Indigo matures, you are introduced to mentors sent to help guide your way. When you first meet these individuals, you feel immediate recognition; it is as if the teacher has been waiting for you. This phenomenon of crossing paths with highly profound people who end up pointing you toward the trail head of the next phase of your journey is standard throughout the Indigo experience. The information and insights these teachers bring into your experience shape and mold you along the way and allow you to gain perspective on how your life fits into a larger context. Again, disguised under the veil of synchronicity, you experience situations and events that are integral to understanding that there is a larger drama playing out within your experience. You soon learn that nothing is an accident.

For the first three years of high school, I didn't think about applying to a college, still doubting that I could get in. So at the beginning of my senior year, when it was time to apply, I was directionless. Not much help came from my parents, and it didn't occur to me to ask. Mom had just left teaching and launched an aerobic dance company of her own. Dad was always more than busy. I felt bad about requesting more of his time, considering he was still my official paper proofreader.

My friends scattered to colleges all over California and I followed Mary Strutner to San Diego State. Nothing went right for me. As my depression deepened, my interest in studying faded. I found solace in eating large boxes of Post's Honey Bunches of Oats cereal, dry, in my car between classes. It was the only place that felt familiar. Even though I continued to run, I was well on my way to the infamous "freshman fifteen" weight gain—in my case, more like the freshman thirty-eight.

When I got out of the car at Christmas, my parents were visibly shocked. I had indicated nothing over the phone about my depression and the school situation. We spent the next few days talking about it at last. I was honest and told them I hated San Diego State.

A few days later, when Mom and I were sitting on the floor of my bedroom, now devoid of squirrel cages and snake terrariums, wrapping Christmas gifts, she offered, "Janine, you know you don't have to go back." I looked at her as if she were an alien. Not go back? That would be quitting! I could never, no matter how bad it got, just up and quit.

My response felt old, far older than my eighteen years, and it was as if I had just been invited to abandon my men on the battlefield in their moment of greatest need. It was a revival, after three months of nothing, of the channel to my old memories. By the end of that evening, the crack in the dam that Mom had prompted had become a leak, and then a geyser. When Mom suggested I call the California State University campus in San Jose to see if I could transfer in for the winter semester, a weight lifted from my shoulders.

Everything fell into place, as it usually does when you are back on the right track. I was admitted to San Jose State. As the months rolled by, it became increasingly clear that I had ended up exactly where I needed to be.

In April 1981, while out training for the upcoming Wharf to Wharf and trying to drop the excess pounds, and still nursing chronic low back pain, I severely sprained my ankle. I hobbled home and spent a sleepless night on the couch with my leg and ankle elevated. The next morning, my mother insisted on calling Dr. Trieb, who was now the team physician for San Jose State's athletics programs.

After an hour-and-a-half wait, we got to see the doctor. He examined my ankle, explained what needed to happen, then left the room. The stress X ray showed a huge gap between my talus and lateral fibular malleolus, a complete, grade-3 tear, necessitating a cast for six weeks. I felt as if my life could have ended at that moment. I was being sentenced to a cage of sedentary confinement. I began to cry, though not because of the pain. How would I exercise now? I needed to train for the race and with a cast wouldn't even be able to get in the pool. It seemed like the steeplechase of obstacles placed in my path would never cease. It felt as if the Universe had singled me out to see how much I could take. In fact, that was exactly what was happening.

Dr. Trieb learned quickly that I was not a candidate for a plaster cast. When the swelling went down, so did the pain. I began walking on it and then doing aerobic dance in my mom's classes. I also swam occasionally in the ocean and pool. I just could not help myself. He ended up having to replace the cast every week or two. As Bob, the physician assistant, sawed off the old one, splitting it in half, piles of sand, seaweed, twigs, and debris would fall to the floor, giving him ammunition for a lecture.

Dr. Trieb, Bob, and I became close over those six weeks. When I walked in, Dr. Trieb would just shake his head and point to the cast room.

During the last appointment, after removing the final cast, he asked a fateful question: "Janine, what do you want to do with your life—what do you want to be when you grow up?" It was so direct it called for an honest answer.

I glanced at my mother. I knew she still believed the speech pathologist's recommendations back in sixth grade, that I not be encouraged in scholastic endeavors. I am sure as a means of protecting me, she had always let me know I was just average, in everything: looks, grades, and athletics. If I responded to Dr. Trieb truthfully, a lifelong dream would be pulled from the world of my fantasies, becoming a very real, conscious commitment, one I would not be able to set aside in this lifetime. I looked back at Dr. Trieb and said, "I want to go into medicine. I want to be a doctor of some kind."

Mom looked at me with the eyes of empathy that manifest when watching someone struggle with their last bit of strength in the face of inevitable failure. I am sure she wanted to shield me from further disappointment, but it wasn't working.

A smile grew on Dr. Trieb's face. "You like sports, do you?" he asked.

I nodded. He pulled a notepad from his sport-coat pocket, wrote a name and phone number on a page, ripped it out, and handed it to me. He knew I was a student at San Jose State. "This is the number for Sue Anthony, the head women's athletic trainer at State. She is always looking for bright and motivated students to help her in the training room. She is also the course director for the academic athletic training program where I teach."

I had no idea what athletic training was, but I gave Sue a call and set up an appointment for the following week. I met with her in her office, where she was sitting with two student trainers, both of whom, I learned, wanted to become physical therapists. Sue was a physical therapist herself, as well as a certified athletic trainer. San Jose State's program was not certified, so to sit for the certification exam at the end of the four-year curriculum, a student had to complete 1,800 hours of documented clinical work-study. The academic curriculum was intense. The philosophy behind sports medicine was to return the athlete to competition quickly—period. Many of the student athletes were on scholarships and would lose their privileges if they had to sit out a season.

I could hardly believe what I was hearing. Here was a course of study that blended all my interests and strengths. Dr. Trieb had obviously noticed that I already embodied the philosophy and had told Sue to give me the hard sell. I started right away, working alongside the other student trainers.

In class, we spent hours watching videotapes of athletes getting injured and discussing the forces involved. The program included much of the orthopedic and emergency curricula found in medical school, and it came with a built-in residency program. I would occasionally run into premed students who were burdened with classes like calculus, physics, and chemistry. They aspired to be doctors but were learning nothing practical. On the other hand, because the athletic training program was tied to the athletic department, my official transcripts and diploma were going to read "Department of Human Performance." What medical school in the nation would ever admit a phys ed major?

Yet I knew I was precisely where I should be. The Universal Forces had miraculously landed me at the feet of my second Jedi master, Dr. Trieb. Because I was working with my hands while I learned, my mind could absorb the material the way it naturally operated—in 3-D. This allowed me to synthesize vast amounts of information. As in elementary school, I was once again making an end run around the standard curriculum, learning even higher-level concepts through an applied approach.

The maturity I displayed while working with the athletes did not go unnoticed. Dr. Trieb began inviting me to participate in some of his research projects on postoperative outcomes of knee surgery. When one of our players would pull up on the field and grab his knee, we trainers saw it as a grand opportunity. The student trainer who was on the field first to assess it would be assigned to follow the case throughout treatment until the athlete returned to play. If it turned out that the knee needed surgery, we were invited to observe the procedure in the operating room. Dr. Trieb wanted us to know firsthand each stage of the healing process. There I was, as an undergraduate, scrubbing at the sink with real orthopedic surgeons. Mimicking every motion of proper scrubbing technique, I tried to appear at ease. Inside, however, my stomach felt like it would explode with a roomful of monarch butterflies. I could hardly believe I was actually standing there being gowned by the scrub nurse, making sure to keep my hands raised and not touch anything!

During this time, I decided I wanted to be an orthopedic surgeon, like Dr. Trieb. I had practiced this type of medicine on animals since childhood. Working on people was clearly just as rewarding.

9

A Psychic Reading

All of you Indigos are drawn to initiation experiences that mirror the depths of your beingness. You are constantly searching to discover who you truly are. You sense a vastness of intellectual wisdom combined with a supreme physical prowess not understood well by you or those around you. Characteristically, you seek your personal limits and boundaries, constantly testing your mettle against mortal obstacles in search of the deeper meaning in your experiences.

In the summer of 1982, after listening with fascination to Mary Simoni talk of metaphysics and paranormal phenomena, which she had recently begun to delve into, a certain curiosity led me to seek the advice of a psychic reader Mary had consulted. After making the appointment, it dawned on me that she would most likely ask what I had come for. I didn't really know. It seemed there was something I needed to hear that was too deep in my subconscious for me to access it myself. So far, I had been relying on intuition and old memories. Who was I really? Why was my experience of having access into other realms apparently so unique that with everyone except my father I felt like a freak? Was I on the right track? Could I really one day become a physician? What was the point of this grooming process? For what purpose was I born? I needed validation from someone who could see the bigger picture and how I fit into it.

I met the psychic at her home in Willow Glen. Carolyn answered the door. She was smaller than I had envisioned during our brief phone conversation. Her home was modest and neatly kept, though as I followed her to the living room, I was struck by the unexpected decor. Cool white modern carpeting contrasted with sparse conservative furniture, while images and statuettes representing ancient civilizations from around the planet were arrayed on every wall and horizontal surface. The space looked as if someone were playing a cosmic joke in my grandmother's house.

Carolyn, however, was all business. She had a recorder set up, and after clipping a microphone to her collar, she handed a second one to me and began explaining what she would be doing for the next hour. She worked in the realm of the "fantastic," she said, accessing information by asking guidance from beings in other realms. Anyone could do it. One only had to ask properly and from one's highest self. "You must ask for the highest domain. Anything less and you are going to get lower forms of truth," she said.

I realized she was teaching me how to link up as a psychic reader. She had recognized something in me that until that moment had been only an unconscious fantasy. In fact, I longed to access the realms of knowledge I suspected a psychic knew how to tap, the ones I glimpsed while running and swimming. I had always intuited that fuller access would come through when I turned forty-two, though I did not know why.

Carolyn was explaining that each of us has an energy field that holds impressions of our past experiences and people with whom we have been associated. "I can pick up on your energy field and see that you have lived in a forest," she said. "You were part of a large Indian group during the colonial days and resented the white man taking over the land and shooting all the wild animals. What does that mean to you today? Indians are free. They have vast amounts of land. They relate more to nature, and their gods and religions are uncluttered. So you are drawn to the simple forms of expression rather than the complicated cultural forms of today. This might show up as compassion for people who are being taken advantage of. It might be a love of animals, maybe even forest animals.

"I also see you having lived during the colonial times like Little House on the Prairie. You like to take things apart and start over from the ground up. It could best be described as a tremendously creative, artistic soul tendency.

"You are a very old soul, a spiritually advanced soul. Having had great experiences and lived more than likely in most of the high civilizations, you would be very knowledgeable, very adept, able to breeze through this life. However, another way of looking at it is that souls have various destinies. Some are given superior wisdom because their destinies are greater than others."

She continued, "A psychic reader can pick up on your many lives, the highly cultured ones—Egypt, the Incas, Babylonia, the Renaissance, the Crusades, the Aztecs. Who is to say whether you lived them all, or whether you are living them all now simultaneously, because we can. This is how it happens. Just a fraction of our identity is manifested through physical form. The rest is elsewhere. We are living on more than one plane of existence. We could go into the Lemurian and Atlantean periods with you—the temple of beauty, where there was interest in herbs, dyes, makeup, and design. So you have an architectural, interior design background from way back then—also engineering, and an interest in spacecraft.

"I have to talk about Ireland a bit. I sense your origin is interwoven with that culture as well—the little people, fairies and the wee ones, and interest in plants, harmony, rhythm, the ocean, horses, all these things of nature. I see a tremendous balance in the soul between the simple, the fantastic, and the advanced—simple meaning pagan, down to earth; fantastic meaning science fiction, creative, inventive; advanced meaning higher learning, culture, the arts, acting, the classics, literature. This means there is a lot to draw from.

"On the other hand, you are not all that confident of your abilities. You have a lot of potential that you are not using, which is interesting to me. You do not believe you can make it, you do not really believe it is your fortune. It is.

"You have writing ability and are creative. I think you are sensitive and could be a receiver yourself. You are not functioning on an intuitive level as much as you could be.

"Oh, one more thing. About people you think you have been with before—you have. They could be linked into your other lives or into your original community. God creates souls with certain affinities for one another. We have our soul family, sometimes even a soul mate. The masculine part of you, your ideal mate wherever he is—whether he is down here or up there—you will unite with him when the time comes to absorb back into the Godhead. It is an idealized love, which does not take away from the other loves along the way."

She continued, talking about parallel souls, astral planes, and past lives, then suddenly interrupted herself. "Do you comprehend all of this?" she asked. "Some people just look at me...."

I nodded yes, even though my present-day mind was hearing what she was saying for the first time. The familiarity of the images, the places, the time periods, their connections with elements in my dreams, and the way she was answering my unasked questions left me feeling...unearthed.

She was describing my life as I knew it, as if she could get inside my most personal thoughts and hear the whispered knowings that sailed through my mind without language. How did she know? An image came to mind. I remembered as a kid looking horizontally through the green edge of a laminated glass tabletop, each layer a world of its own yet connected with the one above and the one below, their separateness only an illusion. Carolyn had just said that we live on many more planes than the physical. Why can't we access the rest of ourselves? Why are our past selves so cut off from our present personalities? Wouldn't it be a whole lot easier if we could just pop into a lifetime with all the knowledge and skills we gained in the previous ones?

As Carolyn was coming up for air, I shot a question at her: "What do you see in terms of my destiny this time around?"

"You have a multiple destiny, it seems. The homemaker role is not exactly the ultimate destiny for you. Are you interested in a particular health problem, perhaps mental health? I am seeing brain structures and do not know what to make of it. I see you in any of many fields—psychology, medicine, teaching, research, laboratory work. The possibilities are immense! You can be assured of almost automatic success in these areas. So if you are looking for a go-ahead in these fields, go ahead, because you are gifted in them. You will make some contribution through research or small group work. I almost see a home or community structure where you will be working and studying as a doctor or something—a clinic, maybe, or a rehab center."

Suddenly, she switched topics. "What is going on with you and relationships? I am getting a big blank."

I smiled back. "Nothing."

"It is not yet time. I know you sense this. The heart wants, yet something else is saying it is not time. That something is the intuition. The intuition is very wise. You need to work with it more.

"I think your intuition goes through cycles. It happens when you are open and relaxed. I think you have some recreational outlet, like swimming, hiking, or riding, that you unwind with. When you are doing it, you are open to reception. You unravel a lot of that penned-up energy—which is all earth, by the way, heavy earth energy you pick up from other people. That is the price of sensitivity.

"Just as picking up a radio signal requires clear reception, if you are going to get good channeling, you need to clear yourself out. In later years, you will be drawn to work with the energy centers called chakras. If you know how to clear those centers out, you will be able to receive and also function as cleanly as is possible on the earth plane."

I was nodding my head in understanding even though I had never heard the word chakra before and didn't know what channeling was.

"These are very active times for you. I see you finishing school. I think you are going to go on. You are going to go on. A master's? A doctorate? The soul seems to have a strong inclination to do that.

"Again, I see this great…when I say 'potential'—wow! I am getting hit with electrical impulses!—great potential out here, yet I don't know if you are going to connect with it."

Just as Carolyn called out "wow!" I observed a spark arc from the cord of the tape recorder up to Carolyn's microphone, creating a popping sound that was recorded on the tape. I stared at her, dumbfounded. Was that an accident, or had some other force in the room with us just made an electrical punctuation mark on the subject of potential?

She wanted to know if I was dedicated to my studies or resented the discipline. I told her I was dedicated but that my dyslexia had made it really difficult to learn how to read, write, and do math.

"But you see," she said, "the spirit is gifted. This is not a handicap, it is a gift. You blanket your inner calling because of what society says or because of scars from the past. But knowing the gift is there, as it is there for every one of us, should help you to endure, to prove that you can overcome."

She added that if I saved this tape and played it in twenty years, it would have even more meaning for me. "I feel as though I am talking to two realities," she said, "the intensely mature you and the still-developing you. You are simply unaware of your greater identity and potential."

I jumped back into what was becoming a conversation. "That might explain why ever since I can remember I have felt like I'm being groomed for something."

She stopped me short. "You are!"

Intrigued, I pressed on. "I have to separate myself from what is going on with other people. They seem to have to go through learning experiences that I don't."

She spoke over me again. "That is very perceptive. That is you working on the spiritual plane. You are being taught by master teachers astrally, even though you don't know it."

I asked what else she saw ahead for me.

"I see an animal farm—now that is a strange thing to say. Are you going to be breeding horses? Raising horses, thoroughbreds?"

"I have always been drawn to horses, and one of my dreams is to raise thoroughbreds," I replied, almost disbelieving her uncanny accuracy.

"Wherever you live eventually, I see wide-open spaces, being out in nature and having a lot of animals. I see it on the outskirts, in the foothills—an area by the sea."

The session must have been coming to an end, since Carolyn began to summarize.

"Do you see anything more specific for me?" I asked. "You have given me generalities. Any specifics at all about people, or situations?"

"I see soul destiny in the areas of neurology, the study of the brain, the study of human behavior, which could mean psychiatry, psychology, and related fields. I see you in teaching positions as well. You will be drawn to explore the energy fields of the body known as chakras and how they relate to the energy fields of the planet. You will access these forces and use them in your work.

"I see you also in a city planning type of program where you are researching community trends. This is probably totally out of mind right now, yet it is there. Now what does this mean? It means there could be alterations in our present-day cities, doesn't it? We do not know what those alterations are. Maybe an earthquake. Maybe a whole new restructuring program that involves human behavior. 'Cultural trends' means mind trends, because everything we see manifested first happens in the mind.

"I also see a reluctance in coming into this lifetime. Before your soul took up residence in the fetus, you were shooting through the galaxy with a tail of silver and sparks, heading to another planet. Coming to Earth was a last-minute decision. You were instructed to come here and you obeyed. However, it was not easy for you to slow down your vibration to be in this dense earth energy. This was part of your learning disability when you were young.

"Your brain is wired differently. The circuits are different from those of the humans—now, that is a strange thing to say, my goodness!

"You have come into this time to assist in a great awakening that will involve tremendous change in the human thought field and massive earth changes. It will be a time of great change on every level. Many souls will decide to leave—choosing death, by remaining unconscious, over rebirth into a higher consciousness. You will be part of helping people navigate through these changes, perhaps helping plan for the new cities that will need to be built from the ground up—a whole new beginning."

At that point, I practically had to lift my chin up from the floor. What she was saying matched the glimmers of thought that streamed through my mind constantly, never staying long enough to attach words to them. It was so easy to brush them off. What exactly was she tapping into?

Carolyn, who must have seen how much her last words had shaken me, looked at her watch and politely but promptly ended the session. I vowed to myself that when my studies in whatever aspect of medicine called me were complete, I would immerse myself in learning about the fairies, the wee ones, ancient civilizations, mythology, and metaphysical history. Otherwise, I tucked the session away in my mind as yet another clue as to where this peculiar life of mine was heading.

10

Initiation of "the Third Kind"

Indigo young adults appear to push themselves to superhuman limits, as if the challenges are some kind of game. You constantly drive yourself toward a goal that is yet unknown. It appears to outsiders that you are on a mission to accomplish a task on a hidden schedule. The Indigo agenda is running headlong into the consciousness shift of 2012 foretold by many ancient cultures including the Mayan, Egyptian, and Hopi. This prediction coincides with astrophysical changes scientists are observing as the base resonant frequency of our planet (Schuman Frequency) is increasing exponentially and the magnetics of the planet are decreasing at the same rate. Where these two lines intersect is called "the Zero Point," which will occur sometime during the year 2012. Humankind as we know it today has never experienced this in its short ten-thousand-year history on this planet. No one can predict what will happen. The Zero Point last occurred twenty-six thousand years ago. The Indigos subconsciously know time is running out and their journey here on Earth is to assist those humans who have done their work in the transition from the third dimension of consciousness to the fourth and fifth.

You are the children of the fifth dimension who have been specifically chosen to come in this time, for this purpose. You can feel the planet's energy rising and many of you cannot sleep at night because you sense a change is coming. Some of you have chosen bodies that cannot keep up with these changes and have developed resistance within your "instruments." These symptoms typically manifest *as insomnia, pain, adrenal exhaustion, depression, or a sense of buzzing coming from deep within your body.*

Mom hosted Thanksgiving 1982 at our house. Though ours was a tight Italian tribe, I could never quite shake the feeling of being different and as if I needed to remain in hiding—ever the observer rather than part of the human species. But with these people, I felt as comfortable as I could anywhere. Whenever we were all together, good times were had.

After dinner, the men were strewn across the couches, chairs, and ottomans flipping channels in search of the "best game." When they landed on the replay of the October 1982 World Ironman triathlon competition held on the Big Island of Hawaii, the channel changing stopped. They were transfixed, and so was I. The bodies on the television screen were sleek, strong, muscular, and in constant motion. This was way more than a marathon. The sport of triathlon, still in its infancy at that time, included a marathon, but only after the athlete had completed a 2.5-mile ocean swim and a 112-mile bike race, in this case across scorching lava fields against 30-mph headwinds.

As the announcer called out the standings of the leaders, the program would flip to vignettes about them. We learned that they trained four to six hours a day. Some had quit work; some found flexible jobs that allowed for so much time dedicated to their athletic pursuits. Others just arranged their lives around the training requirements, working out in the middle of the night or at 4 a.m. These people were possessed.

As the competition unfolded, so did a drama between the leading female triathletes, Julie Moss and Kathleen McCartney. Five miles from the marathon's finish line, Julie, the underdog, was enjoying a comfortable lead, looking good on camera with long strong strides, sweat pouring down her face, her white visor rhythmically bobbing up and down. Kathleen was at least a mile behind her, yet still far ahead of the pack. The commentators told Julie's story—how she had entered the competition as a research project for her thesis in exercise physiology, how hard she had trained, how many setbacks she had sustained. She had come to Hawaii to finish—at all cost. And there she was, attaining a goal she had set for herself, knowing the only person who could deliver it was herself.

Julie's story sent a ripple of change through me. With my eyes fixed on the competition, I began a conversation with my heart—not in words, but in images and whispered meanings. What was I made of? How real were the limits I had perceived for myself, or others had presumed? Are there any limits except the ones we impose on ourselves? I already knew what it meant to face and overcome obstacles. School was going well at that point. It had not become easy, but I had a sense of accomplishment and pride. Did I also have what it took to meet one of the biggest physical challenges to the human body?

As Julie closed in on the two-mile mark, her stride began to get choppy, and her face winced in pain. All of us watching let out a collective gasp as her legs began to lock up with muscle spasms. The announcers were commenting on how hot it had been all day, and how difficult it had been for the athletes to maintain adequate hydration and nutrition. I knew from my training that this was heat illness, a serious medical emergency that would quickly lead to heat stroke if left untreated or the athlete continued the activity. Julie continued. Disoriented and spent, she was relying solely on willpower generated from somewhere deep inside.

Half a mile from the finish, with Kathleen now just a few minutes behind her, Julie stumbled for the first time and hit the pavement, scraping her knees. She languished on the ground for only seconds. Regaining her stance on her own, with blood running down her shins, she began first walking, then jogging as her leg control would allow. She stumbled and fell repeatedly, always getting up and persevering, ever so slowly now, toward the finish line. As the tension mounted, I felt an overwhelming sense of compassion for this woman, a kinship with another human being such as I had never known before, as if she were acting out every struggle I had ever experienced.

Just twenty yards from the finish, Julie collapsed onto the hot pavement, apparently losing continence of stool and urine. With her running shorts stained and the evidence oozing down her inner thighs, she began to crawl on all fours. The race officials were struggling as well. Normally, they would have run to her aid and begun prepping her for intravenous hydration, but they held back, since touching her would immediately disqualify her. Even as she crawled, she wavered. She looked like a gangly foal trying to stand for the first time. The crowd was going nuts! The energy from their cheers seemed to help her continue forward. Just ten yards from the finish, Kathleen McCartney sailed past her and took the yellow tape. Then she came back and encouraged her friend the last few feet. Julie did not stop forward motion until she was safely over the white finish line. Crawling on bleeding knees, having defecated in her shorts, delirious with pain and exhaustion, she had done it. She had accomplished her goal without assistance.

Through the tears that come when something touches us in our deepest places, I knew I, too, would take on this ultimate challenge. As the credits of the broadcast rolled on the screen, I made a pact with my spirit. I needed to know if I possessed the grit and will I had just witnessed. This felt strangely requisite to my grooming process.

I wasted no time. The next day I went out and purchased a ten-speed road bike with toe clips, riding shorts and shoes, a water bottle, and a helmet. At school I arranged for a staff card for the swim complex so I could use the twenty-five-meter pool during staff swim times. For spring semester I was able to arrange my classes so I could devote two to four hours per day to heavy exercise. On the weekends I would work out four to six hours a day. I turned out to be a much stronger cyclist and swimmer than I had ever been a runner. It called for speed, power, courage, balance, agility, and cunning. I spent hours alone, challenging myself to the next personal best in time and distance. I grew addicted to the experience of pushing my body to its limits and finding there weren't any.

After about five months of training, I felt ready to find out how I would do and what my split times would look like in competition. I invited Sue, the head women's athletic trainer and herself an avid runner, to participate with me in the Sea World Women's Triathlon on May 5, 1983, as a relay team. I would do the swim and the cycling, and she would finish with the run.

I left the water that day in the first third of the pack, with "the swimmers," those known for their prowess in the water. My swim-bike transition went off without a hitch; I had been practicing it for weeks. The bike route was fairly well marked, and again I felt primed and ready as I attacked the hills. I felt like I was flying. The fifteen-mile bike ride felt like a sprint. I was back at the Sea World parking lot sooner than I had ever dreamed. I scanned the rows of bike stands for my spot, where

Sue would be. With my eyes trained on hers, I squeezed the brake only at the last moment. She reached out, grabbed the baton, and took off toward the running course.

We ended up taking fifth overall out of seventy-five relay teams. Not bad for a first outing. I gained invaluable knowledge of how to conduct a three-leg race that uses different muscles, equipment, and mediums. I was also introduced to the culture of triathletes. They were constantly stopping and helping one another.

Races became tests of how my training was going, but the real juice of this entire experience was always in the training sessions, where I could transcend the limits of personality and access the deepest layers of self. As I pushed ever-faster times and ever-longer distances, my internal boundaries expanded as well.

That summer I competed in three Bud Light Tin Man races, triathlons half the length of Hawaii's Ironman: a 1.5-mile swim, 56-mile bike ride, and 13-mile run. In the early 1980s, these events were used as official qualifying races for Hawaii's Ironman. To participate in that, an athlete had to complete at least five of these races in less than five hours. I achieved this in all three races.

Yet as the weeks and months went by, I had my share of setbacks. With all the vigorous hill training in the mountains, both on the bike and on foot, I developed bilateral Achilles tendonitis crepitans, an inflammation of the Achilles tendon that allows fluid to build up between the tendon and the tendon sheath. It causes a crackling, grinding sound during flexion and extension of the ankle. This was a problem. It meant that the tendon, if stressed in any unusual way, could easily rupture. And a rupture meant surgery and casting for six months. Living in ice was my standard fare; however, the real treatment for this advanced condition was the dreaded four-letter word: rest.

Every time I tried to run, the pain and the grinding made my stomach queasy. I knew I had to stop. That would have been the mature thing to do. But I was so close to qualifying—how could I quit now? There had to be a way to decrease the motion at the ankle joint and train through it while it healed. That was the whole philosophy behind sports medicine. I decided to tape my ankles before running and cycling so as to lock out all possibility of flexion and extension. I could keep going and make my fourth qualifying race, less than a month away. Most athletic trainers would have found it difficult to reverse the pattern of tape strips by 180 degrees, as taping your own joints requires, but not me. My brain had spent its entire life having to reverse everything it perceived so I could function in the "normal" world. For once I could give it full rein to do what it did naturally, think upside down and backward. My reversed tape jobs were perfect—tight, clean, no wrinkles. Every morning I would set off down the street moving more like Frankenstein than a high-level athlete.

My body, I was learning, was simply a reflection of my mind, and a strong will, belonging to spirit, controls the mind. This realization carried over into many areas of my life. If I wanted something to change, I needed to change how I thought about it. With this realization, I began to reconsider the previously far-fetched dream of becoming a doctor. I also began to get a strong feeling that I would meet someone who would see me for who I was and help me achieve this goal. In a journal entry in January 1984, I described him as tall with blonde hair, and named Joseph.

My cognitive abilities were improving. I was sure the triathlon training had everything to do with it. The image of looking through the edge of a laminated glass tabletop came to mind again. The world behind my eyes at any given stage of learning was like a single layer of glass, apparently complete until my mind opened up to take in more layers of knowing and data. I was realizing that our perception of reality is limited by what our brain is able to decipher. And as I was learning in science classes, the entire perceptive spectrum of our five senses, the source of all input to the brain, is but a small fraction of what is actually out there.

Genie shoe and ruler at Seabright beach.

11

A Companion for the Journey

*I*n general, Indigos have a difficult time understanding societal norms and *customs. You see ceremonial rituals as meaningless to your overall mission. As observers of the human experiment of which you are reluctantly a part, you tend to wonder what all the fuss is about. Indigos do not see the point in graduation ceremonies, awards ceremonies, weddings, and funerals. You have such a deep, self-assured core, and feel so out of place in this time and space, that receiving an accolade or celebrating an accomplishment with others holds no joy. Because you are incredibly sensitive to those around you, many of you will participate just to keep the peace. Inside, however, you may be dying. You cannot believe you find yourself participating in these trivial traditions, but if you do not participate, your cover will be blown. You are in this world, but try as best you can to not be part of it. Many of you seem to others to be aloof and above it all. This attitude is difficult to hide, because you are. You have come into this time and space to guide and teach; getting too involved with the natives is on your forbidden list.*

By the spring semester of 1984, I was one race away from qualifying for the Hawaii Ironman in the fall. I arranged my classes so Wednesdays were completely free to do a mock triathlon. I would ride my bike forty miles over an 1,800-foot mountain range to the beach, run ten miles on the soft sand, swim two miles in the open ocean, and then ride back.

At school, I needed one more lower division biology class without a lab to complete my minor. I signed up for Biology 140, Human Sexuality. The first day of class, I sat in the second row of desks that ran from the front of the classroom to the back and watched the students filtering in. It was a shock when through the door walked none other than Maggie Herning-McHenry, a longtime friend of my parents from the beach. Maggie was like a fun aunt to me. I had grown up with her and her kids in the summers in Santa Cruz. Maggie had been a nurse before she got married and was taking some classes to get her feet wet again before retaking her nursing board exams.

The instructor, who had been sitting in the back next to the projector, walked up the center aisle and stood behind the podium, looking down the entire time. The lack of eye contact was a bad sign. You could feel the collective disappointment fill the room. After giving the textbook assignments and exam dates, he walked back to sit next to the projector and asked that the lights be turned off. Each class period was the same; the students would filter in, take their usual seats, and get ready for slides of genetic mishaps such as trisomy 21, Turner's, and XXY syndromes.

Over the days and weeks, one guy began to capture my interest. He always came in late, walked directly in front of the rows of seats, and sat one row to my left and one seat back, just out of my peripheral vision. He stood out for several reasons. He wore muted Hawaiian shirts made with the fabric inside out. As he walked, his shoes slapped on the floor, signaling they were too big for his feet. He had a high forehead and sparse hair, which made his age difficult to guess, though he looked older than most of the other students. Once the lights were out and the slides were being shown, his whispering to my left was a constant distraction. Tuning into the discourse, I realized he was asking questions and answering them himself! I had taken abnormal psychology the previous semester and remembered that schizophrenics hear spontaneous voices in their heads and respond to them. Purely out of curiosity, I started paying attention to see what other strange behaviors he displayed.

One day during the slideshow, I felt a soft tap on my left shoulder. In the dark, I quickly turned my head and there he was, leaning into the row between us and staring directly at me just inches from my face.

"Excuse me, ma'am, I seemed to have dropped my ruler in your book bag," he said, gesturing toward the floor.

I looked down. Indeed, my red book bag was resting with the zipper slightly open next to my chair. Still working with the football team at the time, I was unaccustomed to being addressed so politely. Besides, I had never been called ma'am before. I responded, "Okay, why don't you just go in there and get it?"

He replied, "I could never just reach inside a woman's bag without her permission."

This politeness staggered me. I reached down, retrieved the six-inch plastic ruler, and handed it over. He thanked me and returned to his work. This was my opportunity to glance at his desk. He was working out physics problems, reading the questions aloud to himself, and answering them. Well, at least that ruled out schizophrenia. The clothing still needed elucidation, however.

After class, as Maggie and I walked down the long hallway toward the elevators, I told her what had happened. Based on his strange behavior, did she think he had a personality disorder? She, too, had noticed the clothing and the whispering, but said, "I think he's kind of cute."

I had been too busy trying to figure him out psychologically to notice, but she was right. He was dark-haired and dark-skinned, about five-foot-nine, with a sleek runner's body, big brown eyes, and a graceful gait. Being conditioned not to exude vibes that the athletes could misinterpret, I was not in the habit of looking at men that way. I continued to watch him, however.

As if our professor sensed that his students could not take one more class of boring slides and silence, he announced one day as class began, "Dr. Harry Genant of UCSF will be speaking this Thursday night about AIDS and HIV. I encourage all of you to attend, as it is pertinent to human genetics. I would like to have a class discussion about his lecture next week." He then took his seat in the back and signaled to have the lights turned off.

A discussion, I thought, what a concept. In early 1984, information about AIDS and HIV was just seeping into public awareness, and researchers at the School of Medicine at the University of California–San Francisco were at the forefront of studying the problem. I had noticed flyers announcing the AIDS lecture, but it conflicted with Dr. Trieb's advanced athletic training class. I could possibly pull an A in that class if everything went according to plan. Missing it even once could jeopardize my final grade.

At the next session of our human sexuality class, the guy to my left was wearing a bright ocher and green shirt and blue-and-white-striped shorts with his usual oversized loafers. I tried not to stare as I analyzed his fashion choices. Maggie came in with a big smile and as usual sat to my right. She whispered, "Did you go?" I shook my head. "Did you?" I asked. She nodded, raising her eyebrows and opening her eyes wide to express big news.

Our professor began, "So how many of you attended the lecture?" Hands went up. "What did you think?"

To my surprise, Maggie raised her hand and began speaking even before being called on. "I am a former nurse and I found the lecturer, Dr. Genant, almost impossible to understand. He was pompous and insensitive, completely missing the opportunity to deliver a useful message. This is an important topic, and people need to be as informed as possible, not shown off to."

Wow, I thought, that's a pretty strong opinion. Perhaps I shouldn't have missed it. Just then, without raising his hand, the crazy guy to my left spoke up. His voice was booming, clear, and articulate. The chatting and whispers that had started after Maggie spoke stopped immediately. "I am sorry that you were unable to understand such a well-thought-out presentation on a complicated subject," he said. "I have worked with Dr. Genant at UCSF doing research on DNA gene regulation, and I can attest to his ability to teach to all levels. If his presentation was that difficult for you to comprehend, perhaps it is you who should question your level of intellect and education."

No one dared mutter another word. I was frozen in my chair. I couldn't even look at Maggie, but I could feel the anger welling up in her.

As she and I left the classroom that day, she started venting about being verbally eviscerated by some pompous asshole who was crazy and wore shoes that were too big. I, on the other hand, was completely blown away. He had used language in a manner I had never heard from a student on this campus. It had a familiar ring; he sounded like my father and his attorney friends.

Maggie's scathing comments went on for several more class sessions, until one afternoon as we got up to leave, there he was, walking directly in front of us. As he saw us coming, he held the door, and the three of us ended up walking down the hallway together. It was not long before Maggie started in on him. He came right back, apologizing eloquently but standing by what he had said. The discussion was lively, pointed, and honest, but they did not stop arguing. When I had to turn down another walkway to get to my next class, I interjected, "Will you two be all right, or should I call the campus police to mediate this debate?" They shook their heads, and continued on together toward the student center.

Now he began hanging back after class and striking up a conversation with us. Maggie did not want anything to do with him and would excuse herself into the restroom as we passed it. He would chatter on to me. One day it was about what he had done the night before in the San Francisco bathhouses, a common hangout for gay men. Did he want me to think he was gay? That did not shake my foundation a bit. I had a lot of gay friends, of my own and through my parents. At one point, he invited me to join him in the bathhouses, which was absurd since the bathhouses were for men.

I responded, "No, thanks, I hate everything about being in San Francisco."

For the first time, he actually stopped talking and just stared. I could see the wheels turning in his head as he tried to find his next best line.

This guy is a riot, I thought. He can talk incessantly about nothing in particular, feeling comfortable as long as his lips are moving. He doesn't seem to mind that I just listen, smile, and keep my thoughts to myself. I then blurted out, "What is your name, by the way?"

He looked at me as if I had just run a sword through his chest and stopped talking. He was obviously reluctant to give a straightforward response. "José. José Chibras. What do people call you?"

Feeling like I had just entered a rehearsal for a really bad Western, I replied in my best Texas drawl, "Some people around these parts call me Janine, others call me Coon, and others don't call me at all."

He smiled, appreciating the banter.

The Thursday before spring break, he asked if he could borrow my textbook for a few days to prepare for the exam. I looked at him dumbfounded. I was planning to review the book and my notes over the week long break at the beach house with my parents. "No, I will be needing it to review for the exam. Don't you have your own book?"

He hadn't bought the book, he replied, as he was only taking the class to pass the time until he started school next fall.

What school in the fall? I thought. Knowing that I was being baited to ask the obvious, I held my tongue.

He then asked, "What will you be doing over spring break?"

I hesitated, still wondering if he was a loon. Most kids at State were from working families who could barely make ends meet. If I told him, I ran the risk of sounding spoiled or stuck-up. Just then, out of my mouth it came, "I'll be at my family's beach house."

"Beach house!" he exclaimed. "I love the beach. I graduated from UC Santa Cruz and spent most of my college years swimming and studying in the sand. I know a lot of families who have beach houses over there." Then he started rattling off the names of families who owned the largest houses that hung over the cliffs on the biggest lots. Everybody knew these names, but I had never met anyone who actually knew these families personally. I thought this guy must be pulling my leg in all directions.

He nevertheless kept trying. "What day works best for you, and what time should I show up?"

What? I hadn't invited him anywhere, particularly not to the beach house. Just to keep him off balance, I responded, "Is this like a date?"

He backpedaled. "Well, no, not officially. I am going to meet you at your parents' beach house, and we'll decide what to do then."

Was he thinking my parents wouldn't be there and he might just get lucky? I responded, "Sure, my parents would love to meet you."

At that point, he started negotiating about the book. He would bring me something very dear to him as collateral for borrowing the book for just two days. I agreed, just to see what he thought could possibly equal the value of a well-used, carefully outlined textbook just days before the exam.

The next day, after class, he pulled out a brown burlap bag and removed from it a woman's small leather...genie shoe?...jeweled, beaded, and pointed at the tip. He proceeded to tell me it was one of a pair he had received when he graduated from the Esalen School of Magic Carpet Riding. His carpet was at home, along with the other shoe.

That was pretty creative, I thought. I handed him the book and carefully lifted the shoe from his hand. We exchanged phone numbers, and I found myself writing out the address and directions to the beach house, while part of me watched the scene from a third-person perspective, with narration. "Are you nuts? Why are you giving this crazy guy your number and directions to the house? What if he turns out to be a serial killer?" But something deep inside was urging me to go ahead. Besides, my mind chipped in, this guy was just full of BS and would probably never show up. As I finished writing, I looked up and said, "If you do actually come, bring your swimsuit. I'm in training for the Ironman and will be swimming two miles in the ocean that day. You're invited if you're game."

Not only did I make sure Mom was going to be there, I also invited Mary Simoni, who had just completed her training as a marriage, child, and family therapist, specializing in sex offenders. I figured I ought to get a professional assessment of this guy's mental state before this went any further.

The rapping on the door announced his arrival. Mom, Mary, and I, who had been giddy with excitement all morning, took our rehearsed places. As I opened the door, José nervously shoved a bouquet of flowers in my face. He was wearing navy-blue suit pants, a light-blue dress shirt, and loafers, ones that fit. He looked like he was going to an interview.

He walked in as if he owned the place. Introductions were made, and the conversation was easy. Mom and Mary, try as they might, could not get a straight answer out of him regarding where he lived, his family, or his future plans. All he would say was that he would be furthering his studies in the biological sciences in the fall. They were pleasantly and politely shut down, something neither of these women was used to. They could extract information from turnips. Once the conversation was clearly finished, I suggested that we change and go down to the beach. As José got up, I could not but notice that the fabric under his arms was drenched in perspiration. Perhaps he was not as bulletproof as he appeared.

He had not been ocean swimming in many months, so I did not push him beyond two lengths of the beach. When we got out of the water, I could see he was not used to the water temperature either; he was shaking uncontrollably. We walked back to where we had left our towels on the sand and lay in the sun, trying to warm up. We talked— that is, he talked. Through many convoluted stories and sidetracked thoughts, I gradually learned that he was twenty-five years old, had graduated from UCSC in 1982 as a premed student, had done research at UCSF in the summers, had traveled extensively in Asia and Europe the year after he graduated (his sister was a flight attendant and gave him free tickets), and had spent the last year studying for the MCAT and applying to medical schools. He had been accepted at the University of Illinois at Chicago and was taking six classes between four colleges that spring to get his mind back in study mode.

As he spoke, there was a flicker of recognition in my mind. Here he is, just as I had written in my journal, Joseph, the person who would show me the way to medical school. The only thing that did not match was his height and the color of his hair.

We spent the rest of that semester and the summer together. In the mid-1980s, disco was everything. We would go dancing all night, mixing our two groups of friends. José always insisted on treating everybody. I knew he had not held a job for at least two years, and though he was very refined socially, I sensed that he was not from a particularly wealthy family. I wondered how he did it.

As we got to know each other, I learned how it was for him growing up an intelligent Hispanic boy. He knew all along that he was going to be a doctor, even though teachers and advisors told him not to get his hopes up. But José not only assumed he deserved the best in life, he also demanded it from himself and others. He wanted the best cars, the best clothing, the nicest home, and what he perceived as the best occupation that would demand the highest respect. Having myself been advised all my life to settle for average, I found his attitude inspiring, and infectious.

I watched as he consciously culled only the best into his experience. His cup was not just full, it was bubbling over with possibilities. He knew life was supposed to be fun—and fun we had. We were constantly cracking up about something. I had become so serious, always trying to prove I could succeed. He saw the child in me and invited her out to play. I was amazed, too, at the way he could walk into a room of strangers and in a few minutes have them all laughing and joking with him. After all the years of playing alone, I was learning in his company how to engage people in conversation and make them feel at ease.

His encouragement was relentless. I would tell him about my learning problems, but he did not seem to get it. All he saw was a bright, talented, beautiful young woman who was capable of most anything, even solving common-sense problems like fixing his car or changing a flat tire. He, on the other hand, had a linear, analytic mind. Spatial thinking and manual execution didn't come as easily, but he could calculate a complicated math problem faster than I could punch it into the calculator. He could remember miniscule pieces of data. In conversations, just for fun, he would run circles around a subject, throwing in true facts and figures, and then draw some wacky conclusion. The other person would be so confused by the process and dazzled by the facts, they would not know which end was up.

One day he asked what I wanted as a career. I told him medical school had always been in the back of my mind, but being practical, I had contingency plans. Chiropractic medicine was one option, so was physical therapy or physician's assistant.

Taking all this in, he paused for a moment and then began blasting about always believing in yourself. "Never listen to anyone who says you can't do it. My guidance counselors used to take one look at my brown Latino skin and start tracking me toward wood shop rather than physics lab. If you want something badly enough, Jakey"—the nickname he had given me—"you can do anything."

Before he left for Illinois, he said he loved me. The concept of being in love was unfamiliar ground for me. I knew what unconditional love from my animals felt like. My one experience of it from a human being was with my father. José, on the other hand, wore his heart on his sleeve. I could feel his desperation as he left. I simply didn't possess those kinds of feelings. What, then, was I feeling? All I knew was that I liked José a lot and loved to be with him because he was so damned funny and entertaining.

When we were apart, he was a jealous mad man, and when we were together at Christmas and spring break, he was his jovial, playful self. This rollercoaster of emotion made me question his emotional stability, and therefore my own. How could something be so good when we were together and get so bad once we were apart? I chalked it up to yet another idiosyncrasy of the human psyche, underscoring again that I was not fully one of these beings. I did not feel or behave as most of them did. The feeling of jealousy was so unfamiliar that I could not even begin to try to understand it. It reminded me of being suffocated and held against my will. I flashed back to the scene as an infant looking through the bars of my crib for the last time. Even that situation felt as if it was harkening back to elements in an old memory when I was dungeoned under fraudulent charges. Under no circumstances would my freedom be compromised. I was just trying to get through Earth School so I could get on to whatever I had come into this life to do.

Throughout this time, José kept encouraging me to set my sights on medical school—the first person ever to do so. "You are smart, Jakey. You can do anything you set your mind to," he would say. "Trust me, if I could get in, you can too. I will help you." His efforts were not completely unselfish. He wanted me with him and was trying to figure out a way. We both knew my declared major in human performance, even with the biology minor, posed an obstacle. On exams, even when I knew the information cold, I would often fill in wrong answers. My eyes and brain still could not be trusted to find the correctly numbered bubble in the linear sequence.

One day on the phone, he offered an alternative route. "What if you got a master's degree in public health?" This idea percolated in my mind and dropped into the place where thoughts go to be animated by the spirit. I did not want to work in public health but was more than willing to shoot for the moon and use it as a stepping-stone. I could complete the medical school requirements, a year each of physics and organic chemistry, at the same time. Why not?

Janine leaving the water at the Mt. Madonaa triathlon.

12

Mount Madonna

Being completely connected to the earth and nature continues to be a guiding theme of the Indigo's experience into adulthood. You never seem to lose this connection with the natural world. Your soul or life force is, in fact, the essence of what was previously known on this planet as the high ascendant masters and spiritual teachers. They have chosen to come back into physical form at this time to bring the gifts of ancient wisdom, spiritual guidance, mysticism, and alchemy. You come with centuries-old knowledge from which you naturally draw. At first in your time here, you do not know the source of this knowledge. It is as if you are walking around in multiple realities: the reality that your physical body's five senses describe, and the worlds of intuition and direct guidance, which are just as real to you. The experience of dancing intimately with spirit shows up repeatedly as synchronicity, unquestionably guiding your way. You learn to listen to and interpret these experiences, aware that they are rare and not happening equally to others around you. This makes the sharing of this information impossible, forcing you even further into your personal chasm of feeling lonely, misunderstood, and ever the outcast.

This was an incredibly busy period in my life with little time for reflection. Given my plan to go to graduate school, I had one last shot at the Ironman, in October 1984, to see if I had what it took to meet my demons just as Julie Moss had done. To qualify, I needed to complete one more Tin Man distance race. The Mount Madonna Challenge, held in the late spring, had always held a certain mystique for me. It was a rare point-to-point race; the swim was in the Almaden Valley south of San Jose, the bike route climbed 1,800 feet up and over Mount Madonna, and the run ended at Torro Park in Salinas. It was a killer course. My parents and the Simonis offered to bring a motor coach and park it at the bike-run transition to collect my bike and offer whatever support I needed, including a private bathroom.

With my race entry submitted, all was a go, or so I thought. Three days before the race, I began feeling a profound weakness and uncharacteristic muscle soreness. A headache developed, along with a fever, sore throat, and a cough. I rarely got sick, and now I could barely get out of bed. Yet knowing never to give in to my body's weaknesses, I pressed forward, keeping up my schedule but cutting back significantly on the physical training. In my head, I could hear my mother's voice telling me, as she often did, just to give it up, that it did not matter if I ever made it to Hawaii. "Who would care anyway?"

I cared. I cared a lot. That attitude kept me going. The wounded, bloody warriors still fighting the good fight on the battlefield were a breed apart. I needed to prove to myself that I fit into that category. No matter how my body was feeling, I would do the race.

The day started with a 5 a.m. alarm in order to be at the race by six o'clock and ready to enter the water by seven. I felt as though someone had unplugged me from the universe's energy source. I had chills and a temperature of 102. I could barely move. This was going to be a very long day, I thought, as I loaded the bike and gear into my blue Honda CRX hatchback.

Taking off my warm-up suit and exposing to the morning air my already chilled body, clothed only in a one-piece tiger-print swimsuit, sounded perfectly awful. Diving into a fifty-four-degree reservoir and churning out two miles, while fighting other athletes for room, was almost unthinkable. This was quite possibly the greatest test of will I had yet encountered. At that moment, a smile came across my face. Of course. It was perfect. The challenge was not from outside. I needed to find the strength within myself to shut down the whispers in my head that kept telling me: Just go back home to bed. You're truly sick.

Pampering yourself is okay under these circumstances. Everyone would understand, wouldn't they?

Just then the gunfire brought me back to reality. I ripped off my warm-up suit, pulled on my goggles, and ran into the water. It was dark and murky, the visibility almost zilch. I tried to pull heavy water with each stroke, but my arms protested. I was so cold that I was having trouble staying present in my body. As I kicked and pulled, trying to find an effective rhythm, I was pummeled by other swimmers. Kicks to the face, legs, arms, and head were constant. At one point, I lost my goggles from a flapping foot to the face. I simply could not pull away from the pack. As I bobbed my head up from time to time to locate the buoy turnaround, it seemed I was hardly going anywhere. I decided in that moment that just finishing this race would be my personal Hawaii; all I had to do was survive the course, however long it took.

After what seemed like two hours, I crawled out of the water. It was 8:30 a.m. I had taken an hour and a half to swim a distance that usually took me about half that time. Considering the circumstances, I gave myself a break. Besides, the cold water had broken my fever. I still felt like shit, but at least the chills had subsided. Pulling myself to my feet, I jogged over to the bike stands and pulled on my cycling shorts over my bathing suit, laced up my cycling shoes, and clipped on my helmet. Off I went to see if I had anything left for what was usually my strongest leg of the race.

I quickly quieted my mind and began concentrating on my breathing and the rhythm of my quadriceps and hamstrings, feeling them evenly push and pull the pedals. The miles flew by. I slipped into "the zone" more easily than usual, aided by whatever virus was besieging my body. I seemed to check out completely, transcending both time and physical awareness. The flat part of the route went by unnoticed. I did not check back in with my body until Highway 152 began its gentle uphill incline through the foothills approaching the dreaded Mount Madonna. I automatically flipped the derailer to the smaller gears and prepared myself for the climb.

The road has tortuous hairpin turns. The race officials had blocked off one lane to traffic. I kept my head down and focused on the rhythm of my legs and my breathing. As the resistance increased, I switched into ever-lower gears until none were left. As the mountain showed me its awesome power, I rose out of my seat and pushed and pulled with my last reserves of strength. Battling this more than worthy adversary, I began to weave back and forth, cutting the sheer uphill incline into smaller, more manageable switchbacks in order to stay on the bike.

Soon I became aware of the other cyclists. I was passing one after another of them walking their bikes up the hill. Just then a white four-door car approached, filled with four girls who were shouting words of encouragement to the cyclists. As they pulled up parallel to my bike, their cheers grew louder: "Keep going. It's not far. You can do it." When they were directly beside me, close enough to see my face, they screamed, "It's a girl! Right on! Go, girl! You're the only one we've seen still on their bike. You can do it! Wahoo!" I smiled as they passed. It felt good to be beating the guys at their own games again.

Janine on the bike leg of the Mt. Madonna triathlon.

My mind drifted to elementary school when the other kids thought I was mentally inferior. If they could only see me now, I thought. I had gone to college without relying on books on tape. I had become a valued member of the athletic medical team and had even done research with the team physician. But I still wondered what the point of it all was. Why did I feel such an insatiable desire to challenge myself to monumental feats of valor created in a context of extraordinary circumstances just to see if I could figure out how to persevere? What forces were at work driving me forward? A mission perhaps? A commitment made eons ago, a vow to succeed or die trying?

My mind continued to wander as my legs churned and burned up the mountain. I was able to remain on my bike all the way to the top and make up valuable time lost in the swim. Noticing how easily my mind was dropping into fanciful thinking, I realized that I had not drunk much of my water and needed to pay closer attention. I didn't feel the urge to urinate and I had been racing now for nearly three and a half hours. I sucked on the nipple of my water bottle, hoping it was not too late. Getting behind in fluids could be the kiss of death for a distance athlete nearing the end of a race—especially with the flu.

I remembered the film footage of Julie and kept on sucking. Before I knew it, I had flown through Watsonville and was entering the outskirts of Castroville. The end of the bike stage was nearing and my quads were spent from the heroic effort of the climb. I hoped I would be able to walk when I dismounted. A thirteen-mile run in eighty-five-degree weather on hot, reflective asphalt was not something I was particularly looking forward to; I couldn't help but notice the nausea. Yet considering my performance thus far, I just might be able to pull this one out and finish with a qualifying time.

I saw the motor coach before my supporters saw me. Just as planned, there were Mom, Dad, Rich, and Mary, mixed drinks in hand, enjoying the excitement of the racers coming in and going out. I pulled up, stopping my bike just inches from my father's foot. He almost dropped his drink he was so excited to see me. Questions rang out from all directions: "How did it go?" "How are you feeling?" "Is there anything we can do?" "Do you want something to eat or drink?" It was a party atmosphere, and I felt like a spectator, foggy and disoriented.

As I dismounted and put weight on my feet for the first time, my fears came true. My calf muscles tied up in spasms. As I tried to walk, my quads seized up. I tried not to call attention to the potential danger of the situation as I hobbled up the aluminum steps into the coach to try to empty my bladder in preparation for the run. I had to strain and bend forward to produce about four ounces of urine. As I stood and turned to find the handle and flush, I glanced into the bowl and was shocked to see that my urine was cloudy dark brown. For a moment I thought, "Shit, I've just started my period. Could this day erode any further?" No, I had just finished with it the week prior. What was this, then? Why was I peeing brown?

I would learn much later in medical school that this condition is called rhabdomyolysis. Due to excessive exercise and other conditions such as viral infections, muscle proteins are broken down and then released into the bloodstream. Because of their large size, these proteins clog the kidneys' filtering mechanism, leading to acute kidney failure. Toxins then build up in the bloodstream and cause a number of nasty conditions, including the inability to process information correctly and make sound decisions—and death.

As I ripped off my cycling breeches and pulled on my running shorts, I chose to forget what I had witnessed in the toilet and press on with the business of slaying my next dragon—thirteen long, hot miles that awaited me just beyond the motor coach door. Pat, a training partner who surprised me by showing up, gestured for me to run alongside him. We took off down the road together. He was fresh, and I was on the verge of hallucinating. He knew something was up and kept a close eye on me, trying to engage me in conversation. It was all I could do to keep focused on breathing in and out. I trained my eyes on the white line on the side of the road, concentrating on putting one foot in front of the other. My pace continued to slow and my mouth grew dry. The air was hot and my once-filled water bottle was no match for my body's dehydrated condition.

At the time, I had little understanding of how grave my condition had become. By the five-mile mark, I began seeing large, colorful spots appear and then disappear on the pavement. I asked Pat if he was seeing them too. He glanced over at me with a concerned look. Soon the spots began to come and go and dance in kaleidoscopic patterns; I was becoming more nauseous. Refusing to believe anything was really wrong, I pressed on. Soon I began hallucinating; images of horrific proportions filled my vision. The only thing to do was to shut my eyes and keep on running.

Pat and Janine on the run leg of the Mt. Madonna triathlon.

I asked Pat if he would guide me by the hand as I ran the last eight miles—blind. At several points, my body simply refused to run. Yet walking made me feel as if I had given up and could no longer be called a competitor. After a few brief steps, I would force myself back into a gait that included flight between footfalls. I refused to quit even though my body was shutting down one system at a time. With two miles left to go, uncontrollable dry heaving started. The heat, dehydration, threatened kidney failure, worsening electrolyte imbalance, and continued breakdown of my skeletal muscles drove me into a deeper state of disorientation. Then, all the physical sensations seemed to melt away as my perception changed from being in my body to above it.

I seemed to be floating, watching the action from above with a 360-degree perspective of the remaining run portion of the race. From that aerial perspective, I could see the finish line and the other athletes as they were coming in. To my amazement, I could also see who was behind me. Only one other runner was still left on the course, and she was walking. I realized that I was in second-to-last place. From my unique vantage point (I had never before been jolted out of my body while awake), I started analyzing how amazing it was that my consciousness could actually be teleported to a completely different point from which to view. Rather than focusing on the pain, I kept my mind busy playing around with all the possibilities this presented.

My finish was not like Julie's. Most everyone had left, catching the buses back to collect their bikes. Only a few race officials and of course my personal sag wagon were still there when I came in. Like Julie, I pathetically crossed the white line on unstable legs in clothes stained with body fluids. I finished in seven hours and four minutes, far exceeding the five hours needed to qualify for the Hawaii Ironman. I was not even close. Yet simply finishing the race that day was all I needed. I had transcended physical, mental, emotional, and spiritual pain by simply willing my spirit to access a level of consciousness above anywhere I had been before.

There are no limits except the ones we create in our own minds, the voice in my head said as I lay in the back bunk of the motor coach on the way home that day. Getting to Hawaii was not the point for me, after all. This grasshopper had completed the assignment on this leg of the journey and was now prepared to apply what she had gained to the next level of the initiation process.

That day I consciously gave myself over to the power that had been driving my life from the beginning. I agreed to go wherever was required, do whatever needed to be done, to trust this force with which I was now familiar. I was not in control anymore. What other people thought of me did not matter, the limitations others placed on me did not matter, even the limitations I placed on myself did not matter, nor did the details that seemed to threaten my forward progress.

I could do absolutely anything I set my mind to; as long as the spirit agreed, the body would follow. I fully trusted this knowing. It was a good thing, too, because the next twelve years would be an ultimate test of another kind. I would be immersed in the linear, left-brain-dominated world of science, where the intuitive, spherical thinking that came most naturally to me was discounted and distrusted. So far, I had been able to lean on my hands-on, creative skills. Now I would be venturing into a world where those tools would be useless, or so it seemed. Yet this journey was necessary to complete the bridge across the abyss to connect to who I was.

The summer of 1984 had brought the annual craziness at the beach—the cooking, overeating (and for some, overdrinking), people-watching, and incessant fun that filled the last two weeks in August. The green, red, and white flag was staked, and the usual gang gathered like salmon returning to their spawning place.

Rich had been uncharacteristically complaining of lower back pain for about a year by then. At Dad's suggestion, he had gone to a chiropractor, but the twice-weekly treatments were not making a difference. I watched Rich move. His body position and gait were off. He would take a long time to straighten up as he got out of his beach chair, and his usually fun-loving personality was subdued. He was obviously in pain and trying to be a good sport about it. We went along with him, helping him play it down as if nothing were truly the matter.

Finally, Rich went to see his medical doctor who had recommended a colonoscopy. It turned out that Rich had adenocarcinoma, the most aggressive cell type of colon cancer. With surgery plus chemotherapy, he was given a fighting chance.

The winter of 1985 was not so kind to the Simoni and Talty clans. Rich's blood work came back abnormal and he complained of cramping abdominal pain. Surgery followed. Dad could not go, so Mom, Mary, and I drove to San Francisco to collectively pull for one of our fearless leaders. The waiting room at UCSF Medical Center faced the bay and the Golden Gate Bridge. Beyond the floor-to-ceiling windows, ominous rain clouds put on a fantastic lightning show while torrential downpours slapped at the glass, filling the room with blessed white noise. Talking was awkward. We just watched the rain.

More than four hours later, the head surgeon pushed the door open, while taking off his surgical cap. He made eye contact with Mary and, without a word, gracefully sat down in the chair next to hers, staring into her eyes as he took her hands in his. We waited for him to speak. Instead, his eyes began welling with tears that eventually cascaded gently down his cheeks. He shook his head. I thought Rich had died on the table and the doctor could not get the words out to say how sorry he was for killing him. Then he collected himself and said in a broken voice, "When we opened him up, the diagnosis was clear. There were little islets of cancer throughout the abdominal cavity. The condition is called carcinomatosis and is incurable. We then ran his small bowel and colon for any recurrences of the original tumor—none were found."

My brain had shut down back at "carcinomatosis" and "incurable," only coming back online at "none were found." That sounded like good news—sort of. We peppered this poor man with questions. He explained that there were no other treatment options. The disease would take its own course. Short of a miracle, Rich's chances of surviving more than a year were poor.

I was acutely aware of our small group's emotions, but what struck me most profoundly was the surgeon's display of raw feeling. I had always imagined doctors to be somewhat removed from the emotional impact of their work. How could they do their job if they were constantly crying with their patients and their patients' families? The fact that he was weeping right along with us somehow made it okay to access our own true feelings and begin the grieving process. I was filled with respect for this man. I decided in that instant that if I did become a doctor, I wanted to be just like him.

Rich went home to his house perched over the yacht harbor in Santa Cruz to live out the rest of his life in a progressive state of liver failure. Dad often took afternoons off and drove over the hill to be with his friend. No two heterosexual men could have been closer. Dad would take Rich out to eat, to the hardware store, and for walks on the beach. When he would leave in the evenings, he would always tell Rich to "walk in the light." This was his favorite parting salutation to those he considered members of his "spiritually aware" inner circle. We were never really sure what he meant by it. Clearly, though, he was extending to the recipient the highest-voltage vibration of love.

That August at the beach was profoundly different. Rich could not even walk down to the sand, so Dad bribed Roger, the lifeguard, with food to let him drive Rich in the car down to the Italian flag and back in the afternoons. Rich would sit there with the group but not say much. Watching this made me deeply sad. Life was taking a huge turn toward change—something we all found difficult to face.

On the last day of the traditional two-week stint, I had to leave the beach early. After saying my good-byes, I began walking toward Mott Street. Suddenly, I had an urge to turn back and look upon the scene one more time. The flag was flat and silent; the crescent of beach chairs was broken, as others had left early as well. The sun, low in the sky, was causing glimmers of light to dance on the breaking waves. Dad and Rich sat in silence, gazing away from me out to sea as if nonverbally celebrating the bond they shared in life and would continue to share even with the inevitable arrival of death. I would be leaving in a few weeks for the Midwest to start a new chapter of my life in graduate school. This was quite possibly the last time I would see Rich alive. As this realization hit me, I remember asking my conscious mind to store this visual memory forever.

PART III

The Bridge over the Abyss

Bill and Carol on Janine's porch in Chicago.

13

Trusting Messages

You will be receiving new information that will be wrapped in different packages and come through different channels from those you are used to. Know that you have the circuitry to handle it. Keep your instrument clear and the channels open to access this etheric knowledge as it agonizes to reach you. You will find it difficult to discuss this with non Indigos because they will not understand. Only the few who are on similar journeys will understand this new language in which words have no purpose.

I started graduate studies at the School of Public Health at the University of Illinois, Chicago, in the fall of 1985. Mom and Dad were supportive, as they had been about all of my ventures. They knew I was going partly to be with José. My mom no doubt thought we would eventually marry and have children, and my dreams of medical school, which I had finally shared with them, would naturally fade. They helped me ship my belongings and when the time came, drove me and my dog, Indy, to the Oakland airport to catch the 12:30 a.m. red-eye. We said good-bye in the departure lounge. As I watched the ground crew load Indy in her dog carrier into the belly of the plane, the stark recognition hit that I was standing in the crack between two worlds. The two people who had known me best my entire life had brought me right up to the threshold. Ahead of me was a life that until now I had only imagined.

Even my relationship with my father was shifting. His role in preparing me for whatever task I had agreed to before entering this physical plane was clearly nearing completion.

Janine and José in Chicago in 1985.

School for me included a double major in community health science and health resources management. I took a graduate student teaching job on campus at which I worked full-time for another year after my course work was finished. Spending three years in Chicago was an education in itself. Until then, I had not felt in person the deep gash that racism has torn in the flesh of this country. I was often the only white person in the grocery store and felt the unwelcoming territorial stares from the other shoppers. Before bed, taking Indy out for her last constitutional, I had bottles thrown at me from across the field with yelling from the same direction, "White bitch!"

Our first Thanksgiving there together, José and I planned a real feast: turkey with Grandma Talty's famous pork sausage and sage stuffing, mashed potatoes, veggies, and pumpkin pie topped with real whipped cream. Just as we were coming in the door from the market, our arms numb from carrying all the bags, the phone rang. I felt my stomach tighten.

José must have seen my face change. "What? Are you all right?"

The knowing in my head was saying, *It's Dad, Rich died.* I replied, "Yeah, I'm okay, but I think it's bad news."

He shook his head, still unsure what to make of my precognitions, and went into the kitchen with the groceries. I picked up the receiver.

"Hello...yeah, I knew it was you."

My father described how everyone had gathered around Rich and how peaceful he was as he made his transition. I could feel my eyes tingle and my nose begin to burn, readying themselves for the torrent of tears. Rich had been a second father to me.

Dad went on. "Janine, the most unusual thing happened right before he died. It had been raining earlier in the day, and by afternoon only showers lingered between breaks of sunshine."

I thought to myself, that's my dad—despite his own wrenching grief at having just lost his best friend, taking the time to poetically set the scene when talking about the greatest mystery we know as a species.

He continued. "Just as Rich was taking his last few breaths, the most fantastically vivid rainbow appeared over the harbor. It was a rare complete arch, starting and ending in the water. It seemed to last forever. Everybody present understood that this was Rich's rainbow, there to provide a portal for him to the next world. It was beautiful."

As he spoke, reality hit hard, bringing a flood of tears. Wonderful, witty, irreplaceable Rich was gone. Home would be different now. The crack between worlds widened a bit more.

Not long after this loss, José transferred to another medical school mid-program. Actually, the severe racism he experienced at U of I forced him out. All of the minority programs were set up for African American students. The few Hispanic students were never socially or scholastically included in the cliquish distribution of critical information regarding special programs, study groups, and tutoring opportunities. After working for several months reapplying to other programs, he was accepted at Michigan State University, College of Human Medicine. We had had one glorious, but stressful and challenging year of living in the same town and state. We would not do so again for another four. His leaving was in his own best interests. Watching him go reminded me of when my sick and injured animals were ready to return to their rightful wild places. I was used to saying good-bye.

Completing the master's degree imbued me with a whole new level of confidence. Forced to keep pace with highly trained students, I came through with a solid B average. I had proved that my disability no longer stood in my way. I could now learn anything put before me.

That was not all. Just a few days after I presented my thesis to the faculty and staff, I got out of bed, put on my running shorts and T-shirt as I did every morning, and hit the floor to do my stretches before leaving for my morning run. While I was in the hurdler's stretch, an epiphany slowly percolated into my consciousness. *My lower back did not hurt!* At first I could not believe it. I shifted into the positions that had always caused pain and stiffness—nothing.

When did it go away? I tried to think back. Did I have it yesterday? Was it there last week? What we focus on stays active for us; what we elect to ignore fades away. My ten years of managing pain had taught me this. The discomfort had lessened ever so slowly over the years until it faded completely. I almost felt like an old friend had died. The pain that had dictated the diligence with which I maintained a strict exercise program seemed all of a sudden to be missing. I did not know at the time how valuable my experience with back pain would be in counseling future patients suffering from the same pathology.

The MCAT exam was the last hurdle between me and my lifetime dream. As if training for a triathlon, I mapped out a study schedule, supported by diet, sleep, and exercise, that would have me peaking for my best academic performance yet by the exam date. Through the summer and into the fall, I was possessed. I was going to *kill* that exam, bury it—dead.

Question after question, booklet after booklet, this test took everything I had. I seemed to be reaching even further into the depths of my will than the day I stood out of the bike saddle, switching back and forth, to climb the dreaded Mount Madonna.

When I walked out of the building at the end of the test day, I was unaware even of what season it was. The colors and shapes of the clouds as the sun was setting created a proverbial silver lining around their edges. Suddenly, a hole of light opened up, and a fan of rays beamed down on the landscape below, punctuating the moment. I stopped in amazement.

My scores were competitive enough to earn invitations to interview at four schools. This was a very good sign. Even as I was setting up dates and travel arrangements, cards and letters began arriving from schools to which I had not even applied. One that caught my attention was from the University of Osteopathic Medicine and Health Sciences in Des Moines, Iowa. I looked at it quizzically. What was osteopathic medicine? *Osteo* meant bone, which meant orthopedics, and orthopedics was what I was going to medical school to do.

José explained that doctors of osteopathic medicine completed the same medical school requirements as MDs, passed comparable and equally as rigorous board examinations, and chose among the same medical specialties. The main difference was that DOs included hands-on manipulative medicine in what they studied and practiced.

Wow, I thought, what a perfect blend for someone with my background. Why hadn't I heard of osteopathic medicine before?

In California, DOs were rare, José told me, because under a 1960s state referendum, the DO schools and hospitals were taken over by MD programs, probably because of osteopathy's more holistic philosophy. Ironically, the more a doctor touches a patient, the less status they have among their colleagues.

That was crazy, I thought, remembering Rich's surgeon who had profoundly touched us—in another sense of the word—when he held Mary's hand and cried with us. I did not think any less of him—quite the opposite. I filled out and sent back the return reply card.

What is small sometimes contains the power to change a life. A simple postcard mailer, looking a lot like an advertisement, introduced me to the very thing I had been preparing for my entire life. I interviewed at three MD schools and one DO program.

Two weeks later, the letter arrived. There it was, between my fingers, addressed to me—my acceptance to osteopathic medical school. Once again, the Universe had given me a goal and then, once I was fully invested in attaining it, presented an off-the-beaten-path alternative that had been the real target all along.

Janine and José on Christmas eve 1988 just after Bill announced to the family that they were already married.

14

A Tribal Custom

Young adult Indigos have such a broad perspective of life and reality, they seem separated from the usual trials and tribulations of dating and courtship. You are forever viewing your life from the place of "Symbolic Site," constantly looking for the deeper meaning beneath the surface of every situation and relationship of which you are a part. When you become involved with those who are still unconscious, it can often cause tremendous turmoil. The un-awoken realize early on that they are dealing with another being who does not share their emotional spectrum, reverence for becoming lost in love, and the codependence that falling and being in love often brings. The Indigo feels emotionally incapable of responding as the un-awoken do. You do not understand the need to be part of a couple and resist losing your fierce independence. You intuitively know that you have come here to take part in world-changing events, even though you do not know what these events will be. This causes you to be cautious in making long-term plans that could involve emotional ties to one who remains unconscious, for fear of hurting that person in the process. You are very careful not to cause harm. This is your nature. Your ambivalence in matters of the heart seems out of character for the immense kindness and compassion you embody and demonstrate in all other situations involving loving relationship.

José and I had now been together for four years without a formal commitment. That never bothered me because I was not looking for one, but he was. Ever since the first summer we had spent together, he had been sure I was the one for him. He would be a third-year medical student in Michigan when I started in Iowa in the fall. He wanted to get married now, no matter what the next eight years of school, internships, and residencies had in store for us both.

For me, getting married seemed unnecessary. I knew I was not going to bear children and was not sure I wanted to make a lifelong commitment. Sexuality was absent from my spectrum of available feelings. This had already been an issue in our relationship. I had no sex drive at all. José at times accused me of not loving him. Perhaps in that way I didn't. My body and mind simply did not know how to respond on that level. Deep down, I knew my circuitry was different, not meant to fire during a purely physical experience. I knew I was not deficient in this way, only different. Was I "in love" enough to agree to spend the rest of my life with him? I wasn't sure. Was I simply using him to show me the way to my future? Again, I was not sure. All I knew was that I loved being with him because he made me laugh and see the world through the eyes of a child. Our relationship was thriving even under the stress of two medical educations. Sure, we had our issues, but we had also come to understand what the other needed to be happy and fulfilled in the relationship. Was this love? Perhaps it was.

José continued to push and I was sure that walking down a church aisle in a white dress with everyone staring at me was not going to happen for me in this lifetime—no way, José. We compromised on being married by a justice of the peace and telling our parents the next time we were both home.

The cramming of massive amounts of information for which medical education is famous started right after the first-day welcome speech. The first-year medical curriculum was virtually a review of undergraduate science courses, but this time in exhaustive detail. I gravitated immediately toward the "big worlds" of anatomy and manual medicine. Before long, I was not only earning As, but also was invited to be a teaching assistant in both subjects the next year.

Osteopathic manual medicine (OMM) was just applied anatomy. Again, I was on familiar ground. I had already developed a keen ability to "see with my hands," to assess subtle tissue motion and construct a corresponding three-dimensional anatomical picture in my head. In lab, many students were having trouble with this mental imaging and even more difficulty handling the body parts in question. I would often offer to help. They reminded me of the students who could not sew the proper stitches on the class art project in fifth grade.

Returning home for Christmas was always a high point in the year. Mom and Dad would pick up Indy and me at the airport with fantastic smiles and hugs that lasted for what seemed like hours. This year, however, was going to be different. José and I had been married for eight months, and it was time to tell our parents. He was still living in Michigan and I was in Iowa. On the surface nothing appeared different to anyone, including me. I did not feel married. What was that supposed to feel like anyway?

On the night we had planned to tell them, he arrived at the door, shaking, wary, and perspiring profusely. I invited him in and he didn't move an inch. "Let's just forget it for tonight, what do you think? I can come back some other time," he said.

"I think this has gone on too long already," I replied, reaching for his arm and pulling him across the threshold. "I have always had a very open relationship with my parents, and keeping something like this from them any longer is not an option."

My folks were delighted to see José and offered him a glass of wine. He sipped his wine and chatted in an uncharacteristically choppy way about school. There was clearly no segue in the world from incision and drainage procedures for oozing, purulent skin abscesses on heroin-using skin poppers to "By the way, we got married last April." I soon realized if this job was going to get done, I would have to do it.

Feeling particularly clumsy, I blurted out, "So what were you two doing on April 15 this year?"

My parents clearly thought this was a joke. We all knew that my father always waited until the last second to pay his taxes. On April 15, he would have been hunched over his desk rifling through documents and later walking the two envelopes down the street to the main post office just before the stroke of midnight. Looking blankly at me, they both asked, "Why?" I checked in visually with José one last time—again an empty look. No help was coming from that direction.

"Well, we got married," I blurted out, and watched as the words hung in the air. I hoped José would rally. No such luck. He just stared back at me. This was not going well.

My parents were speechless. Perhaps they thought I had just announced our engagement and plans for a wedding date, except that my words did not match that message. I decided to let José explain, since the timing had been his affair. I waited for someone to say *something*. Finally, the room burst into conversation. I felt as though I were melting into quicksand.

To this day I am not sure how everything got straightened out, or if it ever really did. To say that José got a tongue-lashing when he told his father is putting it mildly. He was in more trouble than a twenty-nine-year-old man thought he could be with his folks over a crime of the heart. His father demanded a meeting with my father to apologize. The next night José, his mother, and his father appeared at my parents' front door. José led them in as if we were having a party. Mr. Chibras went straight up to my dad, took his hands in his, and said in broken English, "Mr. Talty, it is so very nice to make your acquaintance. I did not raise my son to behave this way. Janine is your only daughter, and he should have asked you for her hand before he took her as his wife." This was heavy stuff to these people, I thought. Thankfully, the rest of the evening went better than I had expected.

January came. José flew back to Michigan and I returned to Iowa to immerse myself in this game called medical school. You could set your watch by my daily routine. This lifestyle was an external manifestation of how I had learned to manage my brain. Organization was crucial to being able to focus and succeed.

If the first year of medical school did not break the weak ones, the second year surely did. It was not so much the difficulty of the information as the volume, detail, and speed at which it came at us that brought even the most disciplined to their knees. I was once again thankful for the sport of triathlon. I had already done battle with the dragon that whispers in your ear at the hardest moments, "Quit. This hurts too much. You do not want it that bad."

Feeling sorry for yourself came with the territory. At night I would dream of the life I was missing. Most people my age were securing jobs, starting families, enjoying life—and going to the beach. Oh, how I longed to lie on hot, lumpy sand under a clear California sky! But what I wanted most of all was to watch Rich and Dad perform their crazy antics, tormenting and playing practical jokes on people—something I sadly knew could never happen in that way again.

When I could not take one more minute of medical minutiae, I would reach for the phone and call my dad. He could always bring my focus back, reminding me how hard I had worked to get where I was now. We would speak of places to visit together one day, share thoughts on current events, or talk about the nature of reality. Dad was gifted at seeing through the obvious and thinking spherically. These conversations always made me feel as if I had just gone on a mini mental vacation into other realms, places that felt familiar and reminded me of the "point" of it all.

Once when my brain felt like it was about to short-circuit, I reached for my journal and a pen, even though I could not afford the time. My mind drifted back to when I was little and Dad and I would walk hand in hand while I asked him incessant questions about the world. I now knew the answers. "Why are we warm, Daddy?" Because kilocalories are a measurement of heat. Cellular metabolism turns the kilocalories in the food we eat into energy. A by-product is wasted heat, which our body maintains within a narrow range, based on our metabolism's speed, which is determined by hormones. That is why we are warm. "How do cuts heal, Daddy?" An injury to the skin's dermal and epidermal layers prompts an inflammatory response, which includes chemotactic factors that call white blood cells to the area. These act as building blocks, while cells called "ground substance" hold the white blood cells together like mortar to create new collagen tissue. The collagen tissue matures into new living skin.

I placed a sheet of paper in my typewriter and wrote:

DAD—things have changed. We are not the same with each other as we used to be. When I was a little girl, I would ask you questions and I would marvel at your answers. There was nothing I asked that you did not know.... Now, I am in my fourth consecutive year of graduate school, and when we share time, I am the one with the answers and you have become the one with saucer-sized eyes of wonder. This natural role exchange is evidence that our life cycle together is becoming fuller, with the circle's head now catching up with its tail. I have become who I am because of the person you are. Thank you for this beautiful opportunity to be me. You have been the greatest of teachers.

My creative mind had let out a big sigh. I would not appreciate the full import of what I had written for three more years.

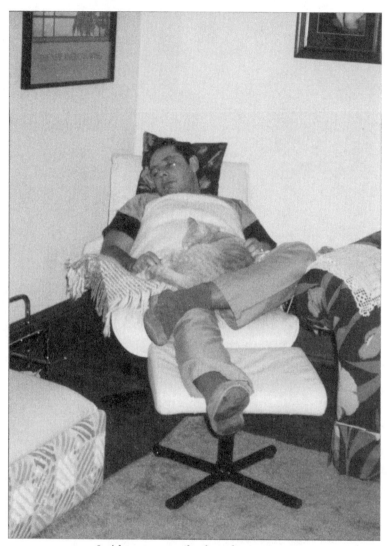

José home as a medical resident in Iowa.

15

Nonordinary Knowing in Ordinary Medicine

It is rare for Indigo adults to have the experience of meeting each other along the way. When you do, these experiences are like none you have ever experienced before. The level of communication you share with your own kind is uncanny. You display immediate telepathic understanding. Words become meaningless and are oftentimes clumsy. You are able to communicate irrespective of time or distance. Similar to Bluetooth technology of today, your spherically designed and equipped brains are like massive radio towers projecting a frequency that connects with other Indigos. These messages are transmitted along the earth's energy grid.

Ley lines surround the planet and act very much like our body's meridian channels and chakras. They contain a flow of energy that is self-sustaining, and where they intersect, a vortex is created. Your physical body has evolved to be able to sense these energies and transmit them through your own system; many are also capable of directing these energies through others. At first you may not understand these gifts—especially those of you who have already reached adulthood. The importance of this trait is just now being understood as the adult Indigos come together in knowing who you are and for what purpose you have come.

José was finishing up his rotations and had decided to pursue a three-year residency in internal medicine. He applied to the University of Iowa, Iowa Methodist Hospital program, in Des Moines. Residency is infamously grueling. In the little time he was at home, he was generally asleep, catching up on hours, days, and eventually months of sleep deprivation. If I hadn't known better, I would have sworn I was observing my first case of narcolepsy.

In January, I began the next phase in my training, sixteen months of clinical medical rotations. My plan was to become an orthopedic surgeon, and orthopedics was one of the most competitive residencies. Not only that, but nationally less than 1 percent of orthopedic residents were female. This was one of the remaining male bastions in medicine, a fact that egged me on all the more.

Based on its academic reputation and past leniency in admitting female residents, I set my sights on Doctors Hospital, an osteopathic teaching hospital in Columbus, Ohio, and succeeded in arranging for a rotation there in early spring. I wanted to have some experience in surgery behind me before I started—we had all heard stories of neophytes passing out at the sight of blood and the nurses waving smelling salts under their noses to revive them—so I landed a general surgery rotation the month before.

The last week of that rotation, I called the medical education department at Doctors and confirmed both my rotation in orthopedics and my accommodations. The woman on the other end of the line corroborated both. She told me how to get to the medical education office, where I was supposed to report at 7 a.m. the first Monday of the month, and where to pick up the key to my dorm room when I got to the hospital Sunday afternoon. Everything seemed to be set.

I said good-bye to José and Indy and headed eastward on Highway 80. I was going to this place to sell myself the only way I knew how, by working harder, lasting longer, being smarter, and demonstrating the highest level of integrity, joyfulness, and gratitude they had ever seen in a medical student. I was once again on the threshold between a world I knew and one that awaited me the next day.

The following morning I followed the directions that came in my packet and used a house phone in the hospital to report in to the office of medical education. After several rings, a woman answered. I introduced myself as a visiting student on the service of orthopedic surgery for the month of March.

The woman, obviously already frazzled this early on a Monday, responded, "Who are you?"

I repeated my name carefully and added that I had confirmed my spot just a week earlier.

"We do not have any record of you for orthopedics, and besides, there are already too many students and residents on for this month. You will have to choose another surgical specialty."

I could not believe what I was hearing. "I am Janine Talty from Iowa," I replied, "and I scheduled this rotation three months ago for the sole purpose of assessing if I was going to apply to your orthopedic surgery residency. Doing another surgical specialty is simply not an option. You have to make an exception."

There was silence on the line. Finally, she replied, "I'm sorry, there's nothing I can do. The two other available surgical specialties are general surgery and vascular surgery." She then volunteered, "I'm not sure if I can recommend vascular surgery with Dr. Bracken. He, um…he is very difficult to work with. Actually, he makes most female residents cry, and most students who end up on his service ask to be transferred by the second week. The only good thing this service has going this month is that our chief surgical resident will be on, and he is a joy to work with."

I barely heard her. I was still processing the concept of not being able to do orthopedics after all my careful planning. The words "difficult" and "makes most females cry," however, had caught my attention. Instead of a challenge in orthopedics, the least I could do for my personal and professional development was to match wits with a known tiger. Besides, I had just done a month of general surgery. No one was going to make me cry. After several tongue-tied moments, the words "I will take Dr. Bracken's service" came forth.

She was hesitant, but gave me the pager number of Dr. Doug Nespory, the surgical resident.

I hung up the phone. How was this happening? What forces were at work here? A big, fat, red universal stop sign had been planted squarely in my path. I forced myself to accept this fact without yet understanding its meaning. All would be revealed in the proper time—though that thought can be difficult to wrap your mind around when your lifetime goals are disappearing from view right in front of you.

I picked up the phone again and dialed the number. The voice on the other end had a slight Midwestern accent and was strong, polite, and somehow familiar and comforting. He said he was doing rounds on the third floor and would be easy to find—he was the only male sitting at the nurses' station. I followed his directions up the stairs and made my way to the desk, where a well-muscled young man in blue surgical scrubs was writing in a chart. I quietly sat down in the chair to his right, not wanting to disturb his thoughts. The moment I settled in the seat, I was overcome by a sense of being encircled by a bubble of comfort and belonging, much like sitting with my dad.

I said nothing. I just sat there basking in the sense of peace and profound kindness, and the awareness that all was well. This was the first time I had felt a knowing coming from my stomach area, heart, and forehead simultaneously. It encapsulated my body like a warm, fuzzy blanket. I watched him as he wrote, sometimes entering a *b* for a *d* and spelling phonetically.

He glanced over at me, then extended his hand. "Hi, I am Doug Nespory. Are you Janine?" As I was taking his hand in mine, our eyes met. My mouth was saying, "Yes, I am Janine. Nice to meet you," but my brain was thinking how utterly remarkable it was that this man had the same deep-iridescent-blue eyes as my father.

He told me about Bracken, how crazy and tough he was, how he drove most surgical residents into the ground, and how few student doctors could keep up with him. He averaged six major vascular procedures a day, including Saturdays and some Sundays. He thrived on excitement and hated weakness. Doug was warning me, if not trying to discourage me outright.

I smiled and said, "Bring him on."

He smiled back and then led me to the surgery department, directing me to the women's lounge where I could change into scrubs for the first case. "Meet you in OR five when you are done." He disappeared down the hallway.

After locating OR number five, I peered through the glass window in the door to see two male surgeons sitting on stools with an anesthetized patient between them. They were working on the left arm. This must be it, I thought. I grabbed a surgical mask, tied the strings behind my head and neck, and pushed the door open as if I owned the place, ready to make the acquaintance of the infamous Dr. Bracken.

The circulating nurse stepped forward and asked, "Can I help you?" I introduced myself, and as she was writing my name in the logbook, Doug looked up from what he was doing and said, "Oh, Janine, glad you could make it." He then introduced me to Dr. Bracken, who was sitting with his back toward me. He did not look up. He just continued to cut and sew, hunched over the patient's arm, saying nothing.

Doug began asking me questions in an attempt to warm things up a bit. "So, Janine, where are you from?"

Thinking he meant what school I was attending, I answered, "The University of Osteopathic Medicine and Health Science in Des Moines."

"Oh, are you from Iowa?" he asked then.

Here it comes, I thought. "No, I'm from California."

Bracken's hands stopped. He slowly sat up and turned around to look at me for the first time. He was a handsome man, or must have been in his day. He looked to be in his early fifties, out of shape and a bit overweight. He too had blue eyes. As he looked at me, I felt as if I were being recognized for the first time in a medical teaching setting; he was looking right into my soul. He turned back, slouched, and began working again. "You don't look like a Californian," he offered.

I smiled, getting the gist. "Were you expecting a blonde with pink lipstick?"

He looked at Doug as if to convey, "She's a spunky one, isn't she?"

The circulating nurse offered me a stool to sit fairly close to where Doug and Dr. Bracken were working. They were placing a Gore-Tex graft on the radial artery of a diabetic patient for renal dialysis access. The arm was exposed and the skin and muscles were retracted. It was a very clean surgery with very little blood. As Doug continued to make small talk, I felt myself becoming warm and faint. The next thing I knew, the nurse was waving a vial of smelling salts under my nose as I slumped against a nearby wall. How could it be? I had just finished a month of general surgery, my hands often in blood and guts up to my wrists, and never once been bothered by it.

Bracken looked over at Doug and said, "This is going to be a fucking long month."

And that it was. I observed more surgery that month than some surgical residents see in their entire residency. Morning report was at

6:30 a.m. in the surgical lounge, where Doug would report to Bracken how the previous day's patients had done overnight. From there Bracken would do rounds. His patients loved him. He was a warm and deeply caring man with a hint of childlike mischief and the air of a master wizard. He moved like a cat chasing a mouse, darting in and out of patients' rooms, teasing the nurses, and obviously having a magically wonderful time. He was the quintessential surgeon, completely aware that he was 100 percent full of himself. If you did not keep your eye on him, he would be off down the hall to the next surgery, leaving his residents and students in his wake.

In the OR, he was the master showman. After meticulously scrubbing at the sink, he would blast through the OR doors, shouting, "It's show time!" The nurses bowed to his every request, no matter how absurd. He insisted on blasting Mozart, Bach, and Beethoven while he was working, quoting the research showing that patients exposed to classical music during surgery had more favorable outcomes. He often conducted both his private and professional business on the phone, broadcast over the OR public announcement system for all of us to hear. He would order birthday cakes for his kids, speak to his wife about airline tickets, call the cleaners to find out when his extra-starched shirts would be ready, and even call other physicians with whom he had bets on upcoming pro basketball games. Life was his oyster, and he was digging for all he could get.

It did not take Bracken long to begin trusting me. He could see I was authentically interested in surgery, despite our rocky beginning, and I was fully capable of handling his sort of bully. Working in men's athletics had taught me well. After we had scrubbed and entered the OR with our hands in the air, he would tease me for not twisting in the correct direction as the nurse held the waist tie strap to "gown" me. My dyslexic dragon was raising its ugly head. I would always spin the wrong direction, pulling the gown away from my torso instead of wrapping me in it. Both he and Doug would stop in the middle of draping the patient to see if I would turn the correct direction, cheering when I got it right, teasing me through the rest of the case when I got it wrong.

Not to be outdone, I would come back with quips such as "Dr. Bracken, is it okay for so much hair to be sticking out of your cap?" A moment of self-doubt would pass across his face as he scanned the walls for a mirror. He was easy to handle—really. He even considered my opinion when discussing the logistics of the surgical and rounding schedules. He would make comments to Doug as if I weren't there: "She does make a good point. How do you think she knows so much about the business of managing a surgery practice after having been here only two weeks? I think there is a wisdom here beyond her current level of medical training."

During morning report the Tuesday of my third week, I was assigned to admit Professor Emirates Salvay from Ohio State University. She was scheduled for a lumbar sympathectomy for severe peripheral vascular disease. I had not heard of this procedure, so after morning rounds with Doug, I stole away to the residents' lounge to read up on it. The goal was to cut the sympathetic chain of the autonomic nervous system that fed the lower extremities, so the arteries in the legs could not constrict as part of the sympathetic nervous response. The sympathetic chain controlled other vitally important mechanisms, however, including the lymphatic system's ability to return fluids to the central circulation. If this mechanism were knocked out, the patient could experience massive edema in the lower extremities. I glanced up from the books, pondering why in the world a surgeon would even offer a patient this procedure. What was Bracken thinking? My gaze landed on the wall clock above the coffee station. It was already 7:30 a.m. The patient would likely be up by now. I raced down the hall to do the pre-op admission note before her 9 a.m. surgery.

Professor Salvay was a sixty-eight-year-old fireball of a woman who obviously missed teaching. She immediately picked up on my being a student and, rather than being put off by that fact, welcomed me. After getting all her medical information, I sat on the edge of her bed, put aside my papers, looked into her eyes, and asked if she had any questions. All patients, no matter how learned, are frightened before medical procedures, especially ones that involve an incision lengthwise down the belly and then a blunt dissection of vital organs to get to a bundle of nerves lying on the anterior spinal column.

Her eyes softened as she reached out and took my left hand in hers. "Are you going to be there?" she asked.

I smiled. "Of course. I have to show these guys how to do this one."

She giggled and patted the top of my hand. "I feel more comfortable with a woman assisting. We tend to feel a deeper level of compassion for each other. I know you will take care of me in there."

I was blown away by her comment. Even after excusing myself to rejoin the team, I could not get her expression of raw trust out of my mind. This sort of link with another being came from the heart, the way I had always communicated with animals. For a moment, I wondered if, in fact, I had been reading her thoughts rather than hearing her words.

Doug and Bracken were elbows deep in a bilateral ilio-popliteal bypass graft when I rejoined them. I scrubbed in and entered the OR in the usual posture, arms up, allowing the water to drip down off my elbows until a nurse handed me a blue towel, before going through the dreaded gowning ritual. As usual, they both stopped to watch the waistband-turning show. I spun the wrong way initially just to entertain them, and they burst out in boos and hisses. I then quickly reversed my direction and said, "Gotcha!" These little rituals had brought us closer; we were now working as a team.

Bracken was talking constantly, as usual. He was clearly trying to recruit Doug to do his vascular surgery fellowship the following year. Evidently, vascular surgery was a prized surgical specialty, and Bracken's program was famous throughout the DO surgical domain. He received hundreds of applications each year. For Bracken to offer the spot as he was doing with Doug was unheard of. I just stood listening to the incessant chatter.

Once the Gore-Tex grafts had been sewn in and all the bleeding had stopped, Bracken stepped back and yanked off his gown, a sign that the master had finished the commissioned artwork. He was off to the pre-op holding area to greet his next patient, allowing his "Dougy" to close.

On most days, with Bracken gone, Doug and I would chat freely. He told me about his wife and two kids. He taught me all kinds of suture closings for the different layers of abdominal fascial planes and the skin. I had naturally good hands, he said, and should consider going into a surgical specialty. I told him about my aspirations in orthopedics, and he agreed, except for one thing. "Those guys have no finesse. What patients fear the most after surgery is having huge railroad-track scars as reminders of their brush with mortality." Because of this, he had spent many months of elective time with the plastic surgeons, learning how to knit the living skin lovingly, creating beauty rather than disfigurement.

After the final suture was thrown, we were off. As usual, I tagged along as he wrote the note and prescriptions for post-op pain meds and dictated the operative note into the hospital phone system. We usually met up with Bracken in the surgical lounge or out in the hallway, but that day he was nowhere to be found. Something was up. Doug paged Bracken and finally the operator patched him through. Looking into my eyes as he listened, Doug dutifully nodded his head, offering the occasional, "Uh-huh." When he hung up, he said, "He is down in the ER with Mr. Porter. We did an abdominal laperotomy and resection of a foot of small intestine for adenocarcinoma on him three months ago. He has been hypotensive and complaining of a constriction in his esophagus. He cannot get food down." I waited for more. "That's usually a sign of constricture of the esophagus. With his history of cancer, it doesn't sound good."

As he was speaking, we were walking out of surgery down the hall toward the ER. Hitting the metal automatic door opener on the wall and blasting through the double doors into the hub of the emergency department reminded me of those old television doctor shows like *Marcus Welby,* M.D. Bracken was at Porter's bedside, surrounded by a sea of Porter's family members. Bracken seemed relieved the moment he saw Doug enter. He quickly but politely reintroduced Doug to Porter and his family, then slipped out of the room, handing off the dirty work of completing the admission for surgical workup to Doug. Bracken motioned for me to follow him.

In the surgery department, after stopping at the cart to put on our blue paper booties and caps, we headed for pre-op holding to meet Dr. Salvay. Bracken plastered on his half-genuine pretty-boy smile as he approached her gurney. Her face lit up at the sight of us. Her saviors had arrived to do battle with the unsuspecting sympathetic chain ganglia hiding deep in her belly. Because this was a relatively easy procedure, Bracken said I would be his first assist on this one while Doug was busy tucking in Mr. Porter. My stomach went into a knot. Me with Bracken—alone?

I thought back to the phone call to the office of medical education just over two weeks earlier. I had come a long way in taming this tiger.

As we scrubbed, he dropped into a rare moment of seriousness. He asked me what area of medicine I wanted to go into.

Not wanting to sound unappreciative, I said, "Why, surgery, of course."

He looked at me with a hint of surprise. "You would be good. You are tough and don't scare easily. I seem to have a reputation of being, shall we say, difficult to get along with. Can you believe that? All I ask is that people show up, do their work, show interest, and stay until we are finished." He went on and on as we shut off the water with our knees, held our hands up, and pushed through the metal doors of OR five. The nurses were surprised to see me alone with Bracken. "She will be my first assist on this one," he assured them. The scrub nurse asked what size gloves I wore. I responded, "Size 6.5 brown with talc, please." No one blinked an eye.

I accepted the nurse's help in putting on my gown and this time spun the correct direction on the first attempt. I could see Bracken paying attention to me as he was applying the surgical drapes, something Doug always did. In that moment, I suddenly saw him in a different light. The mystique of Bracken fell away and I saw him for who he was: a man, a person, a student of life just like the rest of us.

I took my place directly across from him, holding the smoke suction device in my left hand and clean gauze in my right as he made the six-inch incision to the left of the umbilicus longitudinally down the belly. He had his scalpel in his right hand and the cautery device in his left. He would cut and cauterize, and I would dab and smoke-suck. It was considered bad form to have the OR smelling of burning human flesh. A quick, on-the-ball smoke sucker was worth his or her weight in gold. There I was with Bracken, dabbing and sucking like a third-year surgical resident, my full attention on tracking his every move.

He quickly bisected through the nine layers of the abdominal wall. Using only his hands, he carefully separated the omentum that anchored the small bowel in layers of ribbon-like terraces, giving it both stability and a blood supply. As he positioned the wet, jelly-like contents behind the large metal alloy retractors exactly where he wanted them, he would give them a slight shake and let go. The shake was my cue to grab them and hold them in place. I followed him like a cat stalking a rat. I could feel our timing coordinate as if we had been working together for years. Mind you, while all of this was going on, he continued to chat not only with me, but also with the other members of the surgical team.

The hole grew deeper until I was barely able to see down the shaft Bracken had created. He finally reached the abdominal aorta where it bisected into the right and left iliac arteries. This signified vertebral level three or four, where he could begin his dissection search for the sympathetic chain ganglia.

After a while he stopped and said, "There. Can you see it?" I stood on tiptoe and looked deep inside the ever-narrowing hole. The lumbar vertebrae were exposed. Overlying them was what looked like yellow globular fat within slimy-looking tissues resembling what you encounter when skinning a chicken. That was it? I thought. Contained within what looked like waste material lived one of the most complex and magical workings of the body. How divinely paradoxical.

After simply snipping the nerve chain with his long-handled, gold-tipped surgical scissors, Bracken grabbed the retractors from my numb hands and allowed the bowel contents to regain their usual positions. He put his hand out flat, expecting the loaded needle drivers to be slapped onto his palm by the scrub nurse to his right. As he was finishing closing the peritoneum, Doug came through the doors. Without looking up from what he was doing, Bracken sounded, "So what do we have?"

Doug began the report. "I scheduled Porter for a CT scan as well as an endoscopy to visualize the inside of the esophagus."

"Good," said Bracken. "When do we do it?"

"This afternoon, but there is one more thing. Mrs. Becker is becoming more and more hypotensive, and over the last twelve hours the nasogastric tube has produced over a liter of fluid." I had no idea of the scale of nasogastric tube secretions, but one liter was clearly way too much. Mrs. Becker, the eighty-four-year-old mother of Dr. Tomlinson, one of Bracken's colleagues, was suffering from a bowel obstruction from an unknown cause and had recently been transferred from an outlying hospital specifically so Bracken could take over her care. He was known to have a sixth sense when it came to sniffing out disease. Doug added, "Dr. Tomlinson wants to speak to you immediately, and our next case has been waiting in pre-op holding now for two hours."

With that, Bracken looked up from what he was doing, stared into my eyes, and handed me the needle drivers and pickups. I reached out and grasped them reflexively. He then stepped back from the table, grabbed the front of his surgical gown, ripping it off, and said, "Okay, Talty, you close. Come on, Dougy, let's rock and roll!" And off they went.

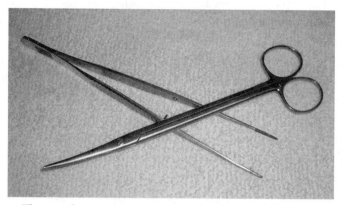

The actual surgical instruments Dr. Bracken handed to Janine to close Dr. Salvay in the operating room.

The meaning of his words at first did not register. There I was, standing in the operating suite holding surgical instruments, with the scrub nurse, the anesthesiologist, and the circulating nurse all staring at me. Someone had to continue Dr. Bracken's closure of Professor Salvay's abdomen. I began trying to collect my thoughts. The scrub nurse asked, "What suture do you want to use, *doctor?*"

I was obviously out of my league, and the wisest approach seemed to be honesty. I peered at her over my glasses and said, "Look, both you and I know I have no business doing this, so why don't you help me decide, based on your long career of assisting Dr. Bracken. What would he normally use in this situation?"

Reviewing in my mind what I had studied in the surgical textbook several hours before, I began to identify each fascial layer, using reabsorbable suture with a curved driving needle to run a continuous stitch. Layer after layer, working from deep to superficial, I closed up Dr. Salvay. When I got to the skin, I was home free. This was the only tissue I had practiced with in the past. I took special care not to bind the skin between stitches so there would be no dotted scars on either side of the longitudinal scar. Millimeter by millimeter, the moist red insides gradually disappeared. I buried the end and tied it off, and then dressed the wound as I had assisted Doug in doing for the previous two and a half weeks. The only thing left to do was write the post-op note and nursing orders.

Going through the motions, feeling as if I had done this all my life, made me wonder if, in fact, I was destined for a career in surgery. I had one major reservation: my back was not cooperating. Even though my constant low back pain had resolved spontaneously five years earlier, my back was not liking the endless hours of standing in one place stooped forward. On several occasions, I had even excused myself and broken scrub in order to squat forward to relieve the crushing pain that radiated down my buttocks, backs of the thighs, and around my entire pelvis.

We finished with the scheduled surgical cases at eight that night, just in time to grab a bite to eat before racing back to the ICU to ponder with Dr. Tomlinson what to do about Mrs. Becker. She was in no condition to undergo major abdominal surgery, but if he did not proceed with an exploratory laperotomy to find the cause of the obstruction, she would surely die. Not wanting to appear disinterested and certainly not feeling unwelcome, I stayed until I could barely keep my eyes open. I looked up at the wall clock: 1:05 a.m. Bracken saw my glance and said, "Shit, Talty, don't you have somewhere else to be?"

I smiled, thinking of my bed in the lonely dorm apartment, and replied, "No, sir. I am exactly were I need to be, following you around until the day is done. As far as I can see, this question has not yet been answered."

With that he commanded, "Doug, put her on the surgery schedule first thing in the morning. We are going in at first light." The relief on Sue Tomlinson's face confirmed that this was what she had hoped to hear.

After only a few hours sleep, I got up to do my morning run before rounding on Dr. Salvay. Relieved to find that the incision had remained closed overnight without any sign of infection, I ran downstairs to meet up with Bracken and Doug in the surgical lounge. As I pulled up a chair at the table where they were sitting, Bracken said jokingly to Doug, "We just can't seem to shake her, now, can we?"

I shot him a sarcastic smile and offered, "I just checked on Dr. Salvay, and her abdominal incision is doing just fine."

Bracken's eyes widened as if he had totally forgotten that the previous day he had left an unsupervised third-year medical student to

close a case, a task usually asked only of surgery residents. I was reminding him of his possible indiscretion, which turned out to be one of
the most memorable experiences of my entire training. I would check
on Dr. Salvay's incision at least twice per day until she was discharged
from the hospital. She was actually glad to know I was the one who had
sewn her up.

After opening up Mrs. Becker, we had our answer, or at least Doug,
Dr. Bracken, and Dr. Tomlinson, who scrubbed in for the case, did.
The entire peritoneum and its contents were covered in small islands
of grayish tissue—carcinomatosis, the same pathology that eventually
killed Rich Simoni. They lavaged the peritoneal cavity, manually "ran
the bowel," palpating for unexpected lesions, and then closed her up.
Everyone present knew there was not much else to do.

Bracken's schedule never let up. Day after day, his service was a
three-ring circus. Doug and I often discussed whether he should do the
fellowship. On one hand, it was an honor; on the other, all he wanted to
do was to get out of training, pass his board exams, and join a surgical
practice that had been recruiting him in Joplin, Missouri, close to his
hometown. I tried to help him weigh the options, and he would listen
intently. We had grown extremely close. There was an unspoken trust
and an intimacy the likes of which I had never experienced before. It
was not physical or sexual, but more a soul understanding and recognition. He seemed to know me on the same level as my father did, as if our
story together had not started only three and a half weeks earlier.

Perhaps the book I had just devoured, *Out on a Limb,* was influencing
me. Shirley MacLaine spoke openly about her experiences concerning
past lives. This was my first exposure to an outside source that essentially explained what my childhood old memories were. It also helped me
understand better my relationship with my father, and how our long-ago
conversations about sharing other lifetimes might, in fact, have been
right. I wondered what would happen if Dad ever met Doug. Would
they, too, have an immediate understanding of each other? And for what
purpose were Doug and I meeting in this time and place? My time with
him was quickly coming to an end. We might never know, I thought. A
nagging understanding in my subconscious told me that one day Dad
and Doug had to meet—it was a matter of order.

On the last Tuesday in March, Doug and I were charging down the hall after the nurses caring for Mr. Porter had paged him; Mr. Porter had just spit up another unit of blood. Quite out of the blue, in his gentle farm-boy accent, Doug turned and asked, "Talty, do you ever see auras?"

There it was. He had been picking up the same vibes from me as I had been from him. I laughed out loud, not wanting to reveal myself too quickly. "You are undoubtedly asking me this because I am from California, right?" I shot back. His face wore a look of complete vulnerability. He had just taken a huge risk. I knew then that he was completely serious. "Why are you asking me this?"

He responded, "I don't know for sure. I've never felt comfortable enough to ask anyone before."

My mind reeled. In a hundredth of a second, all the mysteries I had ever pondered came flooding in—old memories, past lives, telepathic communication, learning difficulties that were sometimes gifts, the search for my life's purpose. I had never discussed such things with anyone either, except my father. We stopped walking and faced off. "No, Doug, I do not believe I have ever seen an aura, but that doesn't mean I haven't felt them." I watched him take a deep breath; his boldness had just paid off. "Why do you ask?" I inquired again.

He started slowly. "I have seen auras since I was a kid. The first time was with my grandmother at a prayer revival when I was three. I asked her why everybody up on the stage had colorful lights around them. She understood what I was seeing and told me that I was a very special child and that one day I would understand what that meant. She encouraged me to use this gift to help people, but to be careful who I spoke about it with. I've kept it to myself until just now."

This opened a virtually nonstop conversation that filled our last seventy-two hours together. I think we discussed every metaphysical concept that had ever crossed our minds. I told him of the feeling I'd had the very first morning sitting by his side at the nurses' station. His energy seemed to blend with mine, like two old friends meeting. He responded that when I had sat down that morning, my aura had almost knocked him over, it was so large and bright; it had even caused his brain to momentarily short-circuit and his dyslexic traits to resurface. He had almost asked me right then about auras. Instead, it had taken him this long to get up the courage.

Doug could not believe I had never seen a person's auric field, and I couldn't believe that he, too, was dyslexic. He described Bracken's aura to me. It was huge and filled with different colors on different days. His face changed as a thought came to his mind. "I have an idea. Next case, you stand across from me, we'll both look at Bracken at the same time. I will try to modulate the auric field vibration so you can see it with me."

"You can really do that?" I shot back.

He said, "Sure, with your help, of course. All you have to do is gaze with 'soft sight' at the center of his forehead and concentrate with pure intention. You'll be able to see it, too."

The opportunity presented itself at the 11 a.m. case on Thursday. Dr. Bracken and I started the case while Doug was finishing up the previous patient. When Doug joined us, he nonchalantly approached the table and stood to watch. Bracken was talking a mile a minute as usual, about nothing in particular. The rapid-fire chatter increased after Doug's arrival. Bracken loved his Dougy and he needed him to make a commitment about the fellowship soon. We dutifully listened. He always spoke on what I would understand much later as the first and second chakra levels—money, sex, and power. Not once did I hear him contemplate the great mysteries in life.

After a few minutes I glanced up at Doug. He was already staring at me. Our connected gaze communicated: *It's time.* We both turned to look at Bracken. I commanded my eyes and visual cortex to shift into soft sight, where peripheral vision and central vision blend together. To my surprise, I started seeing a blue and green haze swirling around Bracken's head, gradually expanding outward until it occupied the space two feet around him. I was seeing his aura. Just like that. I stopped breathing, I was so surprised by its beauty.

Bracken himself suddenly stopped both his hands and his verbal chatter. He looked up at Doug, as if realizing that he had just been seen in a completely different way. He seemed to draw in all of his immodest energy and shrink in size. When he spoke again, my perception of the aura faded. "Doug, you are already a good surgeon. I want to make you an extraordinary one. There is something I want to teach you that only I can. And that is to know when things are going to go bad before they do."

Doug and I glanced at each other in utter disbelief. We were witnessing a phenomenon.

Bracken went on. "I have an extraordinary ability to sense when a patient is going to crump. I have saved countless lives this way." ("Crump" is medical slang for decompensate.) Bracken then launched into telling us a story that happened to him during his residency. He had used his intuitive skills to help save countless lives at a multiple vehicle car accident. "That's what I want to teach you, Dougy," he said. "This sense is a gift and it can be taught to others. We all have it. This is why I'm at a teaching hospital. It's my duty to pass on this skill to others, and I want to teach it to you over the course of next year. What do you say?"

What had we just done? Doug's face was mirroring my astonishment. Our directed gaze with the intention to connect with Bracken's energetic system had opened a portal to his inner being. Even though he was not accustomed to speaking from the heart, he found himself doing so. A sacred space had formed, which allowed an inner wisdom to show up and connect the three of us in a way not possible before. We had unknowingly created an energetic alchemy that together was much more powerful than the sum of each of us alone. Over these past few weeks with these two men, I had come out of myself as a student, stepped into the role of mentor, and offered insight beyond my conscious perception. Our camaraderie held a spark and an energy all its own that contributed to the fullness of the experience. Bracken's "sky's the limit" attitude resonated with Doug and me and it was the probable reason why he let his guard down with me so early and felt compelled to teach Doug what he dared not reveal to the rest of the medical community.

Doug ended up choosing Dr. Bracken's fellowship and becoming a highly skilled general and vascular surgeon. We kept in sporadic touch through medical training and setting up our practices. On occasion, he would suddenly pop into my conscious awareness. Invariably, soon afterward, I would be paged overhead at the hospital and know it was Doug calling. This sort of telepathic communication continues between us to this day.

Raff shortly after we found him.

16

Guidance from the Elders

"**W**hen the student is ready, the teacher will appear." This ancient Chinese proverb was never so true as it is for you. The Universe continues to assemble the most highly developed and advanced light workers who have spent their lives preparing to usher in the next generation. Their cell tissue recognizes you immediately; it is burned into their DNA. They have readied the nest to nurture you to the next level. As they hand over the treasures of their knowledge gleaned from this existence, they can only hope their efforts have been great enough.

To you, they feel like the mentor/protector from your youth. This is how you recognize and trust them immediately. You appreciate the power these relationships will hold for you and for the mission you have come to complete. As you become facile in the art of letting go, you are constantly amazed at how you are protected and coddled in the warm and loving understanding that you cannot fail. You have unselfishly chosen to participate in this reality at this most crucial time. Your agreement to do so is appreciated beyond what you can ever imagine.

I was accepted at Lansing General Hospital, the training facility for the College of Osteopathic Medicine at Michigan State, for what is widely known among medical students as hell year. As an intern, you are available twelve hours a day, seven days a week, to do anything you are asked by anybody, including the janitors. Even they rank above you. The purpose is to expose the intern to every aspect of medical care. In other words, they did not want us to miss anything, especially in the middle of the night while the attending physicians are sleeping.

I prepared myself to give up what little personal life I had left. José and I had not gone out to dinner or to a movie in four years. The only television I watched was the news while scarfing down my dinner between reading assignments.

The intern class that started July 1, 1992, consisted of five members, two of whom, James Extine and Peter McAndrews, made it known that they, like me, were vying for the two coveted orthopedic surgery first-year residency positions the following year. Both had done rotations at Lansing General, which put me at a huge disadvantage. They told me there was one female ortho resident, Denise Williams, who was in her first year, the first female accepted in the program—ever. My chances would unfortunately depend on how she performed. They also told me the ins and outs of how to land a spot; the current ortho residents had coached them.

Some of the guys had purchased for an attending physician a two-year membership at the new Michigan Athletic Club just off campus. Others had shown up at the attendings' homes on the weekends and washed all the cars in the driveway. It didn't stop there. We also needed to win over the surgery residents. Jim and Peter gave me one more piece of advice. If I wanted to look interested, I needed to show up Monday mornings at 6 a.m. for the radiology report conducted by the residents who had been on call over the weekend.

I could barely believe what I was hearing. Nothing seemed worth going to those personally humiliating lengths. If I was going to land one of the spots, I decided, I would do it honestly, by outperforming these guys.

During orientation, we were given our schedule of monthly rotations for the entire year. The month considered the easiest was the one spent half in OMM and half in radiology. Ideally, that rotation would be placed strategically after a difficult month, like nights or ER. As I looked over my documents, however, I saw that OMM and radiology were my first rotation. That meant no scheduled break in the middle of my upcoming year.

On the first Monday, I made it to the 6 a.m. radiology conference after a one-mile swim in the YMCA pool. The "Resident Only" section of the lot was already filled with cars. Not just any cars. Every one was a brand new sports sedan, a monster SUV, or a sports car. Driving my little Honda through the sea of BMWs, Porsches, and Land Rovers, I wondered if I had made a wrong turn into "Attending Physician" parking. No, the sign was correct. Wow, I thought, these guys are either doing a lot of extra call or going out of their way to impress each other.

Locating the room was not difficult. It was the only one at that early hour filled with people. The room was filled with young men dressed in designer Italian silk suits and loafers of fine hand-sewn leather, and adorned with gold—lots of gold. They had gold bracelets dripping from their wrists, huge gold rings on several fingers of both hands, and heavy gold necklaces. They looked like boxers on television before their fights in Las Vegas. These outward displays spoke of one intention among this group: to make a lot of money. I had almost forgotten that orthopedic surgeons are among the highest paid physicians, so the field attracted those whose goal in life was financial wealth, no matter what needed to be done to get there. Taking a seat between two young men, I turned to each of them and introduced myself. They barely paid me any attention. Well, I thought, I wonder which of them had kissed the butt of which attending physician to earn a spot in the residency?

The moment I had crossed the threshold of that room, a feeling of suffocation in my chest spread simultaneously both south and north through my torso. My entire energetic system was screaming at me. As the meeting got under way, I grew anxious, a feeling that eased off only when an absolute knowing dropped into my conscious awareness like an anvil falling from the ceiling. If I wanted to become an orthopedic surgeon, I would either have to be initiated into this tribe with whom I had nothing in common or fight my way in and be forever an outsider.

Just as clear as this knowing was the awareness that it was not coming from me. I was receiving the most direct guidance yet. Some external force was grabbing me and trying to shake me awake. I sat there dumbfounded, having my own personal moment, as the senior resident went over the cases. The meeting lasted until seven. I left the room feeling as if my entire world had just been ripped away from me. In Ohio, it was a scheduling fluke that had directed me away from orthopedic surgery. This time the message was more visceral. My own system was telling me that what I thought I wanted was not to be, after all.

For the first time in my life, I did not know what I was going to be when I grew up. As I walked across the hospital and down the corridor to the attached medical office building that housed the outpatient manual medicine department, a thousand emotions and thoughts streamed through my consciousness. As my hand turned the doorknob, I decided to put all this aside for now and just enjoy my two weeks in a familiar subject that had always brought me acclaim.

I had been assigned to Drs. R. G. Curtiss and Sherman Gorbis, both specialists in osteopathic manual medicine. I introduced myself to the receptionist and she waved me through the clinic door. On the other side was a slight, dark-haired, middle-aged nurse named Julie who greeted me with a big, warm smile. She even knew my name. Then she walked me down the hall to meet Dr. Curtiss. The hallway and treatment rooms were empty, as this clinic did not start seeing patients until 8 a.m. Dr. Curtiss had come in early specifically to meet me.

Dr. Curtiss looked up from his desk. He was a mature gentleman whose demeanor was immediately friendly, warm, and soothing, like a favorite overcoat recently rediscovered at the back of the closet. He motioned to the chair next to his desk. "We have some time before the patients start coming in."

I realized I was in the company of a grandfather, a tribal elder. Dr. Curtiss was a throwback to an era when a physician was expected to handle every aspect of healing, using few resources other than steady hands, a tuned-in gut feeling, and a good mind for science. As we spoke, I felt my insides soften and meld with the delicious comfort emanating from this gentle soul.

Finally, the conversation swung around to manual medicine. He wanted to know if I was interested in the subject or was planning just to observe. A mere 1.2 percent of DOs practice manual medicine, he shared, and many fear that it is a dying art. "The students these days say manual medicine takes too long in a busy clinical practice, and remembering all the diagnostic positions and their treatment techniques is too hard," he added.

I disconnected from our mutual gaze and looked down, gathering my thoughts. "With my background in sports medicine," I said, "I took an immediate liking to OMM as a medical student and felt comfortable practicing it from the beginning. I was asked to be a TA, and eventually I was teaching the lab sessions. For reasons I have not yet shared, I seem to have a natural aptitude for the three-dimensional thinking it requires."

Looking up to read how my words had landed, I saw on his face something like a Cheshire cat smile. "What?" I asked. "Please say what is on your mind. Nothing is off-limits this morning. I have just come from the ortho radiology rounds meeting, where I received the intuitive message loud and clear that I won't be pursuing a career in orthopedics, even though that has been my goal since undergraduate school. I sit here right now open to any possibility. Actually, part of this feels really good. I've been so driven all my life; for the first time I can remember, I am free of it. Maybe I'm here at Lansing General for a purpose I don't yet know." The words rolling off my lips were startling in their clarity, as I had not yet registered all this in my mind.

He gazed at me, entirely aware of what was happening. This time it was he who looked down before speaking. "How interested in manual medicine are you?"

"Well," I said, "what do you mean? Like a career or something?"

He shot a glaring look directly through my pupils. "Yes, like a career."

I raised my eyebrows. "Well, I am not sure I have ever considered it before. Why?"

"A few professors in the Department of Clinical Biomechanics at Michigan State University, College of Osteopathic Medicine (MSU/COM) have been fiddling around for the past ten years formalizing a residency program in Osteopathic Manual Medicine (OMM.) They only need to get it approved through the American Osteopathic Association and get it funded. The other element, of course, is to have ready, willing, and interested candidates." Before I could say anything, he continued, "I will write them a letter to formally introduce you. This, I am sure, will spark them to move forward on the project before we all croak and have no one to replace ourselves."

At that point, Julie came in and announced that his first patient was ready in room one. As we walked down the hallway together my mind was spinning. In the first two hours of my first day of internship, the gods were hard at work spinning the wheel on which my destiny was being shaped.

Before my two weeks in radiology had ended, I received a letter from the Department of Clinical Biomechanics thanking me for my interest in the OMM residency program, along with a statement and application form. Dr. Curtiss's letter must have had an impact and these guys were wasting no time. The statement described three options. The three-year option was the two-year program plus all the requirements for a family practice residency, as well as forty-five graduate credits in biomechanics and research design. There it was, I thought, my next Mount Everest: option number three—two residencies plus the equivalent of a second master's degree. This program would leave me with a solid foundation in general medical knowledge in addition to the OMM training. As a tribute to Rich Simoni, I had vowed never to lose touch with the broad view of medicine even while developing a specialty.

In October, I was invited to a meeting of the Department of Bio-mechanics. In attendance were some of the who's who of osteopathic manual medicine. Dr. Ward took the lead, introducing himself as the future residency director.

He went on to explain the program. As the meeting was drawing to a close, Dr. Jacobs, the head of the MSU sports medicine department asked if I would be interested in teaching in the on-campus OMM labs for first- and second-year medical students.

I responded, "I would love to, but I don't know if I can get out of my duties at the hospital."

He smiled coyly. "Leave that up to us."

I never ventured back to the Monday morning radiology meetings, leaving the heated competition to Jim and Peter. And in early Decem-ber, I received the official letter from Dr. Ward. I had been accepted. In five short months, I had gone from thinking I had journeyed to East Lansing to become an orthopedic surgeon to sitting with the knights of the Osteopathic Manual Medicine round table, called into their service. Moreover, my seemingly unrelated and even contradictory interests, skills, and talents were beginning to weave together, like multicolored threads in a tapestry. OMM coupled left-brained understanding of bio-mechanics with right-brained, three-dimensional thinking and kines-thetic sophistication. Thinking back, I had been preparing for this field my entire life. Almost taking for granted my artistic and observational skills as a child, I had honed them, spending hours out in nature with my sketchpad and sculpting with clay and other media my mother would bring home from her art classroom. I now had permission to bring these abilities into the medical context. All of this was part of a grand scheme to mold me into a kind of physician that had the mind of an artist and the hands of a sculptor.

Now that the die had been cast for my immediate future, I could sit back and enjoy the rest of the abuse that came in internship. Actually, it never did hold up to its billing. Even the dreaded month of "nights" I found enjoyable. It was difficult to sleep when the sun was up, so I would go home, take a two-hour nap, and have the rest of the day to do what I chose. This proved dangerous. We were living in a rural location surrounded by farmhouses and paddocks filled with horses and cows. With all this unscheduled time on my hands, I could start to contemplate what in life outside of becoming a physician brought me joy. It was horses!

José's best friend at MSU, Janos, had a sister named Maria, who was breeding, training, and showing dressage horses and lived not too far away. On one of my trips out to her place that month, she showed me a horse-trading book that listed all horses for sale locally. I took it home and perused it at first just for fun. But as the weeks rolled by and I found myself at home after nights in the hospital doing rectal examinations on little old ladies with fecal impactions and attending to disoriented elderly gentlemen who repeatedly pulled out their urinary catheters, a thought began to sprout. I shared the book with José who, in his best "the world is our oyster" attitude, responded, "Why don't you get your own horse?"

That was all the water the seed needed. Without realizing it, I was about to manifest another childhood dream. Or was it a precognition? As a child my favorite drawing subject was a chocolate brown horse with black mane and tail, white socks, and a white blaze running down his nose, standing in a grassy paddock. Scanning the pages of horse ads left me emotionless, until I turned to the second-to-last page. The ad almost knocked me out of my chair. "Twelve-year-old bay gelding Arabian 14.3 hands, well broken, used in English and Western show, great on the trail. Price negotiable." The familiar heavy feeling in my gut told me I had to meet this horse. Even through the print in this small book, I recognized my old friend. I dialed the number immediately.

When we pulled in, we could see a skinny, mangy white horse, caked in mud but obviously excited that someone had shown up, standing in a small filthy corral. As we got out of the car, it darted inside a tiny makeshift lean-to that was barely high enough for the horse to clear the ceiling, wrapped in layers of old tarps in an attempt to make it waterproof. The owner arrived in his pickup, and after the obligatory greetings, went in the shed to bring Raff out for us to see. He emerged through the opening, pulling on the rope as if he were trying to land a huge sturgeon on deck. The other end was not moving.

Raff and Janine in Michigan.

I instinctively began making a clicking sound, the sound cowboys make when asking their horses to move forward. With that, out came one of the sweetest faces I had ever laid eyes on. Looking exactly as I had drawn him a thousand times, he had a beautifully angular face with huge, kind brown eyes, black bangs hanging down between two alert ears set apart on a broad forehead, with a white blaze running down to his muzzle. He spoke to me immediately. As he reluctantly came out into the overcast light of a Michigan April afternoon, I could see the evidence of his story.

He looked like a Dachau victim, his shoulder and hipbones sticking out with woolly brown fur covering what looked like empty space beneath. I trudged over and politely took the rope from the man's hand as I reached out, offering to stroke this beautiful creature's emaciated neck, all the while communicating that I was there to help and that his suffering would soon be over. In his skinniness, he dropped his muzzle into my palm and laid his forehead against my chest in an act of pure trust. In that instant, I knew my mission was to save this old friend.

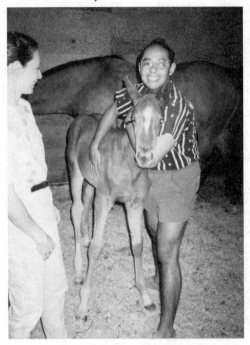

Maria, José and Tickle at four months old.

But that was not to be all. Maria's three mares all foaled that spring. I tracked the foalings with interest, and began forming a relationship with a filly named Tickle Me Pink, a beautiful chestnut with white socks on her two right feet and a narrow white blaze emanating from a star in the middle of her forehead. Tickle's birth had been traumatic, and she was born with back legs that were deformed. She and I developed a special bond during her first few months, as I would stop to play with her on my way home from the clinic. As her broom-bristle mane grew, it fell evenly to both sides of her long and graceful thoroughbred neck. When she galloped, it looked like two wings flapping up and down— as close to my old friend Pegasus, the mythical winged horse that had haunted my dreams in childhood, as a real live horse might ever get. In the course of a few months, I was the owner of two horses.

Janine and Tickle as a foal.

VINTAGE
Etude
Pinot Noir
CARNEROS
240 BARRELS WERE CELLARED AND BOTTLED BY ETUDE
RUTHERFORD, CALIFORNIA • ALCOHOL 13.5%

17

The Wine Bottle

*T*he relationship that you the Indigo Child establish with your special mentor is one of the most profound and long-lasting you will experience with another human being in your lifetime. Often these bonds are multidimensional and have been shared over many lifetimes. As it is with the twin soul concept, the mentor and the Indigo are so similar it is uncanny. It is as if they are the same person who was split into two separate bodies. This is why the mentor is such a fierce protector of the young Indigo early on. Expanding your vision of who you really are is required. Your essence, your life force, exists simultaneously on several different planes. It is like a radio tuned to a specific station on a specific channel or frequency that creates a perceived reality that is exclusive from all the other stations broadcasting at the same time.

While I was away in the Midwest sowing my educational wild oats, much was happening on the home front. The Santa Clara Valley went from some of the most agriculturally fertile land to silicon. San Jose mushroomed from a peaceful suburban community to a burgeoning city.

As the population swelled, so did the legal field, and my father's business along with it. Over the years, he had developed a stellar reputation among the attorneys but was a poor businessman. My brother was a visionary who graduated from college with a degree in business and a vow to make his first million by the age of thirty. He went to work for my father to clean his fiscal house. This took a huge pressure off my dad. He could go back to doing what he did best: being the nice guy, schmoozing with the attorneys and their staff, and doing the business of court reporting.

Dad and Mike developed a passion for wine, even making their own in the garage.

Mike enrolled in the viticulture and enology program at the University of California at Davis. As his knowledge of biochemistry grew, so did the quality of each year's vintage. The family business was getting back to its bootlegging roots. They would have made my Nebraskan great-grandmother proud. Mike and Dad talked about one day owning their own vineyard. Because Mike had done such a great job of making the business financially solvent, Dad and Mom began making plans for their retirement. Dad was in his mid-fifties by then and would fantasize about living in Tuscany with Mom six months of the year. They were laying the groundwork to make it happen.

While my parents were looking ahead to their retirement, I was busy shaping myself into something the world had never seen before—with a lot of help, of course. Even though Dr. Ward and the director of the family practice residency, Dr. Carol Monson, had been in negotiation for months about combining the two residencies, it turned out that the family practice department's new chair, Dr. Robert Marcereau, would have the final say about how the rotations and electives of the two residencies would dovetail to satisfy both programs. He lived near Detroit, ninety miles from MSU, and was going to be commuting every day. At our first meeting, he admitted that no one was sure how this double residency experiment was going to work out, he said. I would need to remain flexible and patient with the process.

I assured him I was well aware of this. "Actually, I could be considered a risk taker. The adventure of it all appeals to me."

"A fine attitude to have," he responded, "for our first guinea pig with a zipper."

A smile crossed my face. I liked the image.

Dr. Marcereau gradually directed the conversation to get to know me as a person, starting in all the usual places: school, interests outside medicine, and family. The conversation took on an added spark when I mentioned that my brother and father were garage wine makers. "I love wine and have been an avid collector as well," Dr. Marcereau offered. He went on and on about his favorite varietals, growing regions, and vineyards. "What types does your family produce?" he asked.

"Zinfandel, cabernet, and chardonnay," I responded, "and they have played with Nebbiolos and pinot noirs."

"Pinot noir," he asked, "what's that?"

The question startled me. As a wine enthusiast, had he never even heard of pinot noir? I hated the taste of wine and couldn't give him a rundown on pinot, but I shared that wine tasting was my father's favorite sport, and going along with him to the wine country was a gastronomical event. I then began describing the special relationship I had with my father, how he had been my greatest teacher, and how lucky I felt to be his daughter.

Marcereau sat back and listened with a soft, understanding smile on his face. When I was finished, he began describing a similar relationship he had with his eldest daughter. The bond between us was now solidified. An idea took seed in my subconscious, though it would not actually push through into the sunlight of conscious awareness for a few more months.

José and I had purchased a small farm near our house where we could keep Raff and Tickle, renting out the farmhouse itself. Stopping every night on my way home to muck stalls and feed the horses kept me sane. Watching Tickle grow was a magnificent experience.

For the first time in almost eight years, I was not going home for Christmas. Because I was going to be working through the holidays, I insisted that José attend a wilderness conference in Lake Tahoe to which Janos had invited him. My parents, who loved Janos as their second son-in-law, offered the beach house to them to recoup after the chill of the Sierras.

That autumn, Dr. Marcereau had attended many late-afternoon and evening meetings on my behalf as the biomechanics and family medicine departments sorted out communications about my residency, often not making it home to Detroit until late at night. I felt guilty, though I was sure, if the tables were turned, that my father would be extending the same courtesy to his daughter. I knew my father would want to thank him for his extra efforts and I knew the perfect gift. Before José left for California, I meant to ask him to request a bottle of pinot noir from my dad's private wine collection for my surrogate father here in Michigan. But in the midst of the usual last-minute packing and preparations, I forgot. Oh, well, I thought, there would be plenty of opportunities to ask Dad over the phone before José returned two weeks later.

December 14, 1993, started like just another day. I woke up and headed out the door with Indy for our usual jog around the lake, then showered and made it to the hospital by seven. I was engrossed in the fast-paced lifestyle of an ER rotation that month, performing procedures and sewing up lacerations. Even though it was a long, busy day, and the staff hardly had a break, I asked the ER attending physicians if I could leave one hour early that evening, since, with my husband away, I had to feed my animals and then get back to the hospital by seven to take call that night. They agreed without question.

As I was pulling out of the parking lot, headed for home twenty minutes away, my pager went off. Mind you, this was before the days of cell phones. I pulled the pager off my scrubs waistband and looked at the number. A 408 area code. José always managed to page me when I could least respond to the call. There was no time to stop at a pay phone and call him back. Besides, I thought, they are probably out to dinner or having cocktails somewhere, having a great time, and simply calling to rub it in. I was the poor sap still "dragging the plow," as my father called it.

By the time I reached the farmhouse, my pager had gone off four times, all with the same phone number. Man, I thought, is he ever insistent! This was very much in character for him, so it didn't occur to me to be alarmed.

I quickly mucked the stalls, threw grain and hay in bins, then was off to walk Indy and feed her, too. Again my pager went off. Even though the phone was close, I could not spare even one minute to talk or I would be late getting back to the hospital. By 6:45, I was on the road headed back to Lansing General with my pager going off every five to ten minutes. Finally, out loud I proclaimed, "I will call you when I get to the resident call room—I swear!" After parking behind the hospital, I made my way hurriedly down the long hallway. Pushing the door open, I reached for the phone and dialed the number.

It rang only once. José's voice was on the other end. "Hello?"

"Hi, dog, what's up?" I said. "Dog" was one of my endearments for him.

"Why didn't you call back sooner?"

"I was driving back and forth between the hospital and the house to feed everyone. I'm on call tonight, remember?"

"Oh, yeah, that's right. I'm sorry, I forgot." I was fully expecting to hear a complete rundown of the fun things they had been doing, eating, and drinking. Instead he asked, "Where are you now?"

"I am sitting in the call room at Lansing General here on duty," I responded.

He then asked a strange question. "Is there anyone else with you right now?"

The room was all of ten feet by ten feet with a separate bathroom. I scanned the room obediently, knowing full well it was empty except for me. "No, I am completely and totally alone—thank God."

He paused, and started his next sentence with the word "Janine."

At that moment, I knew something beyond the current menu choices was up. He never used my given name when addressing me. He had fired the verbal warning shot, the technique we physicians are trained to use when having to deliver bad news to patients or their family members.

"Janine, your dad had a heart attack today."

I thought he must be joking, even though the subject matter was completely distasteful. "José, that is really not funny.

He tried again. "Jakie, I am *not* kidding. Your dad had a heart attack today."

"For real?" I shot back, immediately flashing on all the myocardial infarction patients I had treated that month alone in the ER who had been hospitalized, worked up, and either sent home or sent straight to the catheterization lab and possibly to surgery for a cardiac bypass. Conceding at that point that this could be what happened, I asked in a detached tone, as if we were discussing just another patient, "How is he?"

This time there was a longer pause. "Janine, he did not make it."

Still feeling as if we were talking about some other person—*any* person other than my father—I could feel my insides begin to understand what my mind was still unwilling to.

"Come on, José, quit joking around. You are sick, really sick."

He tried again. "Janine, he passed away today at about 12:30 p.m. He was at the athletic club on the NordicTrack machine. Eyewitnesses said he fell backward off the machine and lay there with his eyes open at first, but he was not breathing."

I sat stunned, unable to speak, because I was undergoing the largest energetic short circuit I had ever experienced. This must have been agonizing for José, who loved my dad as much as anyone and also knew the profound bond my dad and I shared. I still would not allow myself to take in this information fully. It kept bouncing off my toughened exterior. "Didn't anyone do anything? Wasn't EMS called? He didn't really just *die* …did he?"

It was obvious to José that he needed to go further. "Janos and I were with your brother on our way over to the beach house when Mike's pager went off. It was the office looking for him. When we got to the house, we called and were told to go straight to San Jose Hospital because Bill had collapsed exercising. The entire way, Janos and I were trying to console Mike, going through the usual scenarios of what happens when a patient is brought in with either unstable angina or a true MI, and describing all the options such as following serial cardiac enzymes, treadmill evaluation the next morning, cardiac catheterization, and possibly cardiac bypass. We were sure he would fall into one of those categories. Besides he had absolutely no risk factors, save for being a male over the age of fifty-five, and he had exercised and maintained normal weight his entire life. By the time we got to the ER, we were sure we were going to find him connected to all the monitors, sitting up in bed, wondering what all the fuss was about."

José's words were soothing. They gave me a few more moments of hope. That was exactly my first reaction, I thought. Perhaps I had misunderstood him after all.

He went on. "Jakie, when we got there, the entire ER family bereavement room was filled with people. Some I recognized and some I didn't. All of them seemed to know Mike, and all of them were crying. We went directly up to the doctor who had received Bill for the medical report. He had been in EMD upon arrival. They cardioverted your father three times, he went into asystole, and even though they attempted compressions, there was no response."

Now I really felt as if we were discussing just another patient. But suddenly, the walls came crashing in on me. Emotion welled up from the depths of my being the likes of which I had never experienced before. I was caught in my own personal tsunami, drowning and not even caring to fight to the surface to breathe. The tears then came with the force of a driving hurricane. I was about to fall headlong into an abyss so deep and so dark that it would take years before I would find the strength to crawl my way out.

I am not sure how but I was able to arrange for a substitute for the night, drive myself home, make plane reservations to fly out the next morning, and pack my things. Then I called Dr. Marcereau to tell him I would not be at work for the next few days. I was keeping it remarkably together until he answered the phone. It was 10 p.m., much later than it was respectful to phone a colleague. I realized this would be the first time these words would leave my lips.

"Hello, Janine, what can I do for you?"

"Dr. Marcereau, I am not sure if I am even going to be able to say this." My throat seized up and I could not take another breath. I felt unbelievably weak. I'm a doctor, for God's sake, I should be able to at least speak at a moment like this, I thought. Finding it impossible to hold back the torrent, I started sobbing right there on the phone.

"What is it, Janine?" he demanded. "What has happened?"

Through uneven gasps for air, my eyes pouring with tears, and the mucous membranes of my nose already swelling, all I could get out was a squeak. "My father."

"What about your dad? What has happened?" he insisted.

Trying a second time to speak the dreaded words, I could not, knowing that letting them out would make what had happened real. I just sat in my chair in my basement at my desk staring at a photograph of my dad and me at my brother's wedding rehearsal dinner.

On the other end of the line, Dr. Marcereau continued trying. "Janine, Janine, what has happened to your father?"

Finally, I was able to mutter, "He died today."

"What? Are you serious?" he shot back, displaying as much disbelief as I had at first.

Now that the words were out, I wiped my nose and eyes, and told him the story, painfully and slowly. "He evidently had a heart attack. José is out there right now. He called me about three hours ago. I am calling to let you know that I will be flying out tomorrow and am not sure when I will be coming back. I was hoping you could call Dr. Ward and Dr.

Monson for me in the morning to let them know. I am obviously having a hard time talking right now."

Knowing sleep would evade me that night, I took Indy and drove to the barn to be in the healing energy of the horses. I was reeling from an unfamiliar loneliness in the pit of my stomach, as if I had just been unplugged from source energy. I had always assumed the connection with my father was a profound emotional bond, more than the usual father-daughter relationship but still explainable in those terms. Now I realized, because of its absence, that it had been much more. We were of one essence, one medium, one light. Though we had known there was more to our story, I had never considered that our very circuitry was enmeshed. My solar plexus felt like a gaping slash the equivalent of the Grand Canyon in the earth's surface.

The flight home was ethereal, standing at the check-in counter with cheerful Christmas music playing overhead, twinkling lights and garlands on the miniature Christmas trees on the counters, the airline crew and passengers all happy. They were flying home for the holidays. I cried the entire time, trying not to make a scene. The flight attendants did not know what to do with me.

To this day I do not remember who picked me up at the airport, probably José and Janos, but I do remember pulling up to the house. The street was lined with cars and the house was full of people. Mom and I embraced for what seemed like hours. Melting into each other's warmth and rhythmic breathing felt safe and secure.

When we finally pushed back far enough to look into each other's eyes, she simply said, "What am I going to do with this dog?" She was referring to Holly, the chocolate Labrador Mike and I had given Dad for Christmas a year earlier. We had wanted to give Dad a hunting dog for his birding trips with his buddies, now that Rich was no longer there to bring along his dog. Holly, however, turned out to be an uncontainable bundle of canine hyperactivity. She had spent the year banished to the backyard, where she chewed up the Jacuzzi cover and repeatedly retrieved the pool sweep.

I shook my head in amazement at her comment, but it did serve to break the intense sorrow of the moment. My attention turned to poor Holly, who must have been the most confused creature present, looking in at all the people through the mud-streaked sliding glass door. In that instant, I decided to take her back to Michigan with me.

Mom then made her best attempt at telling me "her story," where she was and what she was doing when she heard that my father had died. I prepared myself for the next wave of emotion that was surely headed my way. She recanted the morning events before he left for work, how it seemed like such a normal day. He got up, drank his coffee while reading the paper, dressed in his own personal room that had been converted into an air-conditioned wine room, combing his hair in the bathroom mirror, jokingly reminding them both as he did every morning, "God! I get better looking every day—how is that possible?"

She had reminded him to drive safely, as it had rained overnight and the weatherman had predicted showers that morning. She continued, "I thought it was strange when he called me around 10:30 to ask if I could see the rainbow. I said, 'What rainbow?' He said, 'Go outside and look north. There's the most vivid and beautiful rainbow I have seen since Rich passed away. It's breathtaking!' So I took the cordless phone out with me onto the driveway and looked north. I couldn't see anything but gray skies. Then he said, 'Carol, this is Rich's rainbow. He is here today—I can feel it.'"

I stared into my mother's eyes, a tingling sensation running through my body, which I now recognize occurs when someone is speaking the truth about the mystery of our existence. My inner being suddenly knew that on some level he had planned his own exodus, his age-old friend Rich returning to assist him on his journey. What were we doing standing around being sad for him? He had simply stepped out of his body, without pain, fanfare, or suffering. We should be celebrating his life, rather than mourning our loss.

Hordes of people continued to filter in; people I had not seen in years showed up, all looking blindsided by the news. We smothered ourselves in the story, over and over again. No one would have considered a guy who was in such great shape and had so much to live for dying suddenly at the age of fifty-seven.

I went outside to be with Holly and try to explain to her that she would not be seeing Dad anymore, he had made his transition yesterday, leaving in an instant. Why? Was he, in fact, finished down here in Earth School? "He must have been," I spoke out loud, safely to the dog, who stared longingly into my eyes. My father must have completed all that he came here to do. That meant that my training with him must be complete. I was now ready to carry on the work alone. *What work?* What was the task that haunted me day after day, year after year? What was I preparing for? Was any of this ever going to make sense?

I knew what I had accomplished thus far was not the end goal. Yet I had nearly completed the biggest step: building a bridge across the abyss of self-doubt and learning disabilities connecting to the physician I already knew I was—something I had been initiated into while tending sick and injured animals in this very backyard so many years ago. Sitting here in this space now, on the very lounge chair I had slept on for a year, protected by my nighttime white owl teacher, next to the pool where I grew up pretending to be a dolphin, with an orphaned dog who wanted nothing other than to crawl inside my body for the heart connection she longed for, I had a strange and premature sense that all was well. Was this message coming from outside of me, I wondered. How could I be feeling peace at a time like this?

Just then Mike slid the glass door open enough to poke his head out and said, "Janine, we need to go to the mortuary and begin making the arrangements. Do you feel like joining Mom and me?" His question felt as if he and Mom thought I wasn't strong enough to face this next duty. Still being treated like the little sister always irked me. José, Janos, Aunt Janet, and Aunt Jayne joined Mom, Mike, and me. My mom's sister and sister-in-law were pillars of strength and together planned the funeral events. José and Janos were a different story. Here were two highly capable medical doctors, one practicing internal medicine, the other ER medicine. Yet both admitted that this death pierced the professional armor they had been trained to encase themselves in. Neither had lost a family member or friend this close before. They sat at the round table in the mortuary office, their skin pale and green, saying nothing.

The first question out of the funeral director's mouth was, "Does anyone here know the deceased wishes?" We looked at each other. What wishes? He cleared his throat and tried again, "Does anyone know if he wanted to be buried or cremated?" That was blunt enough to get us talking. "This is the first matter at hand, as it will determine the type of caskets I will be showing you." I could feel myself slipping away from present time, back to a time and place long before.

I was sitting on my father's crossed leg in the family room of our house on Marina Way, watching a nature show about a lion bringing down a gazelle on the Serengeti Plain, realizing that my father would die one day and leave me alone here in this wilderness, just as the gazelle had left her fawn in the tall grass near by. A lightning bolt of recollection jolted me back into present time. I said with conviction, "He wanted to be cremated."

The talking stopped immediately. Mike, who had been taking the lead in family decision-making, looked at me, bewildered. "How do you know, Janine?"

I paused, briefly querying my ability to remember such a thing. "Because I know," I continued. "He and I talked about it many times. He wanted to be cremated." It came out of my mouth again with boldness as if channeled from some other source.

I was fully aware that no one in our family had ever been cremated before. All of our relatives had ended up at Santa Clara Mission Cemetery on Lincoln Avenue. My devout Catholic aunts looked especially knocked off their seats. I looked at Mom. She was expected to make the final decision. She did not look capable of deciding whether she preferred coffee or tea, let alone considering whether to enclose her beloved husband's dead body in a metal, worm-proof box or torch him to be spread at some later date.

The funeral director's monotone voice broke the silence. "Which will it be?"

José asked, "Jakie, are you *really* sure?"

I gave him a piercing glance. "I have never been more sure of anything in my life."

With that Mom spoke up, sounding relieved. "Okay, then, cremation it will be."

The group let out a collective sigh. At least one decision had been made.

None of the other decisions mattered to me. Sitting in this dimly lit room with its gold lamps and musty, outdated wallpaper, I realized Dad and I had been preparing for this moment our entire lives. We were transitioning into a new kind of relationship. I would now need to rely entirely on the uncanny silent communication we had shared. That pure exchange of thought had come naturally with him, just as it had with the animals. The sweetness of consciously communicating that way, alongside the words and gestures of normal embodied conversing, is what I would miss the most, I reflected. As my mind spun off into another tornado of grief, I grasped for anything to soften my landing. I pulled in the thought of Doug, the only other person on the planet with whom I knew this sort of communication was possible. Now I would never know if Dad and Doug would feel a connection with each other as I had with each of them. Perhaps their meeting was never meant to be.

Sleep did not come easily to me that night, though I was exhausted. José and I were in my old bedroom, still decorated in the same wild 1970s white-and-green birch tree wallpaper. Naturally awaking at 4:30 a.m., staring at the Casablanca ceiling fan on the ceiling, I felt compelled to be with my dad. I was already missing his wide, handsome, playful smile and those mischievous eyes. The one place in the house that was all his was the wine room just down the hall. If his essence was still with us, it would be in there. I left the warm comfort of the bed, grabbed my journal and a pen, and slipped down the hallway.

It was still dark as I turned the doorknob, letting myself in. My searching hand found the light switch and flipped the lever up. The cold air hit my body as the light brought the room to life. I took a steadying breath, not sure if I would be able to do this. The walls were stacked floor to ceiling with built-in cubicles, each large enough to hold twelve bottles of wine. Some were full and others were not. On one side of the room were stacks of wooden cases with names like Opus 1, Charles Krug, and Rafanelli burned into the exposed sides. The closet was open. Dad's clothes hung there as they had three mornings earlier. Next to the closet was his desk, cluttered with papers in a loosely organized mess, where he would sit and pay bills or fill out tax forms, submitting both at the last minute—two elements of life he would surely not miss. I sat on the floor, leaning against the protruding bottles, to write his epitaph for the funeral service scheduled for the next day, as my aunts had requested. Where to start? Instead of thinking, I simply put pen to paper. The words came cascading forth.

The scene at the Rosary (the wake the night before the funeral) was like an outtake from *The Godfather*. Droves of people streamed in. We had no idea the numbers of people my father had touched. A huge man Dad had played racquetball with for thirty years at noon at the YMCA collapsed in tears at the sight of him in the casket and had to be physically helped out of the chapel, his arms over the shoulders of his two sons, his body limp. Dad's UPS man came in, still in uniform, sobbing while telling us how Dad never forgot him at the holidays. A Jewish contractor friend of Dad's told us that for the past five years he had had a standing lunch date with Dad every Thursday. He proceeded to set up a table of finger food and main dishes for the ever-expanding crowd, reminding us that it was Thursday, and he had missed his lunch with Dad today. I stood, an empty shell, in the family receiving line, dutifully reaching for people's hands as they filed by, avoiding the hugs that lasted much longer than a normal embrace with someone you didn't know. Unaware of it at the time, what I was trying to avoid was them taking what little life force I had left. Their sorrow mixing with mine was eventually too much to take. Feeling trapped and anxious, I faded into the darkest, quietest corner, and sat sobbing with my face in my hands.

If the Rosary was like *The Godfather,* the funeral looked straight out of a royal event. The chapel was a fairyland of photographs, mementos, flowers, and food. In an unprecedented move, the chief circuit court judge had closed the San Jose courts from ten to one to allow the judges and attorneys as well as the bailiffs, secretaries, janitors, and parking attendants to attend. Pavarotti's passionate rendition of "Ave Maria" played while the eventual 1,300 people filed up the center aisle. Many brought their favorite bottles of wine, Italian cheeses, olives, bunches of herbs, or bright red, yellow, and orange bell peppers and eggplants. Some brought fishing poles, some brought framed photographs of my dad and them going down rapids in river rafts or hunting or sailing, honoring his passion for life. With each gift placed at the altar, the fabric of my innards tore just a little bit more. The capacity of the church was no match for this phenomenon. Those who came late squeezed into the rectory or onto the steps of the entry.

Many people had prepared readings and presented them to the audience. My cousin Paul read mine. I was a mess. So was Kathy Simoni, Rich and Mary's oldest daughter, who sat behind me sobbing so loudly she was making a scene. We had chosen two songs to end the ceremony. The first was Bette Midler's rendition of "Wind beneath My Wings," one of Dad's favorites. The second we thought would express Dad's gratitude to people for having been a part of his life as they exited the church: Dionne

Warwick's "Friends." It was eventually put on repeat, as people instead just stood listening, the lyrics evidently describing their feelings.

Sunday night, Aunt Jayne and Uncle Les invited Mom, Mike, his wife, Katie, and me over for dinner. José and Janos had returned to Michigan the day before. Mom suggested that we bring the customary couple bottles of wine with us. Her words every time he brought another case of treasured liquid home—"Bill, you will never live long enough to drink all of that wine!"—reverberated in my mind as Mike and I stood in the wine room, taking it all in. His presence loomed there for me. Mike was busy going through the cubicles, making the selections for the evening. When he was finished, I followed him out of the room, turning off the light and shutting the door behind us.

Mike proceeded down the hallway to the kitchen. I turned the corner into the hall bathroom that shared a wall with the wine room to brush my teeth and comb my hair before we left. As I was mindlessly spitting out the toothpaste and rinsing, I heard a loud thump and saw the mirror momentarily expand toward me, distorting my image, and then snap back. I was stunned at first. Perhaps Kayla, Mike and Katie's two-year-old daughter had come down the hallway, fallen against the wall, and bumped her head with a loud bang. I poked my head out the door and scanned the hall for signs of a small child about to wail. It was empty. Without really deciding to, I turned the corner toward the wine room, opened the door, flipped on the light switch—and found myself in the presence of one of the most profound experiences of my life.

There, in the middle of the room, was a bottle of wine standing upright on the carpeted floor precisely where I had been standing just moments before, its label facing me. I knew in an instant all that it represented.

I burst into tears and said out loud, "You asshole, you actually did it!" I looked up to the ceiling, half expecting to see Dad hovering above me, mischievously grinning from ear to ear.

I knew before I looked that it was the bottle of pinot noir I wanted to take back for Dr. Marcereau. The request I had never verbalized to Dad or to José had just been granted anyway. In doing so, Dad had fulfilled the vow we had forged so many years earlier. This was the sign, which only I would recognize, that confirmed it was all true: we do live many times, and he and I had shared many lifetimes. The greatest mystery in life was put to rest in that one sweet moment, and there was nothing else to question. Our essence does live on, and he would still be with me, communicating through thought and synchronistic messages, even though he was no longer in physical form. He had taken away every doubt I had ever had and with it every question connected to death. There is no death. I could now go forth and live life to its magnificent fullness, knowing there was nothing to lose—not even my life.

I lifted the bottle from the floor, trying to focus through the cascade of tears. The label read "Etude Pinot Noir."

Alex and Carol.

18

Crossing the Bridge

*Y*ou are learning the art of "Letting go and letting God." You are now *trusting the Universal Forces who take you where you need to be and never fail to deliver the most delicious of this realm's pleasures. It saddens you to observe others who continue to anguish over every decision as if it were going to be their last. For you, it is easy to recognize the open doors and open windows that allow you to pass freely into the next adventure. "If it is easy, it is meant to be" is becoming your anthem. Let go of the details; that is not your work. Live in the moment but keep your eye on the horizon. Trust in the knowing that your course has been set from the beginning and, as long as you continue to heed the signs, you will continue to be shaped and polished in this fast-running river of light. As you make your transition from one stage to the next, your passage will take on mythic qualities. Recognize the ever-present "feathered nest" that is always waiting for you, assuring the direction of your next move.*

Returning to my work as a first-year resident that winter was a monumental challenge. Crushed under the sheer weight of the responsibilities and expectations of the two residencies, I was now missing part of the will to continue. I would reflexively want to reach for the phone to share my daily discoveries with Dad, and then remember that he was gone. Each time this happened, the wind was knocked out of me again. I felt alone, but in a different way from all the other times I had experienced loneliness. This was the loneliness of the orphan. Even though I had never felt as if I belonged anywhere, at least I had always had my dad, who understood and would comfort me with the message that he was always with me, my constant companion and relentless cheerleader. I felt so small, so weak, and so completely vulnerable. José, though he tried, could not do enough or say the right words to console me in my growing isolation. Nothing could fill the cavity that this loss had created.

Each day, driving to work in the silence of my car, I would reach a certain street corner and burst out in torrential tears, unable to control myself. Going through the motions of my day drove me deeper into a numbness that eventually led to a complete mental and emotional breakdown. My short-term memory was gone. I grew so confused. I had no business masquerading as a physician. I was the one who needed consoling and time to heal. In the messy business of doctor training, however, that opportunity never came. Instead, making my own diagnosis, I collected two sample bottles of the antidepressant Zoloft from the resident clinic and started my own treatment.

Over the months that followed, I found it comforting to spend time with my surrogate grandfathers in the department of biomechanics/ OMM. Dr. Ward was my closest confidant and also my greatest challenge. This master in the field of myofascial release technique would lay his large hands on a patient's back and slide the skin around, speaking of "creep" and "inherent tissue plasticity." Also a master anatomist, he tried to teach me to visualize into the tissues with my hands. After hours of trying to understand cognitively what he was talking about, I decided to tune out the words and simply observe what he was doing. The two were entirely different. This simple shift allowed me to get into the "Zen" of learning manual medicine—shut off the verbal chatter and let the tissues under my hands guide me intuitively, manually, and three-dimensionally. Once I understood that I could do what came naturally to me, my skills advanced tremendously.

The transcendental quality of Dr. Ward's clinic was in sharp contrast to the analytical, left-brained style of Dr. Greenman. Phil was the master body mechanic. He had good hands, of course, but the true grail lesson that he offered was the ability to describe in engineering terms every spinal segment restriction we were treating. He was a magician at diagnosing and treating ailments of the body. People would come from all over the country and Canada to see him. Nothing came into the clinic that these master wizard manipulators could not fix. I would stand against the wall and watch, marveling at their skill and confidence. I wanted to be exactly like them one day, able to identify and treat absolutely any somatic problem a patient could present with.

Sadly, one year after Dad died, I was forced to put my constant companion Indy down. She had developed a tumor in her abdomen and was telling me she was in pain. When I had found her as a puppy at the pound in 1982, I had promised her that we would one day live on a farm with horses and lots of open space. I had made good on my promise—sort of. At least we had a farm and horses nearby, and she always accompanied me there. She had been my soul mate from college right through my medical training. Losing her was just one more rip in the fabric that had been torn by grief.

During one of my last rotations in orthopedic surgery, I had the chance to be the first assist in a lumbar microdiscectomy procedure with the head of the department, Dr. Kennedy. The orthopedic residents were attending a daylong workshop, and the attendings were used to inviting me in when they needed an extra pair of hands in the OR.

Jumping at the rare opportunity to participate in a surgery under microscope, I scrubbed in. Dr. Kennedy asked if I could see all right or if I needed a stepstool. I looked through the eyepiece of the microscope and decided that I could see just fine. I knew my initial job would be to dab the blood from the skin incision with the gauze four-by-fours and to smoke-suck. Everything about this procedure was in miniature. The incision was only two centimeters long, the instruments were one-fourth their usual diameters, and the hole where we were working was six inches beneath the skin's surface. Every motion of my hand was magnified twelve times. I quickly learned to modify every muscle command to match the miniscule field. As he cut and cauterized, I sucked. A talkative, flirtatious man by nature, Dr. Kennedy was not one to question residents on the anatomy they were seeing or alternative procedures, which are favorite board questions. He was more concerned with what cars they were driving and which nurses they had recently dated.

At one point, after leaving his narrow metal poking tool leaning up against the hole, he suddenly stopped, looked over the eyepiece at me, and said, "Dr. Talty, have you ever done this before?"

I thought what I was doing was annoying him. Getting ready to defend myself, I puffed my chest up and answered, "No, sir, I have not. This is my first time working through a microscope."

He looked at the scrub nurse with whom he had worked for years and said, "Barney, I cannot believe this. She is acting like a fourth-year orthopedic resident, anticipating my every move like a cat."

He looked at me strangely and smiled. Then he stepped back and asked the radiology tech for the fluoroscopy C-arm to take an X ray for positioning purposes, all the while going on about how he wished his orthopedic surgery residents had such incredible hand-eye coordination. "Do you have any interest in orthopedic surgery?" he asked.

I smiled, thinking back to the first day of internship some three years earlier. "Well, sir, that was my intention in coming to Lansing General in the first place."

"Why didn't you apply? I would have loved to have your skills around here."

I took a deep breath and considered my options. Do I tell him the truth, or do I circle the airport a bit and give him the story with the happy ending? I began slowly, having never said this to anyone before. "When I got to Lansing, I realized that I loved being in the clinic figuring out the orthopedic diagnosis more than standing in the cold OR technically fixing the problem. My first rotation as an intern was in OMM, where I found my true calling, you might say. I am very happy with my decision."

He just stood there with a blank stare, most likely thinking, "What a moron. Does she realize how much more money she could make? And how little OMM docs make?"

Once the X ray had been projected on the screen, Barney went to work repositioning the microscope, using my side eyepieces to focus it onto the field. He leaned over, looked through it for a split second, then jumped back. I was quietly standing behind him with my bloody hands clenched together to avoid contamination. He turned around and looked squarely into my eyes. "Have you been looking through these the entire time?"

"Of course, I have," I responded, confused. "Why?"

He turned both the eyepieces 180 degrees. "Now try that." He moved aside as I craned my neck to look. Then he raved to Dr. Kennedy how not only did I demonstrate an unusual ability to do microsurgery, but my field of view had been 180 degrees upside down. I shot a lightning glance at Dr. Kennedy, knowing my secret had just been revealed.

Dr. Kennedy wasn't interested in the reason, however. Instead, for the rest of the procedure, he went on and on about what unbelievable skills I possessed. I just continued to follow intuitively what he was doing, having long ago stopped trying to figure out if my dyslexic brain was a curse or a gift. When we were finished, he stepped away and left the OR, heading for the dictation room, leaving me to close the incision and tuck the patient into the recovery room. Doug and Bracken had trained me well.

It was noon when I finished, so I headed for the cafeteria, collected some lunch on a tray, and pushed through the door into the doctors' lounge. As I made my entrance, the room filled with a rare vibe. Everyone was smiling at me and began to clap. What on earth were they doing? I turned around to see if some celebrity had come in behind me. No one was there. In the middle of the cacophony of hooting, whistling, and clapping was Dr. Kennedy, who had just told the story for the third time to the entire medical staff present. I was embarrassed. If they knew the real reason why I could function 180 degrees upside down, they might not be as accepting. I just smiled and nodded my head while the rooster continued to crow my accolades. Yet this incident made it clear that my unusual ability was a unique tool placed in my bag for the journey. What had once separated me from others could, in the right situations, be a genuine asset.

Through our medical education years, José and I had been considering staying in the Midwest. Dad's passing had changed everything, however. José and I thought long and hard about what was truly important. Was it higher economic status and academic accolades? Or was it our relationships with our families and their need for us to be closer? Now that Jose was working as a hospital physician, we decided, after much consideration, that when my three years of residency and fellowship were finished, we would move back to California to be with the people we cared about the most. We had been gone long enough—twelve years by the time we would return.

Every time we were home for the holidays, we would look at real estate. Accustomed to Midwest housing prices, we were shocked by the California market and wondered whether, even on two doctor's salaries, we could ever afford a property large enough to accommodate the horses. Moreover, there were few physicians' jobs in California—everybody wanted to live there.

On a Saturday morning in late June 1995, the phone rang. It was Mom on the phone with a real estate agent. She had found our house, she said. It was on seven usable acres south of Santa Cruz.

Mutual friends had introduced Mom to a man, who she was now seeing regularly. The friends had decided after the funeral of his wife some eight months earlier, that when the time was right, Mom and Alex should meet. By spring, their relationship was all I was hearing about on the home front. The only one who hadn't met him yet was me.

I finally met Alex when José and I flew out in May to put up the horse fencing at our new house. I was dressed in my best torn jeans with a tattered T-shirt. Alex was seeking my mother's hand, and I am sure he was thinking our meeting might be difficult. But this six-foot-three-inch tanned man, with his thick wavy gray hair, athletic build, and kind smile stirred something in my mother that had lain dormant for quite some time. Laying eyes on him for the first time, I understood where Mom's schoolgirl excitement was coming from. Before he could say anything, I threw my arms around his huge shoulders and said, "Alex, so nice to finally meet you. I've heard nothing but fabulous things about you." I could feel him relax with obvious relief.

José and I spent the rest of the week looking for jobs. My research led me to Richard Bernstein, a DO who, in association with the local hospital, had just opened an outpatient wellness center. I called immediately.

He invited me to meet with him the next day. The clinic was only seven miles from the house. It was warm and inviting—nothing like a regular doctor's office. I handed him my curriculum vitae and we chatted. He had been recruited by the local hospital and together they decided to start a wellness center that would serve the needs of people suffering from musculoskeletal pain syndromes by providing integrative medical treatment services, supplementing physical medicine and rehabilitation with modalities like acupuncture, massage, onsite physical therapy, psychotherapy, and biofeedback. The building was equipped with a forty-foot aquatic therapy pool, ten treatment rooms, an open-air physical therapy space, and a huge picture window looking out over a grassy field. I was sure I would work in this place at some point. I had no idea I would eventually own it.

On the return flight to Michigan, I was filled with conflicting emotions. I was excited that José and I would be moving back home to the family and friends who were waiting for us. Dad's absence, however, gave the return a hollow feeling. The source from which I had drawn energy all my life would not be there. The sense of being alone and an orphan in the physical world had not dissipated. Being around Mom made me miss him even more.

I had developed rich relationships in Michigan, both professionally and personally. Dr. Ward and his wife had become my surrogate grandparents. My relationship with Dr. Greenman reached a new level when he asked if I would teach in the MSU/COM continuing-education manual medicine courses in both East Lansing and Tucson.

I made sure to personally invite Alex to attend my graduation ceremonies along with Mom. I am certain they wondered how I would deal with such a tremendous occasion in my life that Dad's influence had so much been a part of without him being physically present for its final chapter.

Near the end of the ceremony, Dr. Ward apparently turned to Mom and Alex and said they should be proud of me. In his opinion, I was among perhaps twenty-five physicians in the country who had attained a certain level of skill in the art and science of manual medicine, and he was sad to see me go. If I had stayed, the department members would have recommended me as their next vice chair right after graduation. When Mom related this story, I recognized it as the comment of a proud mentor. But, in fact, it implied much more. The professional impact of our choice to settle in California would become clear as I began seeing patients there. The Universal Forces had directed me to the lesser path, or so it seemed on the surface. But as always, it would lead to far more than I could ever expect or imagine on my own.

PART IV

Another Way of Knowing

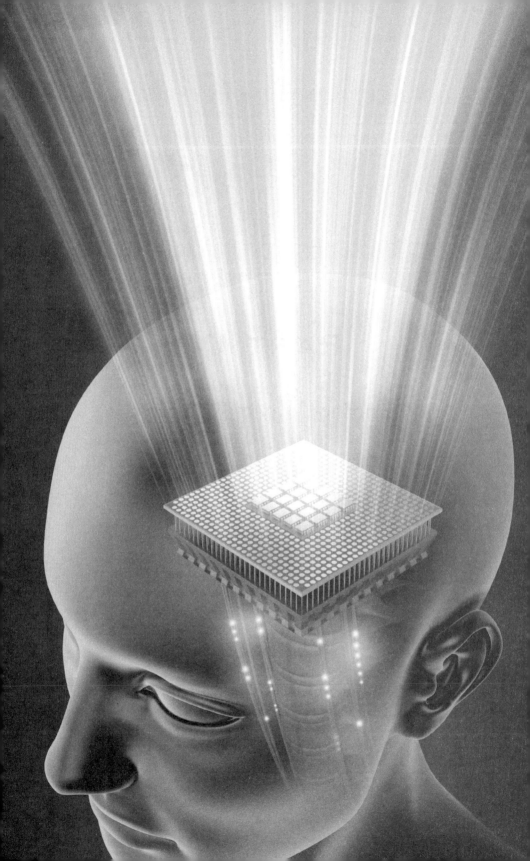

19

Encountering Old Enemies

You are beginning to see with your mind and your heart all that your eyes yet cannot. The lessons of trusting in the process intensify, as do your experiences of the synchronistic interconnectedness it all brings forth. Nothing is inconsequential to your overall curriculum. You are being introduced to the magnificence of who you are and the powers that you have suspected were lying dormant until they were needed. You have completed your lessons well and fought the good fight. Now it is your time to be revealed unto yourself. You are now sitting in the starfighter holding the joystick; your hand is familiar with how it feels. Close your eyes and open fully to the process. Let go of all expectation, for it will only limit you and prevent accomplishment of your task.

It is rare for most people to get such clear messages from the beyond. You have learned to expect it. Creating new ways of doing everything is a lonely business. There is little support for your discoveries. These experiences tend to be more of an internal process, requiring self-validation that the information coming to you is accurate and can be trusted. You are laying down new roads that never existed before. Know that this work is not easy. Be kind to yourself if at first you do not act immediately on a knowing and must wait for more information to support your hunches. Learn from these experiences; they are now your greatest teachers. You have developed far beyond all of your previous mentors and are on the leading edge of knowledge.

We arrived home officially on July 4, 1996, and went to work immediately. José started as medical director of the San Benito Health Foundation and I went to work for the Santa Cruz County Health Services Agency twenty hours per week. This was public health at its finest. Many of the patients were homeless and sleeping under bridges, on the riverbank, or in their cars. I found myself regarding these people with respect for their ability to survive without the basic amenities of life. At the same time, whether by choice or force of circumstances, they were free of the pressures weighing on those in society's mainstream. What a contrast their lives were to mine, I reflected, as I considered the social and financial responsibilities with which I was shackling myself as I stepped into a professional career.

In early August, I received a call from Dr. Richard Bernstein. He was taking a two-week vacation beginning August 15 and needed someone to cover at the Wellness Center, which was already bursting with patients. He asked me to shadow him for a day or two to get familiar with his practice. On the first day, I observed him trying to treat a particular patient and clearly getting nowhere, so I offered to work on her while he went to see his next patient. I could see that she was suffering from a sacral torsion causing a psoas muscle contracture. I performed a quick muscle energy maneuver on the sacrum that allowed the nerves controlling the psoas to let go naturally. The woman happened to be the administrative assistant to the local community hospital's CEO, and she apparently shared her experience back at the hospital.

After Dr. Bernstein returned, I was getting many referrals from the hospital staffers and stayed on permanently part-time—at first. It did not take long for the word to spread among patients, hospital employees, and worker's compensation attorneys that there was a new doctor in town who could not only diagnose and treat mechanical pain conditions, but also describe them in a way the rest of the medical system could understand.

In March of the following year, I received a call from Dr. Ward in Michigan. He was asking me to see a young man who was pretty bad off. He had been contacted by the patient's physician and recommended that he see me first. Of course, I agreed.

Mark Murphy's mother, Mary, phoned the next day. She insisted that her son could not wait the usual six weeks for a new patient appointment, so Mark was scheduled for the following Thursday at the end of the day, so we could take as much time with him as needed. By the time Thursday rolled around, we had gotten the clear message to have the entire clinic on standby for his arrival.

Mary parked on the street right in front of the building. Our sight through the windows was unobstructed. When she slid the van door open, I could see a young man sitting up on a queen-sized mattress in the back. He simply scooted to the edge, put his feet down on the sidewalk, and stood up with what looked like normal movement patterns. I watched him as they walked to the front entrance and then, from a position down the hall, watched the interaction at the front desk between Mary, Mark, and our receptionist, Angela. After the necessary paperwork was signed, Angela escorted Mark and his mother down the hall to my treatment room and then brought me Mark's medical chart. Glancing through our five-page intake sheet, paying the most attention to the medication list and the pain diagram, I gleaned whatever I could from this limited amount of information, reached for the doorknob, and, taking a deep breath, walked through a portal to an entirely new phase of my life.

Mary was sitting in the chair next to the treatment table, with its stack of textbooks, many that I owned and had studied. Mark was sitting casually on the treatment table. I will never forget the sensation that hit me squarely in the chest and solar plexus as my eyes met his. From the innermost part of my viscera, a shriek blasted out to every part of my awareness. Never in my lifetime had I experienced anything like this. I hated him from my core. As that understanding hit me, my mind seemed to split into two separate personalities, the one standing before him ready to help him get better, and the other who was badly misbehaving, as if being forced to stand on burning red hot coals each second I was in his presence. I could barely breathe and my heart raced.

Trying not to seem distracted, after the formal introductions, I sat down on the stool and positioned myself to have eye contact with both of them. The initial interview took two hours. Lean and tall (six foot two), Mark had been a high school star basketball player until lower back pain at the age of seventeen took him out of the game and eventually out of school. His family was wealthy enough to send him anywhere necessary for health care. They went to Stanford Hospital, who sent him to a Dr.

Derby for a discogram, which showed a leaking L5/S1 disc. Surgery was scheduled to fuse the vertebrae, using a rod and screw construct for added stability. Three weeks after the operation, he developed an incisional staph infection. Two weeks later he developed cellulitis. He was hospitalized and placed on IV antibiotics for six days. Finally, the incision was opened and drained.

After five months of excruciating pain for Mark, it was discovered that the hardware inserted during surgery had broken. Mark told me much later that he and his brother had sneaked out one night and wrecked their father's brand new truck by losing control around a curve and slamming it sideways into a guardrail. The horizontal force when they hit could easily have sheared the vertical metal rods in his back.

Being less than pleased with Stanford, the family went to St. Mary's Spine Center in San Francisco to have the rods and screws removed six months after they had been placed. The fusion was still not solid, so the doctors insisted that Mark spend sixteen hours a day for six more months in what is known as a 90/90 chair, a device that keeps the hips and knees bent at 90 degrees, so the bones in his back would be in neutral and sure to fuse. To persevere through this, he needed to be heavily sedated. He also required massive doses of opioids to manage the pain.

It is widely known in medicine that young people, especially males, habituate quickly to stable doses of opioids. The doctors had difficulty finding high enough doses to manage his symptoms while keeping the side effects under control. He was admitted to the Stanford inpatient pain unit for detoxification—twice. When he was released from the chair, his pain was still out of control. Having exhausted all the usual Bay Area medical meccas, the family sought treatment from well-respected community physicians, finally finding their way to Dr. Anderson, who eventually referred Mark to Dr. Ward.

During his examination, I discovered a discrepancy in leg length that had probably caused his original degenerative spinal condition. But this was not causing his current pain complaints—I was sure of that. He was tender all over, only wanted to drink soft drinks, could not bear the thought of drinking plain water, was exhausted and took frequent naps during the day, then stayed up eating carbohydrates all night. Having gained sixty pounds since his surgery, he had developed a terrible self-image and a sense of hopelessness. His mother would sleep at his bedside at night in case he needed something. Their relationship was enmeshed, to put it mildly. Mary never once offered to leave the room during the session. I did not push her.

They finally left the clinic at 7:30 p.m. My energy was so zapped I could hardly finish the note in the chart. This kid was a mess on all levels. Separating his case into categories was the only way I could make sense of it. Taking one presenting symptom at a time, I drew out a flow chart, just as I had done in school when too much information was coming in at once. In the dim light of my desk lamp, a treatment plan began to take shape from the images on the paper.

Mark and Mary returned for the next two months every Thursday to drain me of whatever life force I had left by that time each week. No matter what I did manually or how I tried to counsel Mark on diet and lifestyle or how many bone scans, repeat MRIs, and CT scans we obtained, nothing seemed to help make sense of it. He was an empty shell who was missing the most critical element: the will to heal. As if in compensation, he stole my energy whenever he was in my presence. Even though I could feel what he was up to, I found myself allowing it. On a subconscious level, there was some kind of understanding between the two of us. I had felt that arrangement from the beginning and knew he did as well. What it meant was unclear. All I knew was that after his appointments, I could barely stand. My life force, which is usually more than abundant, was zapped.

One Thursday evening, while I was working on Mark manually, we came upon an important discovery. As I palpated the tip of the sacrum where the coccyx bone and its ligamentous attachments intersect, Mark suddenly blurted out, "That's where my pain is!"

My hand returned to the exact spot he had identified. "Here?" I asked.

"Yes, right there."

I was palpating the coccygeal ligaments. Suddenly, an idea came. "If the pain is originating in the ligaments," I said, "I can do a tissue block with a cortisone injection to see if it will reduce symptoms."

He turned his face to the side and tried to look at me. "You mean give me a shot down there?"

I smiled confidently, relaying the message that he was in the best of hands. Reading my intention, he reluctantly agreed. I gave him the shot.

Not expecting miracles, we ended the session and proceeded out to the empty front desk to schedule his next few sessions. As I was flipping through the appointment book, Mark spoke up, "What was in that shot?" My eyes quickly locked onto his. The first thing that hit me was a sense of presence I had not seen in him before. There was a spark of vitality.

He said he felt like someone had just turned his lights on again. I suddenly realized what I had been missing. The steroid had caused a false elevation of adrenocortical hormones that had been completely depleted due to his years of pain. In an instant, all his symptoms—the carbohydrate cravings, insomnia, tissue sensitivity, hypoglycemic episodes, and weight gain—made sense.

This was one of the most profound lessons of my career to date. I had been tracking Mark's physical symptoms only, disregarding the energetic phenomenon between us as a possible source of diagnostic information. In fact, the message was loud and clear and only needed interpretation: he needed *energy*. His need was physiological and it was real. He had no life force left and needed to draw on someone else's to survive. That is why he was sucking mine.

The question I had not yet considered was: Why me?

Placing Mark on low replacement doses of prednisone allowed him to finally tolerate the treatments he so desperately needed. He started regular physical therapy. He started sleeping at night and staying awake during the day. He agreed to give up his three liters of Pepsi per day and drink plain water instead. Suddenly, protein-rich foods appealed to him again, and his bowels and kidneys began working normally. This offered us a glimmer of hope. Much more was revealed after a massive endocrine workup. Not one value was in the normal range.

By June 1998, Mary had rented a beach house in Aptos so Mark could come in on Tuesdays as well as Thursdays. We tried to have Mark seen by specialists of all kinds—even with my background in family medicine, this case was way over my head—but most of these referrals never happened. After a three-month wait, Mark was seen by a single endocrinologist, who simply discontinued the prednisone, wrote a prescription for Cortef (hydrocortisone), and sent him out the door without a follow-up appointment or a plan. The Cortef caused Mark to immediately gain significant weight, and he begged me to change him back to prednisone. I phoned the endocrinologist to discuss the options but never received a callback or even a consultation report. The message was clear: I was all alone in this.

"See, I told you," he said, when I caved in to his request to change the medication. "You are the only one who can help me now."

Intrigued, I decided to investigate further. "Mark, why do you trust me? Am I not one of *them*?" I meant one of the uncaring physicians he had learned to hate.

Abruptly, with a fire in his eyes that made my heart stir, he said, "No! You're not. You are an imposter, and you know it. There are only three people I trust in the world: my mom, my dad, and you."

I was shocked. What was it about this stranger whom I seemed to know so well? Why did he scare me so? He was harmless in his current state, completely beaten down, unable to handle even his own bodily functions without his mother's help. This entire time, I had kept my emotions to myself, not wanting him to feel how much my soul loathed him, while my presenting personality conducted itself professionally. He obviously had no idea how I felt. The entire time I worked with Mark, I wanted to level with him and open up a past-life discussion that I was sure would answer all these questions. Not knowing how Mary tracked on subjects such as these, and given her constant presence, I held back.

As the months passed, there were small gains, always followed by setbacks. As we ran out of ideas, I began to wonder why the Murphys kept coming. My warrior spirit was seriously challenged, but I had never yet sent a patient away with the parting statement, "I am sorry, I can't help you." It was simply not in my lexicon. All I could hope for was that the Murphys would see the writing on the wall and recognize that either Mark was unfixable or my skills were inadequate.

One Sunday afternoon in August, my precious weekly time off, my pager rang yet again with a call from Mary. Usually, she called to report that Mark had a headache or wasn't sleeping well or wasn't hungry. This time she had a question. "Is it possible for Mark to die from his pain?"

Ever trying to maintain a positive attitude, I responded, "No. No one dies of chronic pain, Mary. Don't even think of such a thing. He is going to get better, I promise you." I said this with such conviction that even I believed it.

Mark and Mary spent the week of the 1998 Christmas holidays in Fremont and dutifully returned the Tuesday before New Year's. Mark was in an especially good mood this day. After treating his entire somatic system, I took my usual place on the stool at the head of the table with Mark lying on his back to balance the cranial sacral system. As my hands settled into the familiar grooves on the sides of the skull and I closed my eyes to focus on the subtle cranial rhythmic impulse, an image slowly appeared to my mind, as clear and real as if I were looking at it through open eyes. Never before had I experienced this while treating a patient.

Before me lay what appeared to be a circular dungeon back in the Middle Ages. Diffuse daylight came through bars of the open stone windows near the thirty-foot ceiling. It was cold and dank. Set into the beige stone walls were arched Gothic-style wooden doors on heavy hinges, each with a huge crossbeam resting in the latch, preventing passage. The person looking through my eyes had apparently been in there for ages and was familiar with each crevice between the stones.

Still sitting on my familiar stool, hunched over Mark with my hands on his temporal bones, lost in a deep meditative state, the still-active part of my brain kept asking: Whose imagery is this, mine or Mark's? I wasn't sure. All I knew was that it felt profoundly familiar. It evoked feelings of being caged and controlled, held against my will, cut off from everything important. For a split second, my mind flashed on the memory of looking out from the baby crib as my dad was setting up my new toddler's bed. I sensed a connection between these two experiences.

The person behind my eyes slowly approached the first of the six doors and with great effort pushed the crossbeam up and out of its latch, clearing the doorframe. I pulled on the door, its ancient rusted hinges shrieked, and the door opened to reveal a wall of red bricks, proving there was no way out. After opening the second door, with the same result, I decided to take a risk.

Using the imagery as a hidden reference, I began, "Mark, why do you think this is happening to you? No matter which direction we head in or what threshold we try to cross, something always prevents our progress. What do you see when you look at this situation?" I was half hoping he would confirm that he was seeing the same scene I was, but he seemed confused by the questions and didn't answer. I waited.

"You know," he finally responded, "I have been bad, really bad, and this...this is my punishment."

Excited, but not wanting to influence him in any way, I went on. "What do you mean you've been bad?"

"I don't want to talk about it right now. All I know is that I am now paying the price for things I have done to others."

My heart raced. How much did he know? It was time to end the session, and professionalism overruled my eagerness to ask anything more just then. Mark was scheduled for the last morning appointment on Thursday, New Year's Eve. I could hardly wait to pursue the topic that had just opened, not only the sense of an old unfinished drama between us, but also the meaning of the dungeon—and for whom.

Awaking to the aggravating sound of my pager ringing on the night-stand naturally gave me pause. My patients rarely had emergencies in the middle of the night. The clock radio read 1:30 a.m. as I reached for the light, hoping not to disturb José. It must be Mary informing me that Mark was not sleeping or had developed a new pain complaint. I punched the scroll button on the annoying device and the message came through, "This is Mary Murphy." No shit, I thought. "Mark is on his way by ambulance to Dominican Hospital. His heart stopped beating and they have been pushing on his chest. Please call Dr. Nelson in the ER."

At first, I lay there thunderstruck. Then I reached for José and shook him awake. "José, José, Mark Murphy is in cardiac arrest. Wake up, this is my first lawsuit."

With those words, he quickly became coherent. "What did you say?"

"Mark is having a myocardial infarction, or the paging service is play-ing one hell of a practical joke on me." Jumping out of bed, I ran for the phone.

Dr. Nelson let me know that Mark had died about twenty minutes earlier. "We finally called it after forty-five minutes of chest compres-sions and bagging him. There was no response. I am sorry, doctor. Will you be coming in to sign the death certificate?"

I had ceased breathing at "We finally called it." Even without airflow to vibrate my vocal cords, I somehow squeaked out, "He's *dead?*"

"Yes, the mother came in with him, and the father and the brother are due to arrive any moment."

"Thanks, I will be right down."

I got dressed, wondering what someone wears to meet a family who is most likely going to sue for wrongful death or delay in diagnosis. Thinking, the hell with it anyway, I pulled on a red turtleneck, jeans, and a cheery cardigan with brightly colored embroidery. I jumped into my car and raced to the hospital. This was my first patient loss. Not even in residency had a patient in my charge died. I had no idea what to say to the family.

After signing the death certificate, I proceeded to the family bereavement room. Mark's father, David, and his brother, Brian, were huddled together on a couch, rocking in grief. Mary was sitting alone in the loveseat. I hugged her. She gave me a "chin up" smile that I wasn't sure how to take. I took a seat in an overstuffed leather chair to her right, and somehow began. "I am not sure I understand why this happened. Even though his physical system was under tremendous stress due to the pain, I'm not convinced that's what killed him."

She looked at me expressionless for several moments, and I waited. Then she simply said, "Do you want to see him? David and Brian just arrived, and the doctor said it would be a good idea for them to see him. Something about completion."

Viewing his blue lifeless body, I waited for sadness or grief to hit, but the only emotion that surfaced was *relief*—it was over for him and me, once and for all. I was not even sure what this thought meant. I only knew that the Universe had brought us together to complete something old and enormous, and now both of us were released and could move on.

We returned to the family room. I half expected Mary to begin accusing me of killing her son. After several silent moments, she suddenly looked at me and said, "I want to thank you for everything that you did for Mark. You stuck it out and never gave up on him like all the other doctors did. He appreciated that."

I couldn't believe these words coming from her bent and broken motherly spirit this early in her grief process. "I'm afraid I didn't help him," I responded.

Her eyes seemed to well with fire. "You did more for him than you will ever know. After each appointment, he was filled with a sense of lightness and energy. That is why he continued seeing you. He was able to take something away with him that made him feel better—at least for a while."

She was confirming what I already knew. Mark had been fighting for his survival and using my life force to do it. What else did she know that I hadn't given her credit for? Thinking back to our last appointment and the dungeon imagery, I had to ask. "Mary, did Mark mention anything about our conversation on Tuesday?"

She absorbed the question with a deep, chest-filling breath. "No, not really, he only said you were trying to psych him out."

To say I was disappointed is an understatement. Mary thanked me again and again for hanging in there with Mark. I kept listening in disbelief, wondering if she had already prepared herself for this kind of ending. Before departing, I encouraged them to have an autopsy done. I felt a sense of urgency that the information might be useful for Mark's brother, who was three years his junior. It could also help explain this, at least on a physical level.

As I drove back home in the midwinter darkness, I realized that the business between Mark and me was, in fact, still unfinished with respect to the dungeon imagery. Unable to go back to sleep, I curled up on the fainting couch in front of the huge picture window and watched the first rays of morning light traverse the sky through the giant redwood trees that line our property. What is this life we are all living? Are we simply acting out parts in a scripted play? Are we here to help each other grow, and if so, for what purpose? Why did I agree to come into this time and place anyway? I was still not sure. I was approaching my thirty-seventh birthday, only five years from the age of forty-two when the answer would apparently arrive in full.

Friday was New Year's Day, and José and I stayed close to home. The weekend brought unusually warm weather for the season. The days were crystal clear and sunny, with temperatures in the upper sixties. On Sunday, as usual, we loaded up the dogs and headed for a morning beach run.

In the three days since Mark's death, the image of the dungeon had tormented me. The fact that I would never be able to ask him if it resonated with his statement that he had been "bad" drove me crazy. The other curiosity was Mary's question about Mark's dying from pain, as if she sensed he might die early. I wanted to kick myself for so flippantly saying that chronic pain never killed anyone. Mark had certainly proved me wrong.

As I ran down the beach, the midmorning sun was reflecting on the waves as they delivered their foam to the sand and then retreated, leaving the sand looking like a mirror. My legs were moving on autopilot and I slipped into a deep meditative state as I traveled over the damp, hard sand. I began imagining one day inviting Mary out to lunch to share with her my personal experience with Mark. As my mind searched for words to express the intense hatred I felt toward his soul without saying it was her son I felt that way toward, all of a sudden my mind once again dropped into viewing imagery, this time with my eyes open.

Whoever I was in the scene, I was most certainly male. I was standing in a field planted in row crops, looking at the village of stone huts with thatch roofs in the distance, near a forest of poplar trees. Near the well, women were chatting as they beat the wheat from the chaff. Their children played nearby, chasing chickens and ducks. I was filled with a sense of wholeness; some great task had been completed for the benefit of these people. No other men were in the scene. Suddenly, I knew they were still involved in a battle, the one from which I had just returned. My body was seriously battered, and I had returned to heal my wounds.

Suddenly, my eyes spotted the color red shimmering through the poplars and my heart skipped a beat. Focusing my gaze, my eyes took in more of the red flashing between the white tree trunks. My greatest fear was coming true. Before the innocents could hear my shouts, the soldiers were upon them. They rode out of the forest into the village in their red-and-black uniforms, fire-tipped arrows at their drawn bows, aiming straight at the rooftops. The women and children ran in all directions, but the soldiers mowed them down with hatchets. My injuries kept me from moving to their aid. I began waving my hands and shouting in an attempt to draw the soldiers' attention away from the few remaining villagers and onto me.

Suddenly, the leader of this mob stopped and looked in my direction. He raised his left hand and the mayhem stopped. The men began to regroup, coming straight for me, riding in pairs behind him. They were coming for me—and suddenly my present-day personality knew why. I was a highly decorated knight, the keeper and protector of vast lands and ancient knowledge, who had led armies into battle against the Crown. As the face of their leader came into focus, I recognized it as Mark's.

At that point, my mind split into two, the one in the "movie" who was about to be captured, and the one living now, who was realizing the meaning of the past year's experience with a young man whose face my soul had never forgotten. In the movie, I was physically dragged behind his horse and thrown into the circular dungeon of beige stone, with the six wooden doors and the diffuse light filtering in from above. Finally realizing that it was my dungeon, not Mark's, allowed the imagery to fade. My awareness returned to the glistening sunlight reflecting off the wet sand in present time, on the third day of 1999.

Suddenly, it all made sense. Mark had been the victor then, holding the power to destroy me and all I held dear, and using it without exception. This time around, it was I who held the keys to the diagnosis, which nevertheless remained hidden so he could not escape. My efforts to help made no difference; the script had been written and the drama had played itself out.

Six weeks later, the deputy coroner's office called with Mark's autopsy report. He died from a rare form of cardiomyopathy that tends to run in families; my hunch that the autopsy information would be useful for Mark's brother proved accurate. The specialist who examined his heart emphatically stated that his death had nothing directly to do with adrenal insufficiency or medications. Other aspects of the report supported my working diagnosis of adrenal insufficiency, however.

I walked away from this experience a changed person and a changed physician. Up to this time, I had approached medicine with the assumption that every pain syndrome had a physical root cause. I followed up the patient's history and physical diagnosis with manual manipulation of the anatomy beneath my hands, visualizing the tissue layers á la Dr. Ward and plugging in Dr. Greenman's biomechanical positional laws. Most of the time I came up with an accurate diagnosis on the first visit, a fact that had made me wonder if my physician's skills were being amplified by something else. Now I began paying attention to my energetic system while evaluating and treating patients, acknowledging the hunches, "gut" feelings, and sensations in my chest.

I began noticing a second line of information arriving, too, this one in my head, a stream of definitive knowing and insight that had a different quality from what my trained physician's mind knew. The experience on the beach seemed to have opened a portal of what had previously been a trickle of intuitive information. It now began to pour in as though through a cornucopia in the top of my head. Listening to these other sources of knowing, alongside my medical know-how and the pragmatics of the person's situation, I would find myself stating a diagnosis and creating a treatment plan with unexpected conviction, which later proved correct.

20

The Energy Tree

*Y*ou are superheroes in the making and do not even know it. You are equipped *in ways you have not yet discovered. As you are introduced to these wonders, do not take yourselves too seriously, for their purpose has yet to be revealed. They may or may not be what they appear. You will rediscover how to use your Lemurian and Atlantean traits and technologies and you will once again become proficient in their wielding. When these inherent qualities are reintroduced to you, you will not be afraid. They will feel familiar and safe. Your systems have been equipped with the prewiring to transmit these frequencies and will recognize these gifts when they are spoken about. This will start for you a quest to search out your other ancient energetic tools that have long been forgotten and unappreciated but are now being reintroduced into this realm. They are all based on the understanding that everything is made up of matter, all matter is made up of energy, and all energy has a signature quantum frequency.*

Within months of beginning work at the Wellness Center, the majority of my patient base had become long-standing worker's compensation patients who had been in the system, sometimes for years, without a proper diagnosis. More often than not, the patient's previous physicians had been MD orthopedic surgeons, who were not trained in what DOs call "somatic dysfunction." Trying to explain that to a furious patient whose symptoms improved dramatically after one or two treatments with me, after having been bounced from doctor to doctor without relief, was a challenge.

One kind of complaint, which I had not encountered at MSU, I found curious, however. The first such case was a woman who had injured her back the year before by rotating her trunk while lifting and carrying a computer. She stood throughout the interview, constantly shifting her weight from side to side. Sitting was not an option. Six months of physical therapy had only made her symptoms worse. Any kind of movement increased her pain. Respite came only when she was lying flat on her back.

While she was putting on a gown for the physical examination, I looked at her films. The fourth and fifth lumbar discs were darkened and dehydrated, indicating degeneration, but I noticed nothing else suspicious. The physical evaluation, therefore, was a shock. I had expected to find significant positional restrictions in the lower torso, but the only thing amiss was a mildly right-rotated fifth lumbar vertebra. When I placed her in the position to reverse it, however, she shrieked in pain. I stopped immediately. I had never before had a patient experience pain with a muscle energy technique.

Over time, I saw more and more patients with the same symptomology. They insisted on standing during the initial interview, and the initial injury was from lifting or pulling something heavy and then rotating the trunk. They experienced a sudden explosion of excruciating pain in the back that slowly engulfed the midsection. The MRIs were always read as negative. And the patients had spent months going from one specialist to another in search of a diagnosis and treatment. I became obsessed with finding the answer. How could I have spent three years with the masters of spinal orthopedic physical diagnosis and not seen a condition that was beginning to fill my practice? In my off-hours, I pored through 1,200-page, multiple volume orthopedic spine textbooks, as well as journals containing the most recent studies.

One afternoon, I suddenly remembered a research paper I had read at MSU. I located it in my stacks of papers. The article described a condition called internal disc disruption, usually caused by lifting and twisting—a tear in the outer fibers of the intervertebral disc annulus. The MRI films were often read as negative. Bang! There it is, I thought. I spent a day at Stanford University Hospital medical library. Returning with a cache of nearly twenty articles on internal disc disruption, I devoured them over the next few nights. A few discussed a subtle MRI finding—a bright white spot in the outer annular fibers that radiologists usually dismiss as normal degenerative change. Reviewing the MRIs of my patients suffering from this syndrome, I was shocked to see, in almost every one, a small white spot in the posterior portions of the otherwise black discs.

Reading through the articles, I noticed the repetition of a name, Richard Derby, MD, who was not only a leader in diagnosing this condition, using a procedure called a discogram, but had also authored many of the articles. I remembered him as the doctor who had performed the procedure on Mark that led to his surgery. When I shared my findings with Dr. Bernstein, he offered, "Janine, Dr. Derby's clinic is in Daly City, just south of San Francisco."

Thereafter, I sent many patients to Dr. Derby. He always made it a point to call the referring doctor immediately after finishing a discogram on a referred patient. When Angela, our receptionist, would knock on the door and interrupt me during an examination, it was usually Dr. Derby on the phone reporting yet another positive discogram. I was always elated to hear the bad news. It meant a definitive diagnosis for the patient that no insurance company could argue with.

After more than a year of referring my patients to him, Dr. Derby popped the question on the phone. "Janine, you obviously understand spine medicine. Why don't you come on up here, and I will train you how to do discograms and other pain management injection procedures?"

I went momentarily mute with astonishment. This man, the leader in his field, was inviting me to train under him. I suddenly realized that my becoming was not quite finished. In fact, it was about to take on a whole new dimension.

By this time, my brother was making seriously good wine and had purchased a seven-acre vineyard on Dry Creek in Sonoma County, just upstream from where we had spread Dad's ashes in the creek a few years before, with the intent of one day building a winery. So the first day I walked into Spinal Diagnostics, after the ninety-mile drive up the stunning California coastline, I brought along a few of Mike's bottles as a gesture of thanks for the care Dr. Derby and his staff had been extending to my patients for more than a year. Thanks to all the communications during that time, Dr. Derby's staff and I were already well acquainted. Each one greeted me with a wide smile and open arms, as if I were returning home rather than meeting them for the first time.

That day, Dr. Bjorn Eek was present, too. Dr. Eek, an orthopedic surgeon now using prolotherapy as his main healing tool, had a practice in Santa Barbara. He would fly with patients to San Francisco on Fridays so Dr. Derby could treat them. Dr. Eek and I were not the only visiting physicians. Dr. Derby was the best in the country when it came to spinal injections for pain relief or discography for diagnostic purposes. The who's who of spine medicine, including the authors of several textbooks I had studied, were walking around in the office that day. Like a wave on the beach, the visiting physicians would lap into a treatment room to observe Dr. Derby perform his magic with needles on a grateful patient, then pull out again into the hallway until the next patient was ready to be seen.

After reviewing the films for the next patient, the visiting doctors waited in the hall while Dr. Derby took a phone call. I went ahead into the treatment room. Jeff, the radiology technician, was in the room setting up. Trying not to get in the way, I leaned against the counter and tried to make small talk. That became unnecessary.

Jeff was reaching into the cupboard next to me above the sink to retrieve supplies when his eyes locked onto mine. The depth of his gaze was somehow familiar. He stopped what he was doing and leaned against the counter, too.

Without breaking the stare, he asked, "Who *are* you?"

I almost laughed out loud. What was he asking? "You know who I am," I replied.

He said, "Yeah, I know your name, and I have heard all about you from your patients. But I want to know, who are you *really*?"

This was not a superficial question. The blast effect of this query traveled to the depths where my greatest curiosities were hidden away. Who was I? Was I just another physician drawn here like a bug to a fluorescent zap light on a balmy summer evening? Why was I here in this clinic—or on this planet, for that matter? I had long ago given up the need to know. I was just following my internal guidance, and the pathway had opened easily for me to be standing in this space on this day.

I answered, "Why…I don't really know—yet. I am still in search of that answer."

He took a huge gamble. "I can see energy, and I have never seen anyone come through here who had what looks to me like a three-foot-diameter tree trunk shooting out of the top of their head through the ceiling."

I stared back. What was he talking about—a tree trunk of energy out the top of my head? Could he truly see what I had been sensing? His comment was obviously sincere, and I could tell he was sane.

He continued, "I know this sounds off the wall. I've never seen this in a physician before."

My mind was a whirl of questions. But at that point, the rest of the team entered as the patient was wheeled into the room.

The medical aspects of the day were just as amazing. With matador-like speed and precision, Dr. Derby could get a six-inch needle into any space or tissue anywhere in the body, cannulating with ease cervical and lumbar disc nuclei, and facet joints deformed by arthritis. All the time, I was wondering if those joints and discs had degenerated due to the loss of range of motion. I could barely keep my hands off the patients, wanting to assess them for positional dysfunction. Drs. Derby and Eek were easy to speak to, so I voiced my thoughts.

Dr. Derby responded first. "When I worked with Phil Greenman, he had the same concerns."

"Really," I replied. "Dr. Greenman has been here, too?"

"Of course. They all come eventually," he said matter-of-factly.

"Would you mind, then, if next week I assessed the joints for motion restriction before you do the injections for pain relief? I would predict that injections would be more beneficial in joints that are not restricted."

"Sure. That's exactly what Phil wanted to do."

I shook my head at the synchronicity. Perhaps I was here in this clinic partially to continue my training where Drs. Ward and Greenman had left off.

At the end of that first day, I found myself looking for Jeff, hoping to continue our conversation. He was in a treatment room putting things away and looked eager to speak with me again.

"Oh, Dr. Talty, I have something for you in my car. Don't leave. I'll go out and get it."

By the time I finished saying good-bye to everyone else, Jeff had come and gone, leaving an audiotape book on the counter with instructions for the nurses to make sure I took it with me. I grabbed the tapes on my way out the door, my head a mass of questions, answers, and inner knowings. There was no denying that I had just met up with my next set of Jedi masters.

Settling into the car seat, I pulled out the first tape, then read the box's cover: *Why People Don't Heal,* by Caroline Myss. My eyebrows rose involuntarily. Jeff's intuition was right on target. For the past six months, noticing curious patterns in patients, I had been pondering exactly this issue. Putting the first tape in the car's cassette player, I listened as I headed back home. Dr. Myss expressed so much of what I had quietly observed about human behavior, emotions, addictions, woundedness, relationships, interactions, and spiritual philosophy, I found it simply uncanny. Being medically intuitive, she could see not only the illness, but also the emotional reason behind it. The patterns she noticed correlated with the Vedic model of energy centers in the body, called chakras, where people store psychosocial and emotional information. With a start, I recalled the prediction by Carolyn the psychic, eighteen years earlier, that one day I would be studying chakras. With that, a flood of recollections of that reading poured forth. Here I was, just as she had said: having bullied my way through higher education, a doctor working in a rehabilitation clinic and living in the wide open spaces of the California coast range four miles from the sea, raising a thoroughbred. If she was able to predict this, the forces acting on us must be real.

As the weeks went by, my relationships with Drs. Derby and Eek deepened. They were not only doing diagnosis with discograms, but were also involved in cutting-edge techniques in treating disc injuries with minimally invasive emerging procedural technologies. I sent some of my patients up to Daly City for these treatments, scheduling them on Fridays when I would be there. Over dinner one Friday night, before Dr. Eek and I made our respective treks home, he and Dr. Derby pointed out that my patients had a 70 percent recovery rate, while those referred by other doctors showed only 45 percent. I had not been aware of this. By the end of our meal, it was decided that Dr. Derby would ask other referral doctors if I could evaluate and treat every eligible candidate before their new procedures. We wanted to see if the statistics would improve for the other patients, too.

My weekly trips to observe and learn from the spinal elders had landed me an unsolicited job. I officially joined the staff at Spinal Diagnostics as a treating physician, and over the next seven years the three of us developed an unusual multidisciplinary approach to treating chronic pain of a spinal origin. Once again, I had been recognized and taken in by masters I did not even know were waiting for me.

On one hand, I was being indoctrinated into the field of interventional pain management, which could fill in where OMT fell short in relieving a patient's symptoms. Drs. Derby and Eek were members of many spine medicine organizations, and they invited me to join. They were always searching out the newest treatments worldwide and traveled internationally to learn from other mavericks in the field. José and I went on some of these excursions. I was being exposed to some of the best if not the strangest medical practices in the world.

On the other hand, my manual medicine training is what allowed me to bring a unique element to the Friday team at Spinal Diagnostics. What José had said long ago about DOs being rare in California was proving true. A DO skilled in manual medicine was even rarer. Referral patients, expecting to see Dr. Derby, were often surprised to see me first. After their session, many would comment: "Nobody has ever examined me like this before," or even "I have been to twelve other doctors for this condition, and you are the first who has ever touched me." Unlike my patients in Watsonville, many of these folks had been referred by the most renowned MDs and surgeons on the West Coast. I was learning that even in the upper echelons of standard medicine, there were sad deficiencies simply because medicine had become so left-brained and objectified.

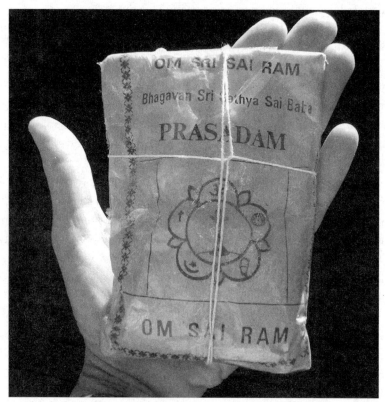

The actual bag of vibhuti, *healing ash from Sai Baba.*

21

Cultivating Intuition

Have you found yourself recently "connecting the dots" from your distant past? Have the hauntings in your gut begun to stir and capture your attention? Has the history of this world taken on grave and added importance as you begin to see it intertwine with your own? Fear not, adult Indigos, this is just the beginning of what you are here to behold. You have brought with you all the wisdom of all the lessons you have collected as you passed through every major culture and civilization that has come before on this planet and others. You contain magnificent experience that will assist as this world transforms, passes through the next portal, and shifts paradigms. You will begin to see the similarities of the mistakes previously made and will wonder why the others do not have the same eyes to see. This will confuse you at first. Remember, they do not think in the same way as you. They simply cannot. Their brains are of the old way, split down the middle, unable to integrate knowledge and information and process it in a new way. Forgiveness is imperative now. Do not point fingers; only make suggestions, and remember to lead by your example.

Even as my career was beginning to blossom, the lessons continued to come through the portal opened by Jeff. As I listened to more of Myss's tapes on my Friday commutes to Daly City, I began to understand certain patterns I had been noticing in some of my patients. The lower back patients tended to be primary breadwinners or single folks who were dealing with loss of personal power and loss of financial stability. The chronic cervical spine patients tended to be women with long graceful necks, which set them up for a lack of muscular stability mechanically, but they were also attractive women who had been treated all their lives as arm pieces, despite being highly intelligent. They also tended to have been physically or sexually abused.

The lower back, I learned from Myss's tapes, contains the first and second chakras, which relate to money, power, one-on-one communication, sex, and the survival instincts. Indeed, many of these patients had lost their jobs because their injury did not allow them to return to work. Some had lost their homes, and the financial stress had caused relationships and marriages to break up. The neck, on the other hand, contains the fifth chakra, which is concerned with self-expression, choice, and the ability to speak your personal will and willpower. My cervical ladies who had been physically abused had not been able to speak out against their perpetrators and had grown up feeling voiceless. How interesting, I thought. Are our bodies really just the physical manifestation of our thoughts and emotions? Can we choose, then, to manifest what we want rather than what we don't want?

About this time, a woman named T'Shala, who practiced an unusual form of massage, walked into the Wellness Clinic and asked if she could work there. Initially, T'Shala wanted both Richard and me to experience her craft firsthand before deciding to hire her. When she invited me to be on the covered floor cushion, however, I was embarrassed. How could I tell her that I preferred not to be touched? I had never really understood why myself. To her credit, I did not have to say a thing.

She knew it as soon as we met face to face, she said. "I am a psychic and can read people," she explained. "I am certified in intuition and use it in my work."

I had not known there was a certification for intuition. Having been exposed to Carolyn Myss's work, I could barely contain myself and had to ask, "Are you medically intuitive? Can you see disease in energy fields?"

"Of course, I can," she replied. We spent the rest of my scheduled time discussing intuition, chakras, auras, and other aspects of her work. T'Shala would tell me years later that she could not believe she was having that conversation with a physician. She knew immediately that she would be working with me for a long time and could see that I was also intuitive but was not using it because I did not yet fully trust it.

In fact, spurred on by curiosity and all that I was learning, I continued to pay attention to my intuition. I began to get feelings about the energetic systems of my patients, which intimated not only the physical cause of their pain, but also the deeper reasons why they had drawn it into their life. My gut was always correct, even though my head could not always rationalize the decisions I was making on the patient's behalf. The answers to some of the most complex situations would simply drop into the top of my head. As I experimented with trusting this inner knowing, my patients' results continued to improve. My intuition was becoming an irreplaceable helpmate in my work.

My listening repertoire on the Friday commute expanded. I was gradually realizing that our physical systems are much more complicated energetically than Western medicine was willing or could admit. The healing techniques of other traditions, such as the Ayurvedic, Chinese, and Native American, give just as much, if not more, weight to the psycho-emotional and electromagnetic components of who we are and the illnesses we manifest as they do to the physical component. My medically trained mind could easily rationalize this by saying these traditions relied on these aspects more because they did not enjoy the advanced diagnostic and treatment technologies that are commonplace in Western medicine now. My gut and my patients, however, were telling me something different: that modern medicine was missing a heart.

In the fall of 1999, I attended a conference, drawn by the advertisement for a pre-conference workshop given by a physician named Christine Page, MD, entitled "Learning to Use Your Intuitive Skills in Medicine."

Dr. Page's workshop began by her discussing the nature of intuition and how we can identify and then use our intuitive skills both in our life and in our work. My soul stirred. For the first time, I was experiencing a live presentation on what to date had existed for me only in brief discussions with a few like-minded individuals or on audiotape. She then led us through exercises that encouraged us to trust our intuition.

In the first exercise, I held the watch of the woman seated next to me and, as directed, reported the first three impressions that filtered through my mind. I intentionally slowed my mind and focused on the color black, which quickly melted into an iridescent indigo, as so often happened when I was doing cranial sacral therapy on patients. It always seemed to be a portal into other realms. The seething circle of indigo turned into a beating heart shape. I took note of it and again closed my eyes and slowed my breathing. This time a cheery yellow color showed up. This, too, was different, so I wrote it down. On my third foray, a lingering sense of sadness filled my chest. I wrote down the word "sadness." I reported my findings to the woman. She responded that she was a physician's assistant to a cardiologist, that the previous summer she and her young niece had painted an entire cottage on Martha's Vineyard a sunny yellow, and that she was indeed sad at the moment, having received a diagnosis of breast cancer just two days prior. We were both amazed. Exercise after exercise, we discovered that all of us had these talents, and that they improve through practice.

Not long after the conference, I saw a new patient, a thirty-five-year-old guard at the Santa Cruz County Jail who was complaining of right arm and shoulder pain. In the midst of a gang conflict at the jail, she had ferociously pulled open a heavy leaded door with her right arm, and felt immediate pain in her entire upper right extremity. She had seen five other physicians and done thirty weeks of physical therapy, but the pain remained.

A full examination came up negative for true tissue or nerve injury but left me with a clear sense of what was going on. This was the first time a knowing was so intelligible on the first visit. I usually waited until a patient's third or fourth visit before even considering deeper questions such as what their injury meant in their life. But because my confidence had been bolstered at the conference, I decided to go for it. I started by asking her if she had a spiritual practice.

Her face immediately lit up. Six months earlier, she had traveled to India and visited Sai Baba's ashram. I had never heard of Sai Baba before. She shared that she wanted to make some changes in her life. She had entered the police force on a whim right out of high school and for the past seventeen years she had regretted her decision. Her words were confirming my impression that she had in fact a soft, sensitive spirit not suited for law enforcement. Moreover, she was clearly hearing the implications of her own words. This was good. Asking one open-ended question had opened up new territory.

I began again. "Sherry, I can find nothing physically wrong with your arm or shoulder. If I can be so bold, I am going to level with you. I see your injury as that of the wounded warrior. The right arm is our masculine; it holds the sword in battle and protects us from our enemies, which is sometimes ourselves. You are fighting a subconscious internal battle that is forcing you to make some difficult conscious decisions. Until you do, your nervous system will continue to provide you with pain messages from your arm." As I spoke, I was astonished, and wondered where the hell this information was coming from. It seemed to flow through me rather than come from me.

Her response was reassuring. She seemed to appreciate the scrutiny on this level. Letting out a deep sigh, she responded, "Now what? I can't just walk out of my job. It pays well and has great benefits."

There it is, I thought, the age-old conflict between security and moving forward into life's creative process. Most people are afraid to step off into the abyss, where the Universe can have its way with them. I had always been quite the opposite. When new opportunities showed up, I loved to take the leap. But this required trust. I suggested that Sherry schedule some appointments with T'Shala. "She is medically intuitive and can help you see what is holding you back and perhaps assist you in cutting the cords that are keeping you feeling so stuck."

Breaking into a smile, Sherry replied, "When do I start?"

On a Friday morning a few weeks after the session with Sherry, I was making the drive up Coast Highway 1, listening to Caroline Myss's first taped workshop on a new subject matter: sacred contracts. Somewhere between Pescadero and Half Moon Bay, as the last tape was coming to a close, the live audience gave Caroline a round of applause. She sounded grateful, almost relieved, that the group had understood the new concept, and she told a charming final story. Each time she had given birth to a new idea and delivered it clearly, "the gods" as she put it, showed their appreciation by having vibhuti show up in her life. Even as I wondered what vibhuti was, she explained that it is a sacred healing ash smelling of roses that Sai Baba in India manifests instantly from thin air.

How strange. Within a few weeks, the name Sai Baba had come into my experience twice. By that time I had learned to pay attention to the law of threes. This was only two; I made a mental bookmark. Just then, I decided to do a little experiment. Thinking if it works for Dr. Myss, it should work for me, I verbalized out loud to the steering wheel and windshield: "If I am on the right track by developing psychic abilities and clairvoyance in order to understand disease on an energetic level, I want confirmation. I want vibhuti to show up."

The following Tuesday, Sherry came to mind during my morning run. The old phenomenon from high school of random thoughts streaming through my head when I was in the "runner's zone" had never quit.

When I got to the office and reviewed my schedule of patients for the day, there she was, at 1:30 p.m. The morning was filled with complicated worker's compensation cases, and I was falling further and further behind on my schedule. After taking a ten-minute lunch so I would not pass out on my late-afternoon patients, I vowed to stay on time through the afternoon. At 1:30, however, Sherry had not arrived. By 1:40, still no Sherry, and I began to get nervous. Just as I was about to tell the staff that if she showed I could not see her, in she walked.

Grabbing her chart and giving her a look that clearly said, "Let's go, we're in a hurry," I charged down the hall with her toward the treatment room. She apologized profusely for being late. I forgave her as we walked inside. We chatted about her sessions with T'Shala, how she and T'Shala had cut the energetic cords holding her to parts of her life that were no longer serving her. She was speaking from a position of power now, which was a shift from her first appointment. Glancing at my watch, I saw that our session had already gone five minutes over. I checked in with her quickly, verifying that she and T'Shala had more work to do together, and stood up to leave.

Just as I reached for the doorknob, she said, "Oh, I almost forgot," and reached for her purse. Fumbling through the bag, she pulled out a yellow pouch tied with red string. "This is for you. It's the reason why I was late. When I got in my car to come here, a voice in my head told me to go back and get this and bring it to you."

I took the pouch, which was the size of my hand and weighed several ounces.

"I only brought back four bags and have been coveting each one. It's vibhuti, healing ash from Sai Baba—he obviously wanted you to have it."

There it was, just as I had requested in the car only three days earlier. What was I tapping into? Could it really be this easy—ask the Universe for a sign, and if your request is in alignment with your destiny, it will simply show up?

Over the next several years, I shared the vibhuti with my patients. When Jeff at Spinal Diagnostics contracted lymphoma and was at the UC San Francisco medical center apparently dying, I sneaked into the ICU, pretending to be one of his physicians, and put some vibhuti on his parched, cracked tongue and forehead before placing my hands on his head to do cranial sacral therapy. He had not come out of his coma in two weeks. That night after I left, I learned, he was sitting up in bed asking to see me. Perhaps it was a coincidence, but I was beginning to abandon the idea that anything is mere coincidence.

Ron Swan, PhD.

22

Becoming an Instrument of Energy

*H**ush, do not be afraid. That which is there for you will burst forth no matter where you go or what path you choose. Follow your heart as it takes you to the
places that will reveal yourself to you. The ancient master that resides deep within
your earthen core will remember and bask in the familiarity of these places. You
have been there and continue to visit often. These places of energy and wonder are
only new in this particular incarnate experience.*

One night in early February 1999 after a Wellness Center staff meeting, I found myself chatting with Ron, our psychologist, whose gentle
manner mixed with a childlike sense of adventure always reminded me of
my father. He reached up and touched the top of the nearest doorframe
to stretch his shoulders, and while his arms were up over his head, I began to get intuitive information regarding his chest, then more specifically his heart. My subconscious mind was busy analyzing the information
flooding in as our conversation continued. I tried to discount it, thinking
my mind might be superimposing my father's heart condition onto Ron,
especially since Ron was fifty-seven, the same age Dad had been when
he died. But when the sense remained strong, I decided to do some fishing. "Ron, when was your last comprehensive physical? More specifically,
have you ever taken a treadmill test?"

He stopped stretching and said, "Well, I've been seeing my doctor recently over my heart murmur issue."

"What heart murmur?" I asked.

"I've been dealing with this since I was fourteen. I have a leaking aortic valve that the doctors keep telling me will someday need to be replaced. It's looking like that time may be coming up soon."

I was stunned by my accuracy. Ron had become my confidant in matters of extrasensory perception. We would take lunch together to hash out the finer details concerning past-life events, synchronicities, and intuitive information, and he had been my supporter throughout the Mark Murphy episode. Until now, I had not received any information about him. "Ron, you have never said a word to me about your heart murmur and, like a beacon, my attention focused right in on it."

"Wow, you are getting good with this stuff, Janine," he responded.

Several weeks later, Ron stopped by to see if I was free for lunch. As we walked down the hallway together, he told me he was scheduled for a valve replacement the following week.

"So soon? What's the rush?"

He said the last set of tests had shown a progression of the blood regurgitating through the valve, and he had begun to experience shortness of breath and early fatigue during exercise. I noticed that the usual pinkness in his complexion had faded to grayish beige. He suddenly looked much older than he had just weeks earlier. I offered no argument. He then asked, "What does your intuition say about my chances?"

His request took me aback. At first I was reluctant to check, for fear he would make this very personal decision based on what I said. But after a few moments, I found myself having the strong opinion, originating from a knowing deep in my chest that he should go forth on one condition: that I treat him, focusing on the rib cage, the evening before his chest was to be opened—or so I thought.

The following Tuesday evening, as I walked my last patient to the front desk, there was Ron, all alone in the waiting room, reading a magazine. The scene struck me as a microscopic allegory of who we are in life. No matter how many people are there to support us throughout life's ups and downs, when you get right down to it, we make the real journey on our own.

We went into the treatment room and I got to work. We chatted about what was to happen to him the following morning. He was a pro when it came to helping patients ready themselves for surgeries. He would take them through relaxation and visualization exercises and had even produced audiotapes for them to listen to right up to the moment they were wheeled into the OR. But this time the healer himself would be under the knife.

The time flew by. Before I knew it, the only thing left to do was balance the nervous system using cranial sacral technique. Taking my usual place on the stool at the head of the table, I placed my hands on the sides of Ron's head. Tuning into the cranial rhythmic impulse and glancing at the sweeping second hand on the wall clock, I counted the number of cycles per minute—ten, an adequate number. I then assessed the position and motion of the cranial bones. Meanwhile, Ron and I were chatting about how his leaky valve had been diagnosed when he was a record-setting high school track-and-field athlete.

As he was speaking, I consciously slowed my breathing and cleared my mind, becoming an empty vessel. I began to perceive the color indigo mixed with black churning and bubbling between my eyes as I slipped into a profound state of relaxation in which I was utterly in the present moment. I finish every treatment this way, and except for the imagery of the dungeon with Mark, nothing much had ever happened—until now.

All of a sudden, a massive tingling sensation dropped into the top of my head and surged down my spine and legs into my feet and then back up again, creating a spherical shape like a giant soap bubble of energy that seemed to empty through my chest, arms, and hands into Ron's head. Once it connected, the circuit came alive, as if a very real electrical current was passing through me on its way to Ron. I was fascinated with what was happening. It felt pleasurable and did nothing to jar me out of my state of deep relaxation. Actually, it reminded me of an orgasm. It's running on those same circuits, I thought.

Ron was about to start his next sentence, but he suddenly paused and said, "I...I...don't want to talk right now."

Then I knew I wasn't the only one feeling this. Its directional nature continued for ten or fifteen seconds and then stopped as abruptly as it had begun. Both of us knew the exact instant it ended. I lifted my hands from his head, and he practically jumped off the table and spun around to face me. We sized each other up with a locked gaze. Not knowing what to say, I let him begin.

"What...what was that?"

Well, that certainly confirmed it. "I'm not entirely sure," I said. I was half hoping that with his years in psychotherapy he would have some context for it. "That's never happened to me before."

I began to feel embarrassed to be in the room alone with him. Whatever it was had felt like an orgasm that fell into the top my head, traveled down my spine, and out my hands into him. Though Ron and I were friends, our relationship had certainly never crossed *that* boundary. I could sense that he was feeling just as embarrassed as I was. We were behaving as if we had just committed accidental adultery and wanted nothing more than to end the moment by escaping out the door. The curiosity of it all held us there, though.

"What did you feel?" I asked.

He took several moments before speaking. "Well, it felt warm and reassuring, filling me with the message that everything is going to be all right. I finally feel at peace with my decision to go ahead with the surgery. What did you feel?"

Several minutes ahead of him in the self-analysis department, I described the directional surge of energy that circulated through my body forming a sphere, and how the energy radiated through my arms and chest right into him.

He was deep in thought as he spoke. "Do you feel any different right now?"

A perceptive question, I thought. All I could offer was that I felt relaxed and confident that whatever this was, it was definitely a good sign for him.

The next day, Ron's partner, Tara, called to tell me the surgery went well. Days later, Ron himself thanked me for connecting him with a force of such magnitude. The sense of peace and comfort had lasted right up to when he was wheeled into the OR and given anesthesia. The sensation was like warm honey encasing him within a protective bubble of reassurance. He summed it up as "pure bliss."

This surge, or energy dump, as I have learned to call it, began to show up now and then with other patients just as unexpectedly as it had with Ron. A few would comment, but apparently most of them didn't notice. I chose to say nothing and simply experience it for what it was. After several months, I experimented with sending healing affirmations into the patient along with it. The diversity of the patients it showed up for also caught my attention. I had wondered if it was a kind of cosmic boost for people depleted of energy, yet it often happened with those who seemed to be quite fulfilled in life and were coming in only for maintenance treatments. I also discovered that if I altered my spinal position, as if I were tuning into a fuzzy radio signal, I could sharpen its directional nature and reduce the "static" on its way through me into the patient.

I began to ask other people who worked with energy about their experiences, but no one ever described what I was experiencing. The next time I was in East Lansing to teach the continuing education courses, I asked Drs. Ward and Greenman over dinner one night if they had ever experienced such a surge while treating patients. They and their spouses looked at me as if I had returned to California and become a nutcase. I decided never again to speak about it professionally.

After three years of declining Helene's invitations to join the girls and dogs backpacking trip, I finally said yes in 2000. Helene was our clinic manager from the hospital with whom I shared an office and this trip was an annual tradition for her and several of her nurse friends from the hospital. It was the first year I didn't have a speaking or teaching commitment during the designated week in September. She guided me on what gear to buy, and reminded me to include a really good book.

Perhaps the biggest challenge was the book selection. Since leaving MSU, I had spent most weekends and nights after work reading spine journals and massive textbooks. José tried to remind me that my residency and the fellowship were over. For him, it may have been. Drs. Derby and Eek had me doing original research and speaking at international spine conferences, and I continually had to increase my knowledge base or prepare a lecture. I didn't even know what people were reading these days just for pleasure.

One Thursday morning in June after completing my run, I was stretching out on the floor in front of the television, which was tuned to *Good Morning America*. The host, Joan Lunden, was interviewing Shirley MacLaine on her newest book. Half listening, my ears perked up when I heard her name announced. My thoughts flashed back to *Out on a Limb*, which I had read during my rotation on Bracken's service. That had been almost ten years earlier. I wondered what she was up to now.

The new book, *The Camino,* was Shirley's personal account of walking an ancient five-hundred-mile Christian pilgrimage trail that begins in France and continues west across Northern Spain, ending at the cathedral in Santiago de Compostela. Shirley admitted that she undertook this trek not so much for religious reasons as for its spiritual history. What interested her was that it traversed a very strong ley line. Ley lines, she was saying, are created where the reflections of the Milky Way and other galaxies fall on the Earth. They are lines of energy crisscrossing the planet, and throughout history humans have built sacred sites along them and where they intersect. When experienced by a human consciousness, ley line energy induces clarity of thought and experience, and the person becomes a more psychic and insightful being, for better or worse.

As Shirley went on to describe being a pilgrim for a month—walking alone, carrying only a light backpack, and staying in the pilgrims' bunkhouses called *albergos*—I sat there spellbound, much as I had watching Julie Moss crawl across the Ironman finish line in 1982. I could imagine the countryside, the driving sun on my neck, the smell of the wildflowers, and the energy coming up through my feet from the ley line. The question of what to read for the girls and dogs backpacking trip had morphed into a bigger question: When would I make this journey myself?

The Mountain Women: top from left to right: Corrine, Julie, Glynis, Sue, Jan, Dede; bottom from left to right: Janine, Donna and Helene.

Spending a week in the Sierras next to a crystal-clear lake with six wonderful women and their dogs—lying in the sun after long morning runs or hikes, eating from plastic bags with our fingers, communing with the elements—allowed my mind to unravel. We partook in heartfelt spiritual conversations around the campfire in the evenings, and at night I cuddled up in my tent with Holly, who was out of her mind with joy, listening to the brush and squeak of the pine trees as the thermals gusted down from the peaks into the valley. I saw what I had been missing—a balanced life. These women, most of whom were at least a decade my senior, were on journeys of personal growth that included literal journeys such as hiking in Nepal, climbing Mount Kilimanjaro, and boating down the Amazon. As they spoke of these adventures, my mind soared. Giving myself permission to take that kind of extended time off still seemed years away. For now, hearing their stories and being in this place was decadence enough.

At the final night's campfire, in a ritual that was part of their tradition, Helene pulled a mini-notebook from her backpack in which on the last trip they had recorded the goals of the group for the year ahead. As each woman's goal was read aloud, she commented on her success at achieving it. This opened up some of the richest discussions I had ever heard. Each woman also proclaimed a new goal for the coming year. Helene scribbled these in her notebook, not to be seen again by a human eye until next year's last-night ceremony.

It was my turn to devise a goal for the next twelve months. Power was proving to be a tricky business between Richard Bernstein and me. I decided to choose realigning my relationship with power as my goal for the year.

T'Shala and I, working together, had been guiding one chronic pain patient after another into a deeper understanding of their symptoms. Energetic and spiritual information about the patient would flood into my awareness even as I diagnosed and treated them physically, and I would refer them to T'Shala to resolve the issue at the energetic or spiritual level. Many patients with chronic neck and shoulder pain apparently had been hanged or decapitated in past lives. Others said their pain felt as if they had been run through with a spear or a sword. I gradually realized that their words, chosen subconsciously, were telling me that it was I who had sunk these implements of death into their flesh, making sure to twist the handles upon impact, in brutal battles over the centuries. In those lifetimes, I had lived by domination—power in its most distorted form.

After the realizations I had that year, reporting on power at the next camping trip seemed so deflated. But I had second thoughts about sharing the other insights with the women around the campfire the next September, even though they were an open-minded lot. When it was my turn to report, I kept it more superficial. My goal for 2002 was to focus on the non-monetary wealth in my life.

That was the year I listened to the Abraham-Hicks material on my drives up to Daly City. As I learned about the law of attraction, I began to view my reimbursement issues in a whole new way. Because my work had taken on a spiritual aspect, I subconsciously regarded it as the work of a spiritual practitioner sworn to humility and poverty. How screwed up was that!

That was also the year I befriended a woman who, like me, would finish her workout at the spa across the street from my office at 6:15 most mornings. We regularly used the women's locker room at the same time, and eventually we started to chat.

Jynel was into all kinds of consciousness-expanding material, including astrology, the UFO cover-up phenomena, and conspiracy theories. I lent her the first volume of my Abraham tapes. She shared with me tapes of Sean David Morton speaking about time coding in the Great Pyramid of Giza, remote viewing, and astrological and sunspot predictions of future events. This exchange started an avalanche of fascinating morning conversations, and my weekly drives to Daly City took on a whole new character. As I absorbed this new material, my outlook on the world shifted. Instead of assuming I had no control over world events that impacted my life, I began to ask why the control appeared to be out of my hands. I chewed up this information, eager for more.

Jynel occasionally mentioned the work of David Icke. I became more and more curious, finally asking her if she had any of his tapes in her collection. I remember her studying me for a moment, questioning whether this fledgling seeker was ready for what he had to say. "Of course, I do," she said, "but you must know that once you hear what he is saying...you can never un-hear it." She lent me a lecture titled "Alice in Wonderland: The World Trade Center Disaster," which introduced me to the notion that thirteen original "bloodline" families are in exclusive control of politics, banking, and the media worldwide. Icke also mentioned the Knights Templar. This caught my attention, since in *The Camino,* Shirley MacLaine had described the Templars as protectors of the pilgrims on their journey to Compostela. Who were these knights? And why did their very mention cause a stir deep in my soul? I had to know more.

Thus began a two-year immersion into world history leading up to the Crusades and beyond. As I finished one book or taped lecture, the next would land in my lap. My interest in medical journals and textbooks faded. Life outside work became a torrent of information that was showing me the world through a different pair of spectacles. I *knew* I was finally connecting to the body of knowledge that would lead to answering the question that had haunted me since childhood: For what purpose was I born?

I began to listen to the evening news differently. Were the networks reporting only what those in control wanted us to know? We had just experienced the largest terrorist attack on American soil that conveniently justified going into Afghanistan and Iraq, and billions of dollars were being transferred into the coffers of transnational corporations controlled by members of the current administration. In light of my reading, these events took on new meaning. We were witnessing the Crusades all over again—Christians doing battle with Muslims over the age-old question of whose God is the real God, even while lands were invaded and pillaged for the ultimate booty: power, prestige, and profit, though this time the cache was heroin and oil. My innards screamed in protest, as if I understood that I had suffered and died many times over in similar scenarios, only to realize over many lifetimes the meaninglessness of such brutality. Perhaps my soul purpose in this lifetime was to help bring this mayhem to an end, once and for all.

That year on the girls and dogs backpacking trip when Helene asked what I had in mind for the coming year, I answered, "I am going to take a month off and walk the Camino next June with José to see what is there waiting for me." The words shot out of my mouth quickly, landing in front of the group, causing the fire to spark and sizzle on cue. Helene quickly scribbled them down. I had pledged a vow to the circle of six. There was no going back.

As we broke camp the next day and trekked down the mountain, the thought came to me that I was in my forty-first year. The following June I would be forty-two. How synchronistic, I thought to myself. It could not have been planned more perfectly.

PART V

The Path to Purpose

Janine on the Camino de Santiago in northern Spain.

23

The Camino de Santiago

*Y*our curriculum has been set. The knowledge you will need will come to you *without much effort on your part. Does it feel as if the interconnectedness of it all is expanding? Do you feel as if you are being led to understand the totality of history so that you can appreciate the mistakes that have been made and the better solutions? You have come into this time to understand the sum total of all that has ever been and then take that knowledge forth to create a new way of being. The tools you will need will be at your beck and call. You will recognize them immediately and be able to intuit their best use. Many who have come before have contributed to the knowledge you will now refer to in order to bring in the new way. Your DNA is strung with the codes that know this. Simply allow your inner being to resonate with the vastness of all that is. Let go and enjoy the ride. You cannot fail—it is law. As you play your role on this universal stage, keep in mind what it is that you seek. You have come to restore balance and peace to this unusual plain of existence. Be an example in all that you do and all that you are. Good teachers never preach; they lead by example, and they never stop being students either.*

José loves to travel but usually in the lap of luxury. When I explained to him the walking while carrying gear, the sleeping accommodations, the food, and the distance, to my amazement he still agreed to go. I spent the next nine months diligently preparing. I purchased the gear we needed:

fleece sleeping bags, lightweight backpacks, good hiking shoes and sandals, head lamps, water bottles, and supplies in case of injuries, blisters, or shoe failures. I also read everything I could find about the Camino.

Helene had recommended Paulo Coelho's *The Pilgrimage,* and I began reading it right after the backpacking trip. Each day I looked forward to getting home and completing my evening chores so I could spend a precious uninterrupted hour reading. One evening I sat at my desk as usual, opened the book in the light of the brass library desk lamp to page 224, and began to read:

> I crossed and recrossed the small city of Ponferrada, looking from a distance at the castle on the hill where I had been bidden to appear. The Templars had always stirred my imagination, and the castle in Ponferrada was not the only mark made on the Camino route by their order....
>
> But as with everything that happens before its time, the Templars came to be viewed with suspicion.... On Friday, October 13, 1307, the Vatican and the major European states unleashed one of the most massive police operations of the Middle Ages: during the night, the main leaders of the Templars were seized in their castles and thrown in prison.... Following a violent sequence of torture, renunciation, and treason, the Order of the Templars was erased from the map of medieval history. Their treasures were confiscated, and their members scattered throughout the world....

The words in front of me triggered the memory of looking through the eyes of a body that had been tortured and then imprisoned. Had that dungeon scene happened during the time of the Templars? Had I been one of the knights? Perhaps the Camino was calling me back to finish something left undone.

At that moment, I glanced up at the calendar above the desk and noticed the date: October 13. How strange to be reading this passage on the same day of the same month that the Templars were arrested. The Universe seemed to be trying to get my attention. I chuckled. It was all happening in perfect order.

Between the practical preparations and my reading schedule, I had little time to contemplate my expectations for the journey. All I knew was that I was being called to do this walk. When Mom and Alex drove

José and I to a hotel near the San Francisco airport to stay over and catch our flight early the next morning, my attention was more focused on whether the house, the animals, and my medical practice would survive my journey than whether my physical body could handle it.

We set the alarm for 4:30 a.m., my normal waking time. Popping out of bed first, I jumped in the shower. No sooner had I finished rinsing the shampoo from my hair and grabbed the bar of soap then my feet suddenly slipped out from under me and I became airborne, heading for the rim of the porcelain bathtub. My left shin and left rib cage hit hard. The recoil of my flexible rib cage caused me to spring back up into the air toward the ledge on the other side of the tub. The right side of my rib cage landed with a crash. I bounced from one side of the bathtub to the other until my body finally came to rest face up, as if neatly placed in a sarcophagus, while the shower water, now pelting my face, threatened to drown me.

My rib cage and left shin pounded with pain, but I was sure there were no fractures. Why had this occurred? In the whole of my life, I had never fallen in the shower. Getting up slowly, I realized how much pain I was in. If this was how the gods chose to gift me before I even left California, I wondered what they had in store for me in Spain.

We traveled for twenty-six hours straight on planes, buses, and trains. My left shin looked like a black-and-blue grapefruit, and my ribs ached with almost every movement of my arms and trunk. We finally arrived late in the evening at Saint Jean Pied de Port in the south of France, one of the three starting points of the Camino. In the morning, after a leisurely carbohydrate load of bread and jam with coffee in the hotel, we set off along the quaint cobblestone streets lined with brightly painted dwellings in search of the pilgrim's office. We picked up the *carnes* (credentials) in which we would collect stamps from every sleeping shelter, hostel, and church we encountered along the way, and headed out of town, our scallop shells on leather strings tied to our backpacks, to signal that we were pilgrims on the road to Santiago.

The asphalt road headed what looked to be straight up. It was late morning on May 31, 2004, and the first leg of the journey, a four-thousand-foot climb up and over the Pyrenees, was beginning. Herds of cows, sheep, and horses grazed in grass pastures bordering the road that undulated along the crest of rolling hills toward the peaks in the distance.

As I walked, reflecting on the land's majestic beauty, I thought of how my father would have loved this trip. In the eleven years since his death, I had often felt his presence. Suddenly sensing the warmth of his love, I wondered if he wasn't there, walking beside me.

Lost in the brilliance of it all, I hardly noticed the grade we were ascending. José, on the other hand, could think of nothing else. His backpack weighed twenty pounds, the heaviest item being his medication bag. Packing like a true internist, he had brought something for every situation. As for me, I had packed athletic training supplies: Band-Aids, moleskin, adhesive sponge pads, a needle and thread to drain blisters, athletic tape, antiseptic cream, and a pair of scissors.

As we climbed, José's breathing became more labored and he had to rest frequently. Yet even air hunger did not stop him from talking. If he was not commenting on our breathtaking surroundings, he was pushing me to the brink of incontinence with quips about how tired and out of shape he was, how he should have listened to me and lost some weight, and how glad he was that he had not read a single thing about this trip, so he wouldn't know what he was getting himself into.

We walked up a forty-five-degree grade for five and a half hours and straight down for another two and a half. On the steep descent, José met his walking stick, a four-inch-diameter branch that possessed a certain character. He leaned heavily on this piece of wood—far too cumbersome for anyone else on the first day of an eight-hundred-kilometer journey— taking one step at a time.

I found it easier to jog the steep downhill. I was wearing my hiking sandals, as I had read that toenail bruises from descending this rocky Roman road in closed-toe boots could haunt pilgrims for the remainder of their trek.

On reaching Roncesvalles, we secured bunks in an eleventh-century church converted into a hostel and located some dinner at the only bar serving food. Filling as the food was, the only thing on José's mind was getting supine as soon as possible.

We awoke to the sound of Gregorian chant echoing off the ancient stone walls of the church. Two deacons were walking up and down the aisles to wake up the pilgrims. How quaint, I thought, as my consciousness crept back into present-time awareness. On this trek, José and I were stepping back to an era without cell phones or pagers, not to mention alarm clocks. For the first time in our lives, we could not be contacted. A calm flooded over me as I considered that fact. I had always hated electronic leashes.

As I stood up from the bed, the tightness in my calves was unmistakable. Walking downstairs to the bathroom, I realized I should have done more stretching after the previous day's eight-hour hike. My shin and ribs were still very sore. We packed our things, fueled ourselves again with bread, jam, and coffee, and headed off toward the next town.

Over the next four days, the pain and swelling in my calves increased. On the fifth day, there was palpable crepitus in both Achilles tendons, and the damage to my left ankle had revived an old injury to that foot and ankle from when I was twelve. By the seventh day, the Achilles tendons were audibly grinding with each step and the muscles of my lower legs had swollen to twice their normal size. It was one of those times as a physician when you wished you did not know what you knew. Tendons this inflamed are at risk of rupturing.

On the morning of the eighth day, my legs barely carried me to the bathroom, let alone another twenty miles. José offered to carry my pack, but my pride would have none of that. I had come on this journey to complete it myself. I would walk, with pack, no matter what. Gritting my teeth, I proceeded on legs that were screaming in pain. Recalling the lessons of my triathlon years, I focused on slipping into a walking meditation that allowed me to leave my body, freeing me from its agony.

There were two routes into Santo Domingo de la Calzada, the day's destination. One split off at the ten-kilometer point along a rural road, adding an additional nine kilometers to the day. The other joined the highway at that point and measured five kilometers into town. Given my condition, we opted for the shorter route, walking on the narrow shoulder of the elevated highway, which ran alongside fields of hops swaying in the breeze. José, now adjusted to the rigors of the Camino, cruised along at a decent pace, while I fell farther and farther behind. As the diesel semi trucks passed at frightening speeds, their tailwinds knocked me off balance.

Lost in my deepening trance, I barely noticed one particularly massive truck barreling toward me. Its invisible wake slammed into me just as I was adjusting my footing to the jagged asphalt edge of the road. My right foot missed the edge, and I fell down and forward, the sweaty skin of my right shin scraping along the serrated edge of the asphalt as I fell headfirst into the scrub bushes below. Top-heavy due to my backpack, weak, dehydrated, and now experiencing a whole new level of searing pain, I looked down to see blood cascading down my leg from hundreds of lacerations, making it look like raw meat. I had new appreciation of the gate control theory of pain. My attention was now on the fresh road rash on my right leg rather than the deep, aching contusion on the left and in my Achilles tendons.

What on earth was happening to me? I had expected to have, like Shirley MacLaine, the most mind-altering, etheric experience of my life on this trip. So far, it was my body that was having all the fun. What had drawn me here, and why? These circumstances were pointing toward serving some sort of penance.

Agonizingly pulling myself back up onto the highway and trying to shut out the wailing coming from my lower extremities, I walked on. José was waiting for me up ahead. He offered once again to take my pack, and again I refused. In truth, I wanted nothing more than to sit and rest, but the guidebook showed only two more kilometers to our destination. I had been to this place many times before, where every cell in your body is screaming at you to stop, and a little voice inside is saying, "If you stop, you will fail the test." Failure was not an option. I walked on.

Santo Domingo de la Calzada was a bustling, dirty, graffitied town with none of the historical charm of other towns along the route. We found a one-star hotel that offered a large room and private bathroom. José went to collect bags of ice while I lay on the bed next to the open window, my massively swollen lower extremities elevated on pillows. The girth of my calves, already well developed from the years of running, was amazing. The continuing pain could mean I had developed compartment syndrome. Would I need a fasciotomy? The right shin, now with dried blood and blue bruising showing between the bits of gravel embedded in the skin, reminded me of grammar school when I would play hard with the boys to prove myself their equal. Injuries had always made me feel tough. This, however, was getting ridiculous.

Lying in bed from early afternoon until the next morning gave me a lot of time to reflect. Rarely getting sick and always enjoying boundless energy, I was now getting a taste of what patients who must be in bed for days or weeks at a time go through. By sundown, as I watched the wind pick up and a thunderstorm building on the horizon, the depression was mounting. I could not stay in this place much longer. I had to think of a solution.

I woke the next morning from a dream in which I was back at San Jose State, taping a male gymnast's badly sprained ankle in a perfect ninety-degree position to withstand the impact of his landings. My consciousness gradually collected evidence that, in fact, I was lying in a bed in a sleazy hotel in a depressing town, with calves the size of tree trunks, a swollen left ankle with a mature bruise on the shin from the fall in the shower, and a lacerated right shin. Priceless, I thought, as I greeted the day.

My subconscious had just provided the answer, however. Sports medicine aims to treat injuries while the athlete remains in the competition, something I hadn't thought about in years. Sitting on the bed, holding my ankle in a ninety-degree position, I wove a tape job upside down and backward, straight on the skin. The fact that the adhesive would cause blisters later was secondary to staying in the game one more day.

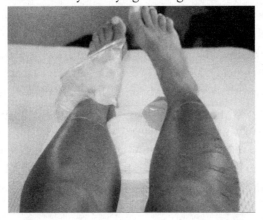

Janine's swollen legs with blisters several days after the fall from the freeway.

The rest and ice had done their work. We completed 21.7 kilometers that day, and I was in much less pain—until the evening, when I cut off the sticky, sweat-drenched tape before taking a shower. Huge blisters had formed everywhere the skin had been covered—yet another challenge. To avoid infection, I skewered each blister with a needle and thread, leaving long thread tails to drain off the serous fluid, relieving the pressure and thus the pain. My legs now looked like those of a worn-out Raggedy Ann doll, with strings sticking out everywhere.

José was nearly hysterical. "If I had any *one* of these injuries, I would be on the first train to Santander! You are *nuts*. What are you doing this for?"

He was right—this was pretty crazy. I took a picture and laughed it off. This Camino had me, for better or worse. What still eluded me was the reason it had called in the first place.

One day melded into the next. Taping my ankles each morning over knee-high nylons, *medias,* to avoid more blisters allowed me to continue in almost no pain, though the swelling remained. The Camino seemed to have decided I had collected enough injuries to my legs and handed me no more.

On day fourteen, halfway through our journey, we walked into Carrión de los Condes, a veritable fairyland of a village preparing to celebrate its very own All Saints Day. The entire population seemed to be pitching in to adorn the main street, which fronted the church, with designs made with fresh flower petals and freshly cut grass. We sat at an outdoor café listening to the church bells pealing, mesmerized by the motion of it all. But once we had our fill of tortas and coffee, and not wanting to take up too much table time, we pushed onward.

Not more than an hour outside the village, the forest along the road opened up to a field edged by a grove of poplar trees that grew increasingly familiar with every step. My soul stirred even before my brain registered what I was perceiving. Here, to my astonishment, was a piece of the awake imagery I had experienced after Mark Murphy died. The soil itself spoke to me in a language I no longer recognized, yet as vibrantly as if I had been here only yesterday. It was here that everything had been taken from me—my family, community, property, and, most of all, freedom. On this very ground, I had been captured. Stopping dead in my tracks, I snapped a picture.

Wondering why I was photographing an open field, José, who had walked on ahead, called to me, "What do you see out there?"

Taking his words to heart, I asked myself the same thing. What was it about this place that required me to revisit it? So what if we had past lives—what were we supposed to do with that sketchy information now?

"This was the field where Mark captured me and threw me into the dungeon," I called back.

He stared at me, speechless for perhaps the first time on this trip. I stood there motionless for a minute, listening for what this place might have to say to me, and then continued on, pondering how my life path had brought me to this place that had evidently left such an impression in some other lifetime, perhaps seven hundred years earlier, perhaps as a Templar. At least I had been right about one thing. The draw to do this trek was connected with the visual download that had occurred while I was treating Mark. I could not discount the validity of what I had just witnessed.

Janine at Ponferrada Castle.

The forest and field were only the beginning. Four days and about seventy miles later, we walked into Ponferrada, the Spanish town Coelho had written about, known for its twelfth-century Templar castle. It was an especially hot dry day, and we were drenched in sweat. After showering, washing our clothes, and hanging them on the communal clothesline outside the albergo, we set out to see the castle. As we wound our way through the streets, following the signs, I felt a heavy constriction in my chest. Thinking it might be from dehydration, I chugged down the remaining contents of my water bottle. The route led us just outside the ancient city walls. There before us was a massive stone structure towering sixty feet into the sky, topped with sharply angled colorful flags flapping in the hot afternoon breeze. The stones were a light sandy beige in color. Complete with drawbridge, circular archery turrets, and a presence that boasted its survival through the ages, this place spoke to the depths of my soul. This structure was one of the old memory drawings of my youth. As that realization hit me, the physical constriction turned to breathlessness and the clear emotion of feeling trapped.

We paid our five Euros and went inside. From the moment I walked through the archway entrance, I knew I had been here before. Over the centuries, the main floor had fallen in, exposing the underground rooms that had held food rations and extra artillery. Long blades of grass were growing high next to catapult stones still lying in what looked like a courtyard. *Ah, yes,* a voiceless voice said in my head, *here men once fought to prove their worth.* The space seemed to echo with battle cries now silenced. As we walked the yellow-roped tourist pathways through the crumbling castle, I felt an ancient sadness for all the bloodshed that had happened here. Had I joined fellow misguided comrades in battle in this place? That thought evoked a very old feeling of despair. As it mixed with my current understanding of the futility of war, I wondered again whether my own soul had learned such lessons over time. Do souls actually evolve, then? Is it possible for human beings to evolve beyond the need to take up arms against each other?

The third and final level offered a spectacular view of the town and surrounding countryside, an obvious point of advantage for the Templar warrior monks. We followed the stone catwalk along the outer wall to a space that even in the ninety-five-degree heat gave me chills. Six stone steps led down to what seemed to be an archery turret—circular, with arched openings laid in with bricks, open at the top where once there had been a ceiling. It was my dungeon, the very scene I had perceived during my session with Mark six years earlier. As with the field scene a few days prior, I was standing again in a real-world spot that up to then I had only known in an imaginary scenario. This time my logical mind sent up a protest—this can't be true. My heart, however, was screaming the contrary. As the two parallel realities collided, my inner skeptic, whose job was to discredit bizarre data, began losing ground. My heart spoke with a clearer voice. It said to go with the experience, to trust in the process that was unfolding. When your eyes are giving you information that matches what's behind them, it becomes difficult to question it. It's what we call *real.*

Three days later, I was again astonished to find myself walking into yet another scene from my waking imageries associated with Mark. The road led into the clouds shrouding the highest mountain ascent of the journey. Walking up the final slope into the enchanting village of O Cerbreiro on the summit, I found before me the exact round stone dwellings with thatched roofs that were set afire and destroyed by Mark's henchmen. The sight took away what little breath I had left from the climb.

Janine at stone thatched dwellings in O Cerbreiro.

Actually standing in these places I had seen in my waking visions seemed to verify that I had lived here in a past life, and that the karmic tie with Mark was real. This was powerful anecdotal proof of the reality of past lives. Yet the meaning of it all still escaped me. What was this land trying so hard to tell me? I pondered this question for the next several days of the Camino.

Certainly, I was getting confirmation that the whispered thoughts and images that arrived in my mind as intuitions carried truth. They could be trusted. I was also getting confirmation that, through many lifetimes, my soul path had morphed from wielding the sword as a warrior to healing people with my bare hands as a physician—including, apparently, those who I had harmed in past lives. This I knew before setting foot on Spanish soil. Perhaps I had been guided to revisit the most agonizing experiences of that warrior's life, the ones most deeply impressed on my soul, to underscore just how correct that understanding was.

We made good time over the next three days and arrived in Santa Irene on June 23, as planned. I wanted to "summit" Compostela on Dad's birthday, June 24. I had felt his presence the entire journey. After an early dinner, we retired to our hotel room. I wanted to get to bed early so I would be as rested as possible for the magical moment of at last coming into Santiago. The sun takes its time to set on June evenings in Spain. I finally fell asleep about 10 p.m., once the sky was fully dark. The next thing I knew, I was jolted awake by a knife of pain slicing up the core of my thorax, along with a putrid taste rising into my mouth. Not even sure if I had time to crawl over José's body from my position against the wall, I lurched toward the bathroom. In the dark, my hands found the porcelain just in time for the contents of my stomach to make their second appearance for the evening.

It was 1:30 a.m. and I couldn't remember ever being so sick in the whole of my life. Once my dinner was gone, I figured my innards would settle down. I crawled back over José and tried to go back to sleep. Within moments, I again shot out of bed, back to the toilet. I hugged the bowl for another fifteen minutes until the violence stopped.

This time I had an audience. "Are you okay?" José muttered, half asleep. "You are making a lot of noise."

Gee, I thought, sorry to disturb you. Every half hour until sunrise, the violent retching, as if from the core of my being, continued. Whatever my body and soul were trying to get rid of, it was very old and putrid.

As the dull light of a dawn under heavy cloud cover filled the room, I started collecting my things. José looked at me from the bed and said, "Where do you think you are going? You are sick. You can't walk today."

I paused to take stock: dizziness from dehydration, hypoglycemia, mounting metabolic alkalosis, chills coursing through my body, involuntary muscle tremors, and profound nausea. With my brow furrowed, I responded, "Well, of course, I can. It's June 24, the day I will walk into Santiago de Compostela."

He shook his head. "Jakie, what is happening to you on this trip? You have completely fallen apart. I was the one we thought would have a difficult time. Look at me. I almost got a blister that you fixed. You, on the other hand.... No one at home will ever believe this."

He was right. My body had suffered greatly. Whether it was a test or a karmic clearing I was not sure. All I knew was that there were ten miles between where I was and where I needed to be. For some reason, among all of the medications José had brought, there was none for nausea. I would finish this ancient journey while looking for the first open pharmacy along the way.

We donned our ponchos and set out into the heavy morning drizzle. By late morning, we stopped at a bar so José could load up on coffee and a snack. Still dealing with waves of nausea, I elected to stay outside, close to the elevated stone planter box in case I needed it.

A few minutes later, a woman came out of the establishment looking for her backpack. Catching sight of me, she looked squarely at me. "Are you okay?" she asked in English, with a slight New York accent.

Though my first impulse was a polite "Yes, thank you," I found myself confessing that I had been up all night vomiting and was still nauseated.

She broke into a smile. "I have just the thing for you." Rifling through her backpack as others began gathering around her, she pulled out a zippered medical bag much like José's. Just then José emerged from the bar, joining us as she handed me a packet of suppositories. "Go in the bathroom and insert one of these. It will cure your nausea."

Janine coming into Santiago.

Walking the rest of the way, barely able to keep my eyes open, was a small price for stilling the waves of sickening fury in my gut. As we finally made our way into the city of Santiago under a high noon sun, I felt nothing except eviscerated. Was this how my Camino would end—slipping into town in a drugged haze? Smiling wryly at my question, I realized that I had quietly been expecting to be greeted like a victor from a battle.

In fact, all I wanted at that moment was to collect our *compostela,* the official certificate for completing the Camino, and find a bed to sleep this one off. Too weak to stand in line at the pilgrims' office, I sat in a chair while José kept our place. When it came time, I mustered enough energy to walk up to the front, produce my booklet of stamps from my fanny pack, make sure my name was spelled correctly, snap a picture, and collapse back into the chair. I still hadn't eaten or drunk anything, and after walking in the driving sun, the dehydration was getting critical. I needed to lie down—and fast.

Janine receiving her compostella.

There it was, my Camino experience. On the physical level, my body fell apart, swelled up, reenacted every sports injury I had ever had, and, to top it off, had a complete cleansing from the inside out. On the symbolic level, I still was not entirely clear what it was all about.

Once I had recuperated, José insisted that we complete every touristy act listed in the Compostela guidebook. First we visited the Cathedral to complete two final tasks of the Camino. One was to kiss the golden bust of Saint James the Lesser, the other was to place our right hands on the marble column carved with the Tree of Jesse, an ancient marble pillar in the church. The depth of the finger marks worn into the hard marble is a measure of just how many pilgrims have passed this way over the centuries. Placing my hand in the deep palm print, I suddenly understood that this was no simple touristy act. My hand adhered to the cold stone as if held by some unseen force, and it took a strong yank to disengage it. What was that about? I watched the pilgrims who followed me. One by one, they engaged their right palm and then pulled it away without effort or delay.

Next I sat down on a pew, taking in the cathedral's vastness. The walls of the central nave stretched up for what seemed like a hundred feet to the ceiling. Directly above the altar was a dome painted with the Illuminati "all-seeing eye," the one that appears on the dollar bill. It reminded me of David Icke's books and videos, warning of the unseen hand that has been controlling us throughout recorded history. Who were the Illuminati, and whose side were they on, anyhow? Were they the same as the Knights Templar? Were the Templars really warrior monks, or was that a cover story to hide a plot to gain wealth and influence? If I had been a knight then, whose side had I been on? Why had I been brought here? What was I supposed to find—and why hadn't I?

It suddenly struck me that perhaps the answers hadn't come because I was closed off to them energetically. I decided to try shifting this, becoming entirely vulnerable in this final moment of being a pilgrim. I began to imagine peeling away one layer after another of my auric field and plastering it on the walls of this colossal edifice. As I did this, for a fleeting moment, I felt an intense, even disturbing, defenselessness. Then a voice began speaking in my head. It was distinct, deep, with, strangely enough, a heavy Scottish brogue. Sounding like Sean Connery doing King Arthur, it said, *"So, my son, you heard the call. You came and completed the journey. For that you need to be commended. You are now released from service."*

But what did it mean—"released from service"? What service? I would be asking myself such questions for some time to come.

Returning home and to the routine of seeing patients was a blessing. I was different; the voltage of what I was able to see, feel, and interpret had magnified. What used to arrive as a feeling I now recognized as a knowing. The "dumps" of energy came through me into the patients more frequently. I even began charting them, thinking that one day their meaning might become clearer. I continued to play around with these surges, altering my spine's position as if tuning into a fuzzy radio signal. I was learning how to wield the cosmic energy that came through me.

Something else kept bubbling up into my conscious perception, too. As I performed manual medicine, my heart was reading dysfunction on a level deeper than that which my well-trained hands could reach. More than psychological, this dysfunction seemed to be on an electromagnetic level and to involve the person's whole being.

24

Ley Lines and Stone Circles

When you think you have arrived, you quickly learn your journey has just begun. As you move into different stages of your life still in search of the instruction sheet that will finally describe the mission for which you have been preparing, your essence begins to be recognized for who and what you truly are. At first, these chance encounters with other highly sensitive beings that have an uncanny ability to see you feel spectacular. They are there to validate you, perhaps for the first time. This begins a processing of all the knowledge you have gleaned in this realm and begins to stir it with the wisdom inherent within you. The blending of the current with the ancient, combined with an innate circuitry that processes spherically, is the unique combination that will produce the paradigm shift into the new age of being. This "new" age is new only to now; it was here and operational in ancient times that humans have forgotten.

Unity consciousness was present here some thirteen thousand years ago in the civilization known as Lemuria. There we existed without the contrast of dualism. There was no dark or light, right or wrong, good or bad. All beings were a blend of both the male and the female and lived in bliss within hermaphroditic forms. You are beginning to remember those times and that place, and long for their return. Those who have returned to this realm, who are on different missions to support this change, have the vision to see you in your concurrent existence while you travel realms other than the one of which you are currently part on the *physical plane. This new set of teachers will come in many different forms. Be careful not to judge. Each one has been sent to you for a specific purpose and you will be changed by the presence of each.*

One evening in April 2005, after completing my chores, I retired to my desk to check the day's e-mails. Up popped an announcement from Christine Page. She was planning a sacred sites tour through the United Kingdom and Ireland. "It will be a journey tracing the history, mythos, and legends of the Holy Grail and Templar lore, in search of the sacred feminine Mary Magdalene, the Arthurian legends, and their connection with ley line energy, crop formations, and the truth behind *The Da Vinci Code*."

As I read, the tingling that usually enters my crown when doing cranial sacral therapy showed up unexpectedly. Visiting these places steeped in the same history that had called me to do the Camino just months before was the logical next step in my own journey. Going was not a choice—it was a command. The trip would begin in London on Saturday, September 24, and end Saturday, October 8, back in London. I didn't care about the dates; in that moment, I simply gave myself permission to go. Convincing José would be easy; after participating in one of Chris's workshops two years earlier, he would go anywhere with her. Even better, he would have twenty-four pairs of ears to bend.

I procrastinated in making our flight reservations, which was quite out of character for me, especially since I was so looking forward to the experience. Finally, one Saturday afternoon in late May, I picked up the phone and dialed American Airlines. We had no problem getting our outbound reservations, but no seats were available on Sunday, October 9, the ideal day for our return. We were going to have to spend an extra day in London and fly home on the Monday.

The day before we left, I had had a session with T'Shala. She reported that my first chakra was now open and I was no longer afraid I might misuse my power. The Camino had been all about pulling earth energy up through my legs. I was now firmly planted on the planet and had agreed to stay awhile. My mission on this trip was to gather "new but ancient knowledge." All my fellow knights were behind me. I had signed on as their earthly representative. My whole life was about accomplishing a task for someone else's greater good. What task? For whom? This trip would provide more answers. At the end of the session, T'Shala told me to pay close attention to my feet, arms, and hands. She said she was told by the knights to say that. Intrigued, I stored that comment in my mind, curious to see what would transpire.

On our first morning in England, the twenty-four of us set out for our first sacred sites adventure. After a relatively short bus ride out of London through postcard-perfect English countryside, Les, our driver, pulled over and stopped our bus. Where were we? All we could see through the bus windows were miles of softly undulating cultivated fields. We were visiting West Kennet Long Barrow, Chris told us, said to be an ancient burial chamber or perhaps a sounding chamber for ritual. The fields that surrounded this sacred place were the very ones where most of the known crop circle formations have occurred and been photographed.

As we got off the bus and headed up the nearest hillside past a wooden gate on a path between recently harvested wheat and barley fields, I looked around as if trying to see back in time. Did I recognize this place? My eyes registered an unfamiliarity that my heart confirmed. As I stood outside the barrow entrance, however, in the same Salomon hiking shoes I had worn on the Camino, I began to notice something peculiar going on with my feet. Tuning in to the sensation was difficult at first, but gradually I determined it was a generalized tingling that enveloped the entire foot. This buzzing sensation eventually traveled up my legs, through my torso, and out the top of my head and shoulders. As it felt something like a shiver, I wondered if I was cold and folded my arms across my chest. The sensation remained.

I left the barrow entrance and slowly walked around its perimeter. The sensation disappeared. Climbing up the grassy mound that covered the barrow, I walked straight down its middle. The sensation returned. What was this? Returning to the barrow entrance, I went inside to find Chris, Leland (Chris's husband), and several of our group toning in harmony. The sound was amazing. As it reverberated off the stone walls, it seemed to go straight into my chest, reigniting the sensation that had run from my feet through my head moments before. Much more intense than an electrical shiver, this could only be described as a surge.

As we made our way to Silbury Hill, I reflected on T'Shala's words: "Pay attention to your feet, arms, and hands." Already the message was making sense. I leaned on the fence, gazing at this largest prehistoric man made mound in Europe, wondering what those ancient people knew and why they had constructed such a thing. Again, without warning, the buzzing enveloped my feet and traveled upward, this time clearly through my chakra system, eventually exiting my crown. Meanwhile, my thoughts drifted to Zacharia Sitchin's books deciphering the Sumerian tablets about ET visitations from the heavens. Could this mound have been a landmark seen from space? I chuckled at the inventiveness of my own thoughts. Yet all bets were off on this trip. I was prepared to at least notice every thought that passed through.

Ever since the Mark Murphy episode, my brain and my heart had maintained a constant debate between rational thinking, on the one hand, and intuitive feelings and knowings on the other. It felt as if I were living in two distinct parallel realities—the one that was the source of intuitions and guidance, and the other, the five-sensory here-and-now—that were sometimes permeable to each other, like two parallel roads that occasionally intersected. Would they eventually join together? My role, I sensed, was to hold the energy of both and be a vessel for their meeting.

The bus stopped just outside the Village of Avebury for us to view the famous standing stones—known as a place where Celts, Druids, Cathars, and even Essenes once performed rituals—and then dropped us off at the village café. While our group was grabbing a bite of lunch, and Jose and several others were ordering beers at the bar, we learned that a real-life Druidic ceremony was going on among the stones outside. José's eyes widened; he loved getting involved with the local folk. Even better, we arrived to find the ceremony being filmed by a crew. If there was a camera nearby, José was usually in front of it, charming everyone with his enthusiasm and brilliant banter.

The modern Druid women were wearing green velvet robes over long purple dresses. The men were in black velvet robes with sheathed daggers stuck into the red sashes around their waists. They had formed a circle around a man and woman in street clothes who extended their arms over a flat stone as a Druid man tied their wrists with a blood-red sash. All of a sudden the intent was clear—we were crashing a Druidic wedding ceremony. When it was finished, the head female Druid, wearing a crown of herbs and flowers, scanned the crowd asking if anyone present wanted to join them and be indoctrinated as a bard.

José turned to me. "What's a bard?" Thank God, I wasn't the only one who didn't know, I thought. I shrugged my shoulders and considered the source.

He then turned to the woman with the crown and asked her. She walked up to him, took his hands gently in hers, and looked into his soft, Guinness-influenced eyes. "A bard is a member of the order of Druids who carries forth their verbal history."

How perfect, I thought. José glanced at me and we both started laughing. They could not have asked for a more appropriate candidate.

As we walked back to the café where the bus was scheduled to meet us, José, the newly initiated Druidic bard, turned to me. "I didn't want to feel stupid in front of everybody, but what is a Druid?" It was hopeless. In his utter brilliance, Jose hated to read books. He honestly had no idea that the Druids were reputed to have used, if not created, many of the standing stone circles, including Stonehenge, the next day's destination. On the drive back to the hotel, José told his story with gusto. The bus erupted into sharing Druidic lore.

We were to meet in the hotel lobby the next morning at 5:45 a.m. for a specially arranged sunrise meditation among the stones at Stone-henge—a rarity. Most tourists must remain outside the yellow-rope bar-ricade that encircles the stones. Chris had somehow pulled the necessary strings so we had permission to walk among these most ancient of relics, tone to them, touch them, and examine the moss that grows only on them and nowhere else on the planet.

As the first rays of the morning peered over the horizon, hitting the eastern faces of the stones, the sheer magnitude of what they must know screamed through my consciousness, as if I could hear them speak-ing in millennial terms. How insignificant we humans are. These stones have been standing here for some five thousand years. Standing in their presence, contemplating their message, I became aware once again of the strange electrical feeling in my feet and legs. It grew and waned in intensity as I moved around the site. At the very center of the circle, it felt like a surge—a direct current coming up from the ground, through the soles of my feet on the grassy earth, and straight out the top of my head. I then realized that here in England I was at last sensing what I had gone to Spain to experience and hadn't. This was the ley line energy that Shirley MacLaine described. It was running *through* me.

The dark silhouettes of the stones as the sun began to illuminate them against the dawn sky were familiar in that subconscious place where the old memories remain. This was shape recognition—our most primitive survival mechanism. For the first time on this trip, I knew I had once before stood in this very place at the same time of day, witnessing sunrise.

Now I was getting somewhere.

We piled into the bus again and headed west to Glastonbury. The group was quiet, staring out the windows at the English countryside. Perhaps it was the early hour, but I think it also had to do with the magnificence of what we had just experienced. On some level, the messages encoded in our DNA understand the messages of these stones, but our modern-day Western-trained psyches cannot decipher the meaning.

How can we access what we already know? I wondered as the bus rolled past the undulating English pastures with stone fences separating the sheep from the cows. This question had haunted me ever since my first undergraduate neuroscience course, when I realized that the study of the brain, which more importantly housed the mind, was an organ studying itself. The answers to life's greatest questions lie just outside our capacity to access, limited only by the interpretive delicate balance of neurotransmitters. I was simply not satisfied with the assumption that the knowledge our soul possesses is inaccessible. As a child, I not only experienced these old memories, but also trusted them and built upon the knowledge they provided me. As an adult, I developed a different relationship with that knowledge. I learned to be skeptical and to question the possibility of past-life knowledge, parallel universes existing simultaneously, paranormal phenomenon, nonordinary perception, and extraterrestrial influence. This trip so far was just more confirmation that there were natural forces acting and behaving beyond our ability to measure them objectively. To personally experience evidence-based proof of these phenomena served once again to quiet the scientific, rational me.

Our first stop in Glastonbury was a late-afternoon visit to Challis Well, its iron-red waters said to represent the sacred feminine here in Glastonbury. We stood in a circle around a pool, which was shaped like a giant vulva—the sacred geometry of the vesica pisces—with many progressive vesica pisces cradling the water on its descent from the actual spring uphill.

Afterward we wandered on our own through the surrounding water garden. As I walked up some garden stairs, the tree limbs seemed to part, revealing the fabled Tor, a five-hundred-foot hill that is the most notable landmark of Glastonbury, standing valiantly above this extraordinarily beautiful setting. According to British pagan and Celtic lore, the Tor—the famous Isle of Avalon—was where the dead passed on to another existence. I stood captivated by its magnitude. Something about it seemed to call to me, pulling at my chest to come forward and stand upon its summit. How strange, I thought, to be summoned by a hill. I pulled out of this trance and continued to explore the garden, said to contain fairy energy. Afterward I felt like I'd experienced a whole-body energetic cleansing, which left me weightless and buoyant.

The next morning, quietly leaving our hotel room in Street, a small Quaker town two miles outside Glastonbury, for my daily run, the lightness I had experienced more than twelve hours earlier was still with me. As I turned right onto the main road to Glastonbury, my legs felt magnificently strong and agile. It was a gorgeous fall morning, the sky just beginning to change from black to midnight blue, the road shimmering from an overnight rain, and breezy gusts causing goose pimples on my exposed legs and arms. I quickly slipped into my space of mental nothingness, not really paying attention to the route, knowing I would end up wherever I was destined to be.

After a while I passed a driveway marked "Challis Well." I hadn't been aware I had headed in that direction. I just kept running, feeling something drawing me forward. A thought crossed my mind: Wouldn't it be interesting to get to the top of the Tor? I checked my watch. It was 6:55. Sunrise was at 7:05. Entering a neighborhood lined with heavily laden large-leaf deciduous trees and lots of bed and breakfast signs, I passed one that said "Tor B&B." It must be close, I thought. Then I passed a street with a "No Tor Access" sign. Not much farther up the road, I noticed a second, unmarked street that rose abruptly and disappeared into the overhanging branches of the trees that lined the street. I turned and ran into the mystery.

The pavement ended at a dirt road that led to a wooden gate and eventually a pathway leading through the grass into the woods beyond. As I reached the gate, the branches above me parted, revealing the magnificent Tor, topped with its tall church tower, peering down like a giant long-necked dinosaur. I followed the labyrinth path that circles around this massive mound. Finally, reaching a paved pathway with stairs that headed directly to the top, I ran up it, and within minutes was standing atop the Isle of Avalon, completely alone in the gusting wind that screamed through Saint Michael's Tower.

All of a sudden I was overcome with the now-familiar tingling, followed by a surge of energy careening through my feet, legs, and body, and exiting my head and shoulders. My consciousness flashed on Lancelot, Arthur, the Knights of the Round Table, the Knights Templar, swords, armor, bloody battlefields, and the well-trained horses. My mind was awash with images and stories as if I had plugged into an ancient circuit that still relayed the frequency of these realities from some other channel of existence. As the wind continued to howl, I faced east toward the rising sun and felt compelled to kneel down. With my hands cupped on my right knee, I bowed my head, imagining that I felt the weight of Excalibur tap my right shoulder and then my left, reliving the act of knighting. The only witness to such a sacred ritual this time was a raven, jubilantly calling as he danced in the wind, repeatedly landing and taking off again, playfully celebrating with me.

Later that morning our group visited Glastonbury Abbey and Saint Mary's Church with its remaining ruin, the Lady's Chapel. Chris explained that this structure is built upon two intersecting ley lines called the Michael-Mary Ley, thought to be the strongest and most intriguing as it serpentines through southern Britain. The points where the two lines cross are often marked by a stone circle, burial mound, or church. Stepping onto the chapel's stone floor, I became aware of a slight tingling in my feet. As I walked toward the inlaid tile line running directly down the middle of the floor, the sensation increased, spreading up into my torso, and then crescendoed as my feet stood on the line, the surge blasting out the top of my head and shoulders. I felt the way Marilyn Monroe looked in the famous picture of her standing on the street vent with her skirt being blown up.

I suddenly realized what was happening on this trip. Beginning with the energy download into Ron five years earlier, my body had become a channel, an instrument, able to plug into subtle energies and transduce them along the neurological circuits usually reserved for the sensations of orgasm. Could this explain my low sex drive and inherent knowing that, at least for me, these circuits were reserved for some other duty? The lower-extremity injuries when walking along the Camino ley line had been a clearing out of the resistance points within my instrument. This trip's engagement with ley lines was a turning on and fine-tuning of this peculiar circuitry. As this realization raced through my mind, I thought of Jeff's description of a tree trunk of energy coming out the top of my head my first day at Spinal Diagnostics. Was this what he had seen? Had the circuitry been there all along, waiting to be activated?

I walked across the floor of the Lady's Chapel several more times, entraining the subtleties of what I was sensing. For the next several days, I paid attention to this now-familiar sensation coming up from the earth as we traversed through gardens and burial grounds, along paved streets, and in ancient buildings. I soon learned that I could pick up the presence of ley lines and track them or the specific coordinates of their vortex points using nothing but the sensation in my feet and legs. I had become a human divining rod.

On our first night walking to dinner in Edinburgh, we turned onto the main thoroughfare, called Rose Lane. The tingling in my feet and legs confirmed why it was so named. It sits atop the Rose Line, the ley line so magnificently fictionalized in *The DaVinci Code*. As we stopped at our first cross street, looking right and then left, suddenly, there in front of my eyes was an image that, like Stonehenge, stirred my old memories.

I was staring at the far-off illuminated cliffs topped by Edinburgh Castle, secure in the knowing that all was well—at least for now. I stopped dead in my tracks, breathless and rigid, as a knowledge locked away deep within me exploded into my conscious awareness. I had died in the name of God and country on the very walls of that castle.

How was it that I knew this? And how could I explain this one to José, who was calling to me from the other side of the street, "What are you staring at?" Forcibly breaking the trance, I pulled my gaze away, mumbling as if to the castle, as I dodged the speeding cars, "You and I are not yet finished. I will see you tomorrow to try to sort this one out."

Arising before first light, and after a long morning stretch, I set out in my running shoes, making my way down the Rose Line toward the castle. Just as in Glastonbury, the ley line energy made my legs feel strong, ready to carry me wherever my heart was directed. I ran up the four flights of stairs, at least sixty steps each, taking them two at a time, to the path adjacent to the road that wove its way to the castle entrance. The entrance did not feel familiar. The message was clear: When I was here last, I had not come as an invited guest. The Brits had held this castle for quite some time, and many a willing Scotsman in the land had fought hard to regain it, some to their death. This history must still bleed from the stones—how else could I be sensing it?

We were scheduled to be the first group allowed back into Roslyn Chapel after it had been closed for filming of the movie version of *The Da Vinci Code*. The film crews were still packing up as we arrived. The famous fifteenth-century structure looked odd surrounded by trucks with satellite dishes, huge cameras, lighting equipment, scaffolds, and reels of cable. You could see José's circuits come to life as we passed a news crew's van. José pushed his way toward the van, demanding to speak to the reporter. José never took no for an answer. As luck would have it, the reporter was looking for someone to interview. It did not even take much schmoozing for José to have an appointment to be back at the van at exactly 10:30 a.m. to be on camera. Meanwhile, the rest of us would be in the chapel listening to the docent's lecture.

The interior of Roslyn Chapel was much smaller than I had envisioned while reading *The Da Vinci Code* one year earlier. The docent explained that nearby Roslyn Castle had played a key role in Scotland's fight for independence from the British Crown in 1303, just a few years before the Knights Templar were disbanded in 1307. The St. Clair family who built the chapel had been Templars and then Masons. The symbols exquisitely carved in stone on the walls of this structure remain a mystery to this day. Some of what they depicted was supposedly not yet known in Europe, according to the version of history we are taught in school. I remembered David Icke on tape speaking about these very carvings depicting stalks of growing corn and aloe vera. Both plant species were found only in North America at the time of the carvings.

If, in fact, Columbus was the first to discover America in 1492, how could these stonemasons have carved these images beforehand? Mr. Icke's premise was that the Illuminati network, which he maintained included Columbus and the royalty of Spain for whom he sailed, knew much more than they ever shared with the public. By altering the real story, they could control the reality of the commoners. He certainly had a point, I thought, as I strained my neck to see these carvings for myself and snapped a photograph.

Templar symbolism was everywhere. There was not one surface in this structure that was not screaming to tell the observer something. A code perhaps, as in Dan Brown's book? Or perhaps something even more exquisite, something about us or the physical laws that govern the world in which we live? Was the Holy Grail hidden here, as many over the centuries have suspected? Or was the Grail, in fact, the knowledge carved on these walls—in plain sight?

We descended into the crypt to find a woman facing the stained-glass window and singing a beautiful Gregorian-like chant. Lingering until she was finished, José asked her what she had been singing. She answered, "Sir, I was not singing. I don't know how to sing." José asked, "Then what were we just hearing?" She replied, "I was simply channeling the music that exists in this space."

Her comment gave all of us goose bumps. Was a mysterious power somehow embedded in these walls? This was much more than a building with an interesting history. It was a portal.

We rejoined our group, several of whom had started toning inside the music nave. The dome in this space is adorned with cubes suspended from the four crossbeams that join in the middle of the dome. Each cube is carved with a different geometric pattern and hung with a corner pointing toward the floor. The beams from which the cubes hang descend to supporting columns, each topped by a figure of a monk in a long-sleeved robe, each with his own hairstyle and appearance and holding some kind of instrument—drum, fiddle, bagpipe, mandolin—like members of an orchestra. As I moved around the space, I soon identified that wherever I stood, the voice of the person standing directly across from me sounded as if it were right above me. This dome was amplifying and redirecting the sound. I stood there wondering if there was a code in the geometric patterns on the cubes and if it had anything to do with what the monks were trying to convey with their unique looks and individual instruments.

Chris had arranged one more stop for us before we left Scotland. Les drove us a short distance from Edinburgh and parked outside an unassuming stone cottage set alone among acres of pastureland where more of Scotland's ubiquitous sheep grazed. The first hint that this was anything but a typical cottage was its crystal-inlaid stone doorstep.

As I crossed the threshold, all my preconceptions about what the interior would look like were exploded. The walls were painted white, the floor was blonde hardwood topped with a candy-apple-red round carpet, and the furnishings included metallic gooseneck modern lighting and a white brushed-cotton half-moon retro-style sofa. Standing on the red carpet, you could look through the small dinette surrounded by a glass solarium to the grassy hill behind the cottage.

Our host, John Reed, asked if we would enjoy a spot of tea. While hauling every mug and cup he owned out of the cupboards, he began telling us about his research. Building on his career as a concert sound engineer, he had taken the study of sound into sacred spaces that have acoustical qualities not previously understood.

"I would like to demonstrate to you what I am doing and show you what happened when I took this technology into the King's Chamber in the Great Pyramid at Giza. However, only twelve people can squeeze into my tiny lab at a time. We will have to do it in two groups," he said, as he poured the steaming hot tea into cups and gestured to us not to be shy about helping ourselves to a cup.

I decided to wait for round two. When the second group filed into the tiny laboratory, I took a chair in the back next to José. John was standing in the middle of an array of speakers, microphone stands, and what looked like stacked stereo components. Behind him, an LCD projector faced a pull-down white screen. In front of him was an elevated Plexiglas drum with a black skin stretched over the top held down with adjustable metal clamps. Above the drum a video camera was suspended with the lens pointed down, its cables connected to the projector.

John explained that his work was based on that of Hans Jenny, who in the mid-1940s had sent various frequencies through a drum skin spread with mugwort seeds. I was immediately reminded of a Gregg Braden videotape I had watched while preparing for the Camino. The video included an old super-eight film clip of Dr. Jenny's seeds shape-shifting into geometric patterns as the tones changed beneath the drum skin. The higher the frequency, the more complicated, ornate, and beautiful the patterns became. Braden's argument was that since the mid-1980s scientists have been measuring a steady increase in the base resonant frequency of the earth, and as it increases, our cells respond in a way similar to the seeds. At the same time that the planet's frequency is increasing, its magnetic field is measurably decreasing. Tracking the rates of change on a graph, Braden calculates that these two exponential curves will intersect at the point of near-zero magnetics and a pulse frequency of 13 Hz toward the end of the year 2012. This date correlates on the ancient Mayan calendar with the end of the current grand 26,000-year cycle, also known as the Precession of the Equinox. Braden reported that one of the predictions was that at that time the poles will reverse and the earth will slow to a standstill and, some hours or days later, start to rotate in the opposite direction.

Caught up in this flow of thought, my mind continued to sort through similar information, finally flashing on Dr. Masaru Emoto's work with water. Distilled water that has been exposed to intended messages of love, gratitude, and peace, then flash-frozen and viewed through a dark-field microscope, takes on complex multilayered lattice-like forms like snowflakes. When the messages are of hate, greed, and fear, the forms are disorganized and messy, barely discernable as patterns at all. Thoughts of love, gratitude, and peace are said to carry a higher frequency than negative thoughts do. I suddenly saw a correlation between the water, mugwort seeds, and our cell tissue: The higher the frequency they were exposed to, the more complex and beautifully structured were their patterns. Emoto's work showed this, and John's work corroborated it. Our thoughts are measurable frequencies and directly affect our physical body—something I had been intuitively trying to teach my patients for years.

My attention returned to the present moment just as John was about to do a demonstration. Rather than using simple frequency tones and mugwort seeds as Jenny did, he used music and sand. Thinly sprinkling the sand on the dark surface of the drum, he told us, "Classical music produces the most complex patterns. I have tried all kinds, of course, from pop to jazz to rap to new age. I've discovered that any sort of percussive beat scatters the sand in all directions. The music must be constant and undulating." He then placed a CD in the stereo. As the music played through speakers set inside the drum, the sand, its image projected onto the screen for us to see, shifted into geometric shapes, changing from pattern to pattern as the frequency and intensity of the tones changed. I thought of Bracken playing classical music in the OR and was immediately reminded of what it feels like to hold a person's cranium between my hands as I palpate for the frequency and intensity of the cranial-rhythmic motion, which carries information about the health status of the person's life force.

As the sand danced on the drum skin, John told us the story of his performing an experiment with this same technology in the King's Chamber in the Great Pyramid. The sound began to reflect the shape of the acoustics of the Kings chamber, flowing into the form of the familiar Eye of Horus, once used by ancient Egyptian physicians to determine the proportions of ingredients when mixing medications, and also the basis of the all-seeing eye, the Masonic symbol found on the American dollar bill and elsewhere.

At that moment, I felt my stomach drop in that old familiar feeling, and milliseconds later the knowledge that had come in through my solar plexus registered in my brain and I felt amazement. Here was this symbol popping up again. I had first heard about it as an Illuminati symbol on a David Icke video four years earlier, then I saw it myself in the cathedral in Santiago de Compostela, and here it was again, part of the yet-unpublished research on ancient Egyptian architecture conducted by this Scottish gentleman. What did this symbol really mean? Was there a connection between these times and places?

John then shared with us that when he played the same music selections in Roslyn Chapel, the sand took on very different shapes. It arranged itself in the geometric patterns that are on the stone cubes hanging down from the crossbeams in the music nave, he said. He then rolled his eyes as if to say he wished he could tell us more. "My agreement with the Roslyn Chapel Historical Society was that I would not share what we discovered in the sand when we took our equipment down into the crypt. Only to say that there, too, the acoustics created images that when analyzed numerically, followed the Fibonacci numeric sequence as it relates to the harmonic golden mean."

With that he stopped, looked at his watch, and asked if we had any questions.

Questions! I could have stayed there all day asking questions. Yet even if that were possible, I would have been at a loss to express within the limits of the spoken word the complexity of the thoughts flooding through my mind. I sat there stunned, lost in a brainy barrage of interconnected concepts that eluded articulation. What was perfectly clear was that for someone with my training and skills to sit in this small laboratory in a cottage in Scotland and witness firsthand a demonstration, one I had first seen on videotape, of how matter responds not only to vibration but also to the unseen forces of intention was no accident.

The next morning we took an early flight to Dublin. After a bite of lunch and a bit of shopping we headed straight for Glendalough, meaning "valley of two lakes," one of the most important monastic ruins in all of Ireland. In the late sixth century, during Ireland's Golden Age, Saint Kevin founded the seven churches that once stood there.

Chris had us feel the energy around the single round tower on the site, which to our amazement seemed to be a swirling directional vortex that the tower collected and then directed toward the lower of the two lakes. Chris explained the accepted lore about the tower, that it is one of many constructed across Ireland in the late eighth century as a place of refuge against attacks by Vikings. It seemed to us, however, that the tower was more like an antenna drawing etheric cosmic energy into the earth's grid of ley lines so it could flow toward water.

On the small piece of land lying between the lower and upper lakes stood a stone circle even more ancient than the tower. Chris informed us that from the air these two lakes with the land in the middle look like the infinity symbol, and that the energy circulating around this shape crosses in the middle like a figure eight, creating a vortex. The ancients had arranged the standing stones to mark this powerful location.

Not far from the upper lake stood the stone ruin of one of Saint Kevin's churches. Chris pointed up the wooded hill and explained that behind the church was the site of the twelve-by-twelve-foot stone cell where Saint Kevin had lived for several years in seclusion. The forest was known for its elemental beings—the basis for the stories of Ireland's fairies, gnomes, and wee ones—each of which takes pride in keeping a particular tree, rock, or fern beautiful.

As we walked silently up the hill, I paid close attention to what my senses perceived while focusing mainly on my chest, knowing that subtle information would not come through my eyes. As I did so, the colors of the leaves, bark, earth, stones, underbrush, and sky grew vivid like nothing I had ever experienced outside of an art gallery. It was as if we were walking into heaven itself. As my eyes registered this magnificent beauty, my body relaxed into a remarkable state of bliss.

Reaching the spot between two trees where Kevin's cell had once stood, I sat on a log and looked out to the lake below. The sky was overcast, which enhanced the colors even more. From this perch some thirty feet above the water level, my gaze zeroed in on one particularly symmetrical tree in the forest on the far side of the lake and remained focused on it for what I discovered afterward was more than forty minutes. As the time passed, I could feel a recalibration going on inside me, as if the fairies had gone to work on my circuitry, just as they scrubbed the trees, ferns, and pathways in this enchanted woodland. A deep, calm, yet joyful effervescence filled me. Time had no meaning. Neither past nor future existed—only now. This was the message, the point of it all. I did not want to leave.

Extending this experience well beyond its time limit, I made my way back down the path, then veered to the left to follow the lakeshore. A stream fed the lake and tree branches, heavy with leaves, hung low over the dancing and glistening water. The youthful summer greenery was just beginning to give way to the brilliant, decaying palette of early autumn. I tried to open myself up to spy a gnome or a fairy sitting on a stone or hiding behind a tree trunk.

Lost in the grandeur of it all, I suddenly experienced an intense surge of energy streaming up my legs and trunk, and flowing out the top of my head and shoulders. I must have been following an energy line out of the woods. I checked my location with respect to the stone circle a good two hundred yards to my right. To my amazement, I was aligned exactly with the circle's mathematical diameter. I had stumbled upon the ley line that shot right through the center of the standing stones and straight out toward the lake.

For me, this experience constituted the "blind study" for which the still skeptical part of me had been holding out. Ley line energy was real, and my ability to sense it was real. I could not have imagined this sensation, and I was not mistaking it for a common shiver or a chill. Yet I had felt it distinctly, before becoming aware of my location in relation to the ley line.

As I made my way across the grassy field to the waiting bus, something even stranger began to occur. Walking on the ley line, feeling the most incredible blissful charge and state of being ever, I observed the sensation turn laterally at my shoulders and begin flowing down my arms into my hands, exiting out my palms. Taken aback by this new directional current, I glanced at my palms, half expecting to see energy shooting out of them like a laser beam. I could see nothing. I could feel everything. I played around, pointing my palms in different directions, almost expecting to hear a whooshing sound as the energy cut through the air.

T'Shala's words came to mind again: "Pay attention to your feet, arms, and hands." How could she have known what would happen to me on this trip? Or was it truly a message from other beings, given to me through her? Was this force passing through because my transducer was now fully open and operational, after years of physical, mental, and spiritual preparation? And if so, what was it all for? Who was I to be able to find a ley line or vortex point simply by walking over or standing near it? Somehow, I knew this had a purpose much bigger than I, even if it had everything to do with the purpose for which I was born. I continued to ponder these questions for the rest of our journey, all the while wondering where this energy was going. Was it being stored somewhere? And what the hell was going to happen when I treated my first patient?

David Icke's boarding pass.

25

A Remarkable Meeting

You can no longer deny what is happening. The evidence cannot be refuted. As you rise to the positions that hold many forms of power, your role will become self-evident. Attracting other Indigos into your experience is natural. You are all on journeys with similar themes. Going about waking the others to the truth is as unique to you as you are to the process. Relish the strengths each of you has. Some of you are the edge of the snowplow breaking apart the hard crusted ice head on. Others of you are here to support the "head bangers" so that they can continue to survive the onslaught hurled at them constantly. You know who you are; your individual role is vital to the success of the awakening to allow for the mass ascension that has been foretold in the ancients' teachings. You should know; you wrote those teachings. Your time is growing short, perhaps shorter than you realize. Can you feel the tension rising? Do you sense something is coming? Something the world has never seen before? This is your DNA programming; it is who you are. You were designed to respond to the vibrational and magnetic changes the planet is currently undergoing, not only to adapt, but also to thrive and to help the others do the same.

Our last day of the trip, Chris conducted a tour of London, where she had lived for most of her adult life. We walked toward Temple Bar, the political and financial center that allowed this small island nation to rise up over others and for a period in its history to rule the world. This is one place where the Templars went underground after the Order was demolished in 1307 and, according to David Icke and others, continued their reign as master manipulators, remaining in control even to this day. Their creation known as the United States holds sway as the last remaining superpower while appearing as a "free" democratic nation.

As we approached Temple Bar, the old familiar pain started in my lower back. I had not felt it since graduate school, nearly two decades earlier, save for the times I had stood in the operating room too long. How strange that it should all of a sudden revisit. A tall monument stood in the median of the busy four-lane road in front of the Royal Courts of Justice. As we approached, my eyes scanned upward and, with a jolt of surprise, recognized the figure on top, a winged dragon. In one of Icke's videotaped lectures I had seen the previous year, he had discussed this very monument as an overt display of Illuminati reptilian symbolism. According to him, the Illuminati are shape-shifting extraterrestrial reptiles who have manipulated reality as we know it via our five-sense, limited-range decoding systems throughout recorded history. They maintain that control today in front of our very eyes by manipulating the media in regards to politics, business, and the banking industry.

As Icke's theory came flooding back to me, without even thinking, I spun and captured Chris's gaze with mine. She knew I had something important to ask even before I did. "Chris, what do you think about what David Icke is saying about the whole reptile thing?"

With that, the group exploded with questions about reptiles, Icke, secret societies, symbolism, bloodline familial control, and the like, most of the group having heard something of such things. Chris spent the next fifteen minutes answering these questions and explaining her direct experiences with reptilian beings. As we continued on to the Temple Church, Chris and I chatted about the darker aspects of these power places. I was reluctant to ask her about my back. She confirmed, however, that this was a large dark vortex, heavy with ancient secrets and modern deceit.

That Monday morning we hailed a cab headed for Heathrow to catch American Airlines flight 87, bound for home via Chicago. José had purchased a wild pair of golf pants in Scotland, a patchwork of bold Scottish plaids, none coordinating in pattern or color. I challenged him to wear them on the flight home to give Alex and Mom a laugh when they picked us up in San Francisco. José not only agreed, but also upped the ante, deciding to wear them with the rainbow-colored shoes he had picked up in Glastonbury. He looked perfectly ridiculous but carried himself in such a distinguished way that people were forced to see beyond their initial judgments of a person's external packaging.

We settled into our seats, José and I on the right side of the fuselage. As the plane taxied down the runway, leaping into the air for an on-time departure, I was looking forward to an extended period of contemplation, pouring my still-processing thoughts onto the pages of my journal.

Not more than twenty minutes after takeoff, with the airplane still climbing and the seat belt sign still illuminated, I noticed a flurry of flight attendant activity to our left. On the other side of the plane, several rows in front of us, four flight attendants surrounded a gray-haired male passenger who appeared to be slumping out of his seat into the aisle. Without even a mutual glance, José and I simultaneously unbuckled our seat belts and bolted out of our seats. Here we go again, I thought. Many times before on a vacation, we had stepped up to assist with unexpected medical emergencies.

Climbing over unsuspecting but cooperative passengers, we forced our way across the middle section. Meanwhile, the flight attendants had the man out of his seat and lying in the aisle. I explained that José was an internist specializing in critical care and I was board-certified in family practice. I glanced down at the man's face and was surprised that he looked vaguely familiar. José positioned a yellow oxygen mask over the man's nose and mouth, then checked his pulse. The man was breathing on his own, had a regular heartbeat, and moderately strong blood pressure. Why then was he unconscious?

Making an all-out attempt to stimulate the patient awake is the usual next step, first by digging your elbow into the sternum, then, if needed, slapping the patient's face with a reasonable amount of force. As José progressed through these procedures, I asked the flight attendants to bring all the pillows and blankets they could find. Propping the man's legs up would encourage increased blood flow back to the brain. Still there was no response. At that point, José decided to "start a line" in order to pass medication quickly if the heart's condition suddenly worsened.

I rifled through the plane's medical kits and pulled out a venous catheter, tubing, IV bag, and other necessary items. The gentleman in the seat behind identified himself as a retired general surgeon who was traveling with his wife, an OR nurse. How perfectly convenient I thought, handing the items to the man, who went to work inserting the catheter as his wife set up the IV bag and adjusted the flow rate. There was not much else to do but monitor his vital signs.

A flight attendant relayed a message from the pilots, asking José if they needed to turn the plane around and head back to Heathrow. Without a moment's consideration, he replied, "Absolutely. I am not willing to spend the next eight hours on my knees with this guy as we head over the Atlantic. Land this plane now!"

Hearing that assured command from a guy in Scottish plaid and rainbow shoes, the flight attendant scurried back to the cockpit with his reply. She then announced to the rest of the passengers that we would be returning to Heathrow.

My first intuitive hit was that this guy had overmedicated with sedatives for sleeping on the flight. José obviously had the same idea; he began going through the man's pockets. From the left pants pocket, he pulled out an unmarked pill container containing two different unmarked white tablets. From the right pants pocket, he pulled out a folded piece of green-and-white card stock, a boarding pass. He unfolded it and read its contents. In a blast of discovery, his gaze shot from the print to me, his eyes wide in amazement. His message was clear: "You are not going to believe this one!"

I mouthed back over the din of the jets, "Who is he?"

This time he spoke. "It's David Icke."

Now it was my turn to look amazed. Suddenly understanding why this guy looked so familiar, there it was again, the weight of this realization landing in my stomach first before my brain registered it. I scanned his hands and confirmed classic ulnar deviation of his fingers, a disfigurement characteristic of rheumatoid arthritis. It's David Icke, my mind repeated to itself over and over again. He was the one person I would have most loved to have run into while in Britain, and here he was, unconscious on the floor of our plane, needing our assistance.

What on earth was going on? My mind raced with a mix of excitement and deepening concern. I thought back to one of his videotapes with him telling the crowd how some people in high places would like nothing more than to see him dead. Had he been poisoned? As the imaginative part of my mind began to offer scenarios, the rational part suggested other, more benign explanations for his state. Could he have slipped into an altered state of consciousness volitionally? Had he been meditating before takeoff and accidentally produced an out-of-body state? I had read stories of such things. I glanced at my wristwatch. He had been unconscious for more than an hour. That was a long time to be out floating in nonordinary reality.

Just then one of the flight attendants touched my arm and told me to take a seat because we were on our final approach into Heathrow. José and another flight attendant were wedging a pillow between the metal seat leg and Mr. Icke's head. I sat in the seat next to the one he had been sitting in and positioned my feet on the outside of his left thigh to prevent him from rolling forward when the jets went into reverse upon landing. With my calves ready to act as clamps, I reached down and placed my left hand on his left hipbone as an added point for stabilization. Almost instantaneously, a massive energy dump came crashing into the top of my head and surged down my spine, left arm and hand, and both legs into him. My entire body vibrated, interacting with the most intense directed energy I had ever received. My energetic system was a mass of intense current. I instinctively checked the time on my watch before directing my gaze between David's eyes. I noticed a myriad of whispered thoughts racing through my mind, mixing with the energy surging through me on its way into him.

Here it was, my first energy dump with a patient since engaging with ley line energy on this trip. The quality of it was proof positive that the experience had changed me. I felt shyness for a moment, realizing that this energy was running on the same circuitry as an orgasm into a man to whom I had never been formally introduced. With my patients, I at least had implied permission to touch them. No, I thought, it must be okay with him. I sensed that he was an active participant in this transduction of energy or it wouldn't be happening at all.

With that settled, my thoughts turned somehow to my father. Eleven years earlier, he had passed out at the athletic club in San Jose with no one there to assist him and had died. The whispered intuitions in my mind began organizing themselves into a message that mixed with the surging energy cascading into him. The words were not ones I would have chosen. The message was: "This is David Icke. He is okay with this sort of thing. You have permission to proceed. May no harm come to him. May he be mentally, physically, and spiritually supported, and may he reach his highest potential." My body vibrated as the massive tidal wave of current continued to surge through me. This was different from my experience with these energy surges in the past. The energy had never before interacted like this with my energetic system.

Moments after the words ceased, Mr. Icke's eyes suddenly flew open, looking directly into mine. Without a hint of disorientation, he attempted to sit up. Shocked, I moved my left hand from his hip to his chest to guide him back to the floor, sensing that the wheels of the aircraft were about to touch down. The moment my hand lifted from his hip, the energy surge disconnected. José then took over, having a much better reach on his torso than I, urging him to lie back down, that everything was going to be all right.

I quickly checked my watch. The energy surge had lasted five minutes—a personal record, I thought, as the tires of the plane hit the runway. The energy surges in the clinic usually lasted five to ten seconds. The fact that this was the most obtunded person with whom I had participated in this way might explain the length of time.

The laser-beam clarity he had initially displayed was only fleeting. He slipped back into a partial state of confusion and continued trying to sit up as the plane rolled toward the gate. Within minutes of arrival, the paramedics were on board and took over. They quickly slapped on electrodes and attached a two-lead EKG to his chest, checking his cardiac rhythm. At that point, he was able to respond to simple questions: "What is your name?" "How old are you?" "Are you experiencing pain in your chest or having trouble breathing?"

After checking the rhythm strip, they allowed him to sit up and then get up off the floor. Helping him to his seat, I found myself standing directly in front of him. His eyes were unfocused, but he was awake and medically stable enough to make simple decisions, so I began to remove the IV port from his right arm. I introduced myself and urged him to let the paramedics take him to the hospital, but he kept refusing. Once the port was out, I excused myself and went to the bathroom to wash the blood from my ungloved hands. When I came out, he was gone.

During our two-hour delay for refueling, I told José what had happened and how David Icke had woken up. With honest sincerity, he replied, "Well, I sure wasn't able to roust him. Jakie, what do you think is happening to you?"

Once the plane was in the air again, I had more than eight hours to contemplate what had just occurred. I had manifested Mr. David Icke— or had he manifested me? I could not get over the level of coincidence. Some great energy surge had just passed through me, acting like an external cardiac defibrillator, to revive a completely obtunded man, the very one who for the past four years had been unknowingly providing me with knowledge so fantastic as to be barely believable, even though it had always resonated in the places where my old memories were stored. My skeptic fell mute. I could not deny any part of this one.

My body continued to vibrate and I could not turn my mind off. Sleeping was hopeless. I thought of people I wanted to tell this story to. Certainly, Chris and Leland, and then there was Jynel, who had introduced me to Icke's work. Smiling to myself as I imagined what I would say, I realized how unbelievable the incident was, and that I had no physical proof to back up my story.

Arriving late in San Francisco, we met Alex and Mom in front of the baggage claim, making sure they saw José in his dazzling colors first. On the drive home, as José's version of the story flowed, at the appropriate moment he reached into his pocket and produced the folded boarding pass with the name David Vaughan Icke inscribed across the top. There was the irrefutable evidence.

I took the boarding pass with me to work the next day. T'Shala, and my office staff, Raven, Mari, and Susan, went nuts; no one else knew who David Icke was. Still buzzing with what I thought was excitement, I sailed through the day, seeing the scheduled patients and catching up on two weeks' worth of paperwork. Leaving the office in the early evening, I still had energy to burn. I raced home to feed the animals and grab a bite of dinner; I could hardly wait to get on my computer and Google "David Icke." I felt drawn to know more about this man.

Logging onto his website, I clicked through to his biography. Before my eyes appeared a five-page account of his life. As I read, I was struck by the consonance between his story and mine—not so much in the facts as in what had influenced him and how he responded to it. At key moments, he, though with skepticism, had let himself be guided by a voice in his head, not unlike the "voiceless voice" I so often heard and followed.

Like me, A psychic had told him that he had been given a mission, and all of the experiences put before him were to make sure that he felt the full spectrum of human emotion. Through this initiation process, he had been chosen to carry a message of a great awakening of human consciousness that would include massive physical changes on the earth. As I read that paragraph, I felt my heart nearly stop. I had been given similar information from the psychic Carolyn nearly twenty-five years earlier.

One passage in particular caught my attention. On the last day of a visit to Peru in February 1991, Mr. Icke had been drawn to a mound along the road near Lake Titicaca, atop which an ancient circle of standing stones stood. Walking to the center of the circle, with the hot sun bearing down on him from the cloudless sky, "Suddenly he felt his feet being pulled to the ground like a magnet. With no decision on his part, his arms raised above his head at about forty-five degrees, slightly outward, and were held there for well over an hour. He felt no pain in his arthritic shoulders or arms until it was all over."

The next sentence practically knocked me out of my chair: "A flow of powerful energy began to surge into the top of his head like a drill down through his body via his feet through to the ground, and he could feel the flow coming back up from the ground the other way via his feet through to the top of his head."

I could barely believe what I had just read. My entire body began to tingle, as if I were standing on the vortex myself. After years of hoping to meet someone who had experienced the same directional energy that I did, here he was. Not only did this confirm the validity of my experience, but that very energy coming through me had revived this person just the day before.

A voice in his head, the account said, told him it would be over when he felt the rain. The energy increased until his body shook "as if plugged into a power station." The Peruvian sky was clear, the sun piercingly hot, but as he watched, a mist formed over the distant mountains, quickly coagulating into a rainstorm that moved in his direction so fast it looked like time-lapse photography. As he felt the first drops of water on his face, "the surge of energy suddenly stopped as if someone had flicked a switch. He staggered forward, his legs like jelly, his shoulder and arm muscles now very painful." His hands and feet continued to burn and vibrate for twenty-four hours, and from that point on, his life was never the same.

After reading this account, I was completely convinced that our interaction was no accident. I had just spent the previous two weeks being exposed to the energies of ley lines and standing stone circles myself. What did all these similarities between us mean? And what about being forced to book that Monday flight as all the Sunday flights were full? That suddenly felt prearranged. I knew I had to tell this man my side of this almost unbelievable story. And it felt important to make the acquaintance of this person whose experiences were so similar to my own. I typed out my account of the events in an e-mail to David Icke.

After clicking the send button, I recognized this as one of my life's defining moments. I was for the first time identifying myself, in writing, as someone who was familiar with and available to these energies. This implied a subtle shift from an observer and student of this phenomenon to a participant and practitioner with it. Whatever lay before me, I felt ready.

Still buzzing with energy, without a hint of jet lag, I continued not to need much sleep. Ideas, memories, insights, and correlations continued to stream through my brain in staggering volume. I was able to see how every event of the past few weeks related to everything that preceded it: what I had done, books or tapes I had read or heard, the people who had recommended them and how I happened to meet them. How it all fit together and led up to the previous day's experience lay open, revealed. Most of all, I could not get out of my thoughts the fact that the energy surge through me had revived a completely obtunded man. I knew this was not a simple accident. I was sure he did, too.

Thursday night I went up to my office and logged on to my e-mail. The name of the sender, David Icke, appeared. With my heart pounding, I opened the message.

Hello Janine,

    It was a bit of a shock to read your letter and realize some of what happened because I have so little recollection. Something very profound happened to me in that deep sleep state, like I was downloading vast amounts of information from "way out." Some is just beginning to filter through. It may well have been that it needed someone like you to "bring me back!" I am leaving the

US today (the paramedics are on standby) and I will be back at work Friday. Do you have a number I could call for a chat about it all?

Thanks for all that you did.

Much love,

David

David and I finally spoke on the phone three weeks later. He launched right into his perception of the events on the plane. He regularly takes a sedative on long flights just as the plane pulls away from the gate. Usually, he does not begin to nod off for a half an hour or so. This time, however, everything was a blank from right after he took the tablet until he came to, lying on the floor on the plane with someone telling him to stay down and that everything was going to be all right. For the following ten hours, his conscious mind was completely "out of it," he said; only his "subconscious brain" had seen him through. Late that afternoon, he left on a British Airways flight to Chicago. Once he got on the plane, he fell into a deep four-hour sleep. When he woke up this time, he felt normal again. He was half thinking it had been a dream, until he discovered a cotton ball taped to his right inner elbow and two little electrodes stuck to his chest. Then he began to wonder what on earth had happened. He checked with his office in England to see if anything had hit the press, as he is infamous in Britain. "Heathrow has its own news agency for such things. It leaks like a sieve," he commented. He found out nothing until he received my e-mail. Until just a few days before our conversation, his body was still buzzing and he could not sleep. He kept seeing images of his brain as a computer downloading massive amounts of data.

I asked him if this energy and buzzing were similar to how he felt after his experience in the Peruvian stone circle. He responded that he considered this his "second Peru."

That comment confirmed my suspicion that our meeting had a significance beyond either of our understanding. Then it was my turn. I described the energy dump and how it seemed to revive him, as well as my experiences in the stone circles and what had been going on with my patients over the past six years.

What he said next offered me a new level of understanding about the meaning of this energy, where it came from, and why it was showing up. He said he does a lot of what he calls "five-sense" research, meaning what's knowable through our five ordinary senses. Intuition often puts him in the right place at the right time to gather such information. Recently, however, information had been coming to him directly, that is, intuitively, concerning the relationship between the chakras of the body and the vortexes of stone circles. The vortexes bring energy from the etheric field into this reality.

"The network, the Illuminati, have sought to close down these vortexes to reduce the amount of energy we are working with," he said. "It is like turning the electricity off, if you like. The same is happening with the chakras of the physical body, through stress, through the way society is structured, and through chemicals in water and food. It all stops this connection. There are people—and you clearly appear to be one of them—who can access this etheric energy field and bring this power in through their chakra system. It is like they are plugging themselves in on an energetic level to bring this energy field through them into other people."

One of what people? I wondered. Were there others who could do this? If so, where are they? Who are they? Why haven't I met them before—or have I? My mind seemed awash with every question, suspicion, hope, and wonder I had ever pondered about who I was and what I was doing here on this planet, seemingly stuck in one reality yet having simultaneous access to others. The image of the green glass tabletop—my childhood attempt to understand multiple simultaneous realities—came to mind. I could not believe I was having this conversation with a man who had spent sixteen years gathering information that seemed as specific for me as it was for him.

"So when someone like you brings energy into someone," he was saying, "they go into a blissful state because they are actually, for that period, reconnecting with the infinite level of themselves, where there is no past, no future, no fear. It is a place of absolute balance; it is just indescribable. Once you connect with it, this world is never the same again. The source of your inspiration is something else."

The conversation then turned to how more and more people are coming into this awareness and how, sixteen years earlier, a psychic had told him a great awakening was coming. It was going to transform life on Earth because of the transformation of people's awareness of who they are and the nature of life. In the ensuing years, the awakening has speeded up. As more and more awaken, it becomes an exponential curve.

I told David that when I was twenty, I had gone to a psychic who had told me essentially the same thing: There would be massive earth changes, and many would not stick around; those who chose to stay, however, would help reorganize society in a different way. I shared that the psychic had identified me as one of those people.

This comment increased the growing blaze between us. David remarked that this conversation was reminding him of when he was just starting to put all the pieces together about his own life. He began talking about his visit to the psychic and how she went into "channeling mode" to receive information from a being of another order. He had written about this psychic reading in his book *Truth Vibrations,* and felt compelled to read the passage to me over the phone.

While he put the phone down and scuttled off in search of his personal copy, I found myself grinning. I felt embarrassed that I had ever questioned his sanity. He was more than in his right mind; he was brilliant. In return, I found myself revealing to him aspects of myself that I usually keep hidden. There was a magnetic attraction and ready intimacy between us way beyond sexuality—more like meeting a twin, someone made of the same fabric, as if every part of the other person feels the same. We were speaking our truth to each other with rare honesty and openness, even finishing each other's sentences, much like my connection with Doug. Back on the phone, David said by way of introduction, "This came through a channeling session I had in 1991. The medium identified the source that went by the name of Magnu." Then he read what I had unknowingly been waiting for forty-two years to hear.

> I feel you are sensing now the energies coming in, the energies surrounding your planet. This is causing many of you to ask questions.... to reevaluate completely your way of life, where you feel you wish to go, what you want to do.... Some of these upheavals are very confusing, very distressing, very disturbing.... You must organize yourselves into groups to support each other.
>
> Now then, my own allegiance with your planet goes back to the Atlantean period. At this time there were many energies being used and information and knowledge being used which

were for particular reasons of safety withdrawn, shall we say, to prevent complete catastrophe, to prevent total destruction of your planet....

At that time, shall we say, this knowledge was distributed only to the few. It was taught in what one would call a temple setting, though I am very careful about using this word. It has connotations, maybe. So let me use that word in the broadest possible sense. There were those initiated into this knowledge. There were grades of initiation, and those who passed the full initiation, these were known as Guardians of the Light and Keepers of the Secret Knowledge. This is the context from which I am coming.

There came a time when this knowledge and the energies were withdrawn. It is very difficult for me to explain to you precisely what I mean by that, so I will let you mull these things over. As the energies around your planet quicken, so these latent energies, these energies which have been withdrawn, will now be phased back in. They will gradually be awakened. As the consciousness level of the planet raises itself, those of you Light Workers who are working together to raise your consciousness, you will be able to hold more and more refined vibrations and so we will be able to use you as a catalyst to be able to feed in more and more energies.

As more of you raise yourselves to meet the challenges, so we can awaken more of these energies. Now, energy is consciousness, and the energies themselves contain the knowledge and the information, which is beginning to surface again in your consciousness, so that many of you will remember the Atlantean times. You will remember that you communicated with, say, dolphins and whales. You understood these other sentient creatures. You could levitate. You could cause quite significantly large objects to levitate. You could manifest things. You could cause spontaneous combustion by not miraculous means at all. Once you know what you are doing, these things follow. It is a matter of *order*.

Now I am looking to a time on your planet when these energies, this knowledge, is reawakened and reintegrated into your consciousness. I am not looking to a time when this knowledge will be for a few, but when your whole planet will be awakened to this understanding, which you have simply forgotten. It is not a matter of new information; it is a matter of remembering who you are and where you come from.

So you are being asked to change.... It is not a matter of small changes, of a little thing here, and a little thing there. You are really being asked to turn yourselves inside out. There is a massive shadow, which must be cleared, and it's up to Light Workers such as yourselves to focus yourselves on that challenge.

Those of you in the forefront of this, you are rather like a snowplow. You are the thin end of the wedge. You really have, how shall I put this? To a certain extent, I suppose, you have the *shitty* end of the job. You have got to do an awful lot, but nevertheless you are capable of doing an awful lot. That is why you have chosen to come. That is what you are here for, to really shovel some shit, and therefore make some space behind you to make it easier for the others.

The channel then spoke about the earth's energy system.

There are...lines around your planet, through your planet, which correspond, I suppose, very much to the acupuncture lines and meridians in your body. Where two lines cross, you create a vortex.... The more lines that intersect, the bigger the vortex. Therefore when you have a chakra you have a large vortex of intersecting energy. It is the same with your planet.... Now you could say the plexus (network) in and around the islands you call the "British Isles" is the hub of the wheel of plexuses and energies which surround your planet. It has acted in other times like a fail-safe device. In order to activate these chakric points upon your planet, the energies must all pass through the central point. They must pass through the heart of the pattern.

He stopped reading aloud and commented, "How interesting you came to England, eh?"

I'm not sure how or if I responded. The passage had lit an inferno under my subconscious mind. As the heat increased, tiny bubbles of recognition were making their way to the surface—a realization was forming.

The channel's message was meant for me to hear just as much as it had been for him more than a decade before. It was dawning on me that the Universal Forces had conspired to bring the two of us together—well beyond sane plausibility—at least partially for this reason.

Suddenly, the realization popped through. David had described to me the purpose for which I was born. Finally, the question that had haunted me since my earliest memories was answered.

It was all there: the connection to the Atlantean period the psychic had spoken about, the connection to dolphins and whales, the withdrawn energies that suggested a misuse of human power, the proof of worthiness through initiation, the increasing access through the years to what seemed to be a secret knowledge, working with the chakra system and being drawn to ley lines and stone circles, learning to conduct flows of energy and be a catalyst for them to be fed into other people and apparently back into the earth's grid, and finally, the sense of having been born for a certain purpose, to help accomplish a very large task.

I had been chosen for this work long before I landed in this physical body, just as I had sensed all along. To prove myself worthy for the task at hand, I had engaged with challenges of many kinds as an initiation into this inner circle that the channel referred to as the Keepers of the Secret Knowledge. My path had been different from anyone else's around me because I perceived the world differently, because I could see it for what it truly is in present time. My lineage hailed from somewhere else on some other plane of existence in another dimension of time. I was here, living as an incarnate being, to help reawaken and reintegrate energies on this planet. And at the same time, my soul had chosen these experiences and was evolving through the lessons they brought me.

I had unknowingly been graced with a wide-open channel, the "tree trunk" out the top of my head that Jeff had described. My neurological circuitry seemed predestinated for precisely this energy download experience. Even the specifics of my medical training were ideal, giving me an in-depth preparation for both understanding and actually using my own system as an instrument for healing and benefiting others. I chose a mind that was open but skeptical, ensuring that I would question the whole of it, in order to remain in the realm of the sane.

While part of my mind was off processing the magnitude of the message delivered through David, the conversation shifted. I then found myself describing to David how bored I had become in medicine, having realized the limitations of the allopathic approach. For the past two years, I had been intuitively sensing that dysfunction of the physical body is held at the electromagnetic level and needs to be addressed there.

He responded by telling me that two weeks before the event on the plane, he had visited San Diego to meet with a doctor and her brother who practiced what they call "quantum medicine." They were using cutting-edge technologies that had the potential to access DNA patterns and clear interference fields on the electromagnetic level. One of the technologies was the EPFX/SCIO, a biofeedback device linked to a computer program that tests the frequency patterns in every aspect of the person—physical, emotional, and spiritual. When it is finished, there on the screen is everything about the patient. The machine can then put the frequencies of herbal and natural remedies and other alternative healing methods into the body, skirting around the need for actual physical treatment.

There it was, like a gift from the gods arriving softly into my experience, slipped in among the many topics in a two-hour conversation: a technology that went directly to the electromagnetic level of patient's system. I was so excited I could barely contain myself. The most important questions I had were answered in this one conversation. Internal circuits I had never felt before had woken up and gone "online" as this discussion progressed. Was this related to the fact that we had so much in common?

David offered to introduce me to the people in San Diego, then went on to relay some of what was in his website biography but added more detail. He had been a loner in school and had never read a book or finished high school because he was so uninterested. Instead he excelled athletically and became a professional soccer player by the age of fourteen, until his career was cut short at twenty-one by the worsening pain of rheumatoid arthritis. Soon after, he became obsessed with learning about the world around him and was reading a book a day, guided by what felt like a specific curriculum of knowledge. He learned, on his own terms, what he wanted to know, not what the educational system was attempting to shove down his throat. I told him that I had recovered from the severe injury to my back at the age of fourteen, from what the doctors considered would be a lifelong disability. If asked, they would have said that I could never recover to the point of being a runner, much less a triathlete. I told him, too, about the challenge of my dyslexia, which had forced me to teach myself how to learn—likewise on my terms. All the while, as we were sharing, I could not get over how similar our lives had been in both theme and miraculous detail.

Pamela and David Icke with Janine, Mt. Shasta, California, 2006.

Michael, Janine and Doug at the vineyard.

26

Discovering Indigo Identity

There comes a time in all of our lives when we remember who we are. The Universal Forces that commanded our presence here at this time left clues in the forest for us to follow. The kernels of truth and resonance led us to know why we have come. This book is one of those clues. You were astute enough to manifest it once you were drawn to the topic of the Indigos, silently thinking to yourself how much their story sounded like parts of your own. This has been the message to you, in hopes of touching that place deep inside of you that knows you have come here for a specific purpose, on some sort of mission in unselfish service to the greater good, willing to put your warrior spirit forth to forge new pathways, sometimes against all odds, to lead this realm back to the place of universal oneness it once enjoyed. Do not despair if you have never before thought of your life in these terms or had a clear past life remembrance. You are not alone. In fact you are one of many who have remained hidden, each unknowing of the others who have made this same journey. You contain the latent circuitry that was waiting to be activated by the experience you have just had in reading this book and the many experiences that will follow.

The mass of children who began coming in the mid-1980s was noticed and described; we earlier arrivals were not. We, the Indigo Scouts, were labeled as "different," to the point that new psychological diagnoses had to be created to describe and categorize our strange new ways of thinking and processing information.

For the next several weeks, I slept little. The stimulation that had started when the energy flowed through me on the plane magnified after speaking to David. I did not have much outlet for it. I tried to journal my thoughts and emotions, though they were sparking off so intensely that writing could not capture all that was pouring through.

I continued to be struck by the similarities between David's life and mine. And he said there were other individuals having similar experiences. What was this phenomenon? At some point during the many hours that I lay awake from 3 a.m. until I hit the trail or the pool at 5 a.m. to blow off some of the amassing energy, that voiceless voice told me: "Indigo Children. Go look up the Indigo Children."

I had heard of these special kids and, a few years back, had seen James Twyman's movie *Indigo* and Neal Donald Walsh's documentary film *Indigo Evolution*. I took at face value that they were psychic kids. Still not needing to sleep, I got out of bed, went upstairs to my office, and Googled the subject. Within a few moments, I realized that on my computer screen lay an exact description of my life, in both theme and in detail—the characteristics these kids possess and the frustrations they often experience. And I learned that the Indigos were not all children. I read how they have been coming into physical form for the past hundred years, perhaps even longer. The older Indigos are referred to as scouts, those who have come to blaze the way for the greater numbers who have followed—just as Magnu's message described. I then flipped to Amazon.com and ordered every book available on the subject.

David had talked about his growing up and the life events that led him to where he is now. I noticed a common pattern. *He was one, too.* The similarities we shared were all Indigo in nature. We were both warriors. I continued to read. Some, who once lived in Lemuria and Atlantis, come from other galaxies, returning voluntarily to Earth at this time, gifted with extraordinary traits and ancient knowledge, to prevent what happened in the past from occurring again.

Was I on the brink of going mad by thinking in these terms?

I then researched the name "Magnu." According to Rudolf Steiner, he was a high ascendant master in Atlantis whose last incarnation on Earth was that of Jesus Christ.

Doug kept coming to mind. I knew instantly that I had to share this story with him. If my conclusion was correct, he, too, was an Indigo.

That would explain our immediate familiarity in the nurses' station, even before we first exchanged words. It also explained why we shared the ability to see Bracken's aura and are able to communicate telepathically across the continent in real time.

I then thought of my father, and recognized the same pattern. The experiences he and I had shared while I was growing up, the closeness of spirit, and the telepathy with him all made sense in this light. Was this why I had felt such a burning desire for Dad and Doug to meet someday?

I bent the ears of Doug and his wife, Sheryl, over the phone with my crazy newfound enlightenment and sent them loads of reading and viewing material. Doug had already intuited our Indigo connection after seeing a brief news report devoted to the subject on CNN earlier in the year. We scheduled a week together in California, which would be in April 2006.

We had several things planned for them in far-out California that their more conservative Missouri friends and family would probably never believe. They each went on the SCIO machine, which I had purchased in January and been practicing with ever since. The SCIO was just what I had been asking the Universe for. With access to electromagnetic levels of information, the reasons why some people were not getting better by conventional medical methods came into crystal clarity. I could begin clearing disease, dysfunction, toxins, emotional baggage, chakra imbalances, and much more with a few clicks of the mouse. I was convinced this was Atlantean technology that had been reintroduced into this dimension at this time. It felt as familiar to me as David did. Interestingly, those who can immediately track with its concept were Atlantean themselves. In this way, it chooses its own kind.

Doug and Sheryl each had a session with T'Shala as well. Sheryl went first so that during Doug's session she and I could drive over to the compounding pharmacy in Capitola before all of us set out for Sonoma and my brother's vineyard and winery. She was experiencing perimenopausal symptoms for which I had prescribed a natural progesterone cream. By the time Sheryl and I left the house, it was 5:15 p.m.; the pharmacy closed at six. Doug's session had started at 4:45, with specific instructions to T'Shala to determine the origin of the connection between Doug and me.

Ray, the compounding pharmacist, loved Mike's wine and I had brought along a bottle of it as a gift for his help over the past several months concocting formulas for my patients.

I had the opportunity to hear all about Sheryl's session as we crawled our way north on Highway 1 in heavy spring-break beach traffic. My heart was fluttering with anxiety. I knew we would probably make the pharmacy before it closed, but I could not talk myself out of an overwhelming sense of urgency. At the first opportunity, I jumped off the freeway, driving like I was at the Indianapolis speedway along equally packed side streets. Zigzagging through traffic, going head-on at one point with oncoming cars, skidding around corners, and finally pulling into the parking lot, I checked my watch. It was 5:45 exactly. We burst out of the car. Sheryl headed for the pharmacy as I opened the car's backdoor to retrieve the bottle of wine in its bag. As I reached in, I was suddenly overtaken by a wave of what could only be described as vertigo. It felt as if my entire perception had been yanked to the right. Standing upright with the bag in my right hand and closing the door, I tried to shake it off, yet I was staggering to the right as if I had just had a stroke or suffered an aneurysm. I called out, "Sheryl, I...I'm dizzy."

Just then, out of nowhere, a second massive pulling sensation yanked me once again to the right. Visually, the world looked like a Salvador Dali painting. As I lurched to the right, the world skidded to the left. I attempted to take account of my condition. I had no head pain, no arm or leg pain, no numbness or tingling, and no loss of consciousness. What the hell was going on then? I could hear Sheryl calling my name. "Janine! What is wrong?" Just then I received the final blow. As if my head was magnetically drawn to the asphalt, down I went, the right side of my head first, as the wine bag flew out of my hand, landing hard on the parking lot surface. I could not move yet I was fully awake.

Sheryl, an OR scrub nurse, grabbed my right wrist and started searching for my radial pulse.

I looked up at her and said, "Sheryl...I'm okay, really, I'm fine."

She looked at me with immense concern. "Janine, you are not okay. You are lying in the middle of the parking lot holding up traffic, unable to get up. This is not okay."

I certainly could not explain why I had gone down, or why the right side of my head felt incredibly hollow. I did sense with perfect confidence, however, that I was going to be fine.

After a moment or two, I was able to get up, collect myself, and walk leaning to the right like a drunken sailor to the pharmacy door, where the receptionist was standing, having witnessed the entire event. "Should we call for an ambulance?" she asked as we made our way in.

This looks really great, I thought, as I handed Ray the unbroken bottle of wine. Feeling the need to explain, I said, loud enough for the receptionist to hear, that I don't drink the stuff.

We completed our business as I leaned heavily against the counter, reassured by the fact that all four extremities were moving on command and my thoughts remained clear and consistent. I kept asking myself, "What the hell is this all about?" Each time, the answer came that something was happening on an energetic level.

Sheryl insisted on driving home. Though knowing that I would do the same if the situation were reversed, my hardheaded self was still unwilling to relinquish control. My persona had changed into one that remembered having to remain strong even after being wounded in battle. On the way home, I turned to Sheryl and insisted that she not tell the guys what had happened.

"Are you nuts?" she exclaimed. "Janine, you just passed out in the parking lot for no apparent reason. If you don't tell them, I certainly will."

"If you tell them," I responded, "we will be spending the entire evening in the ER getting CT and MRI scans, which will all be normal. We will never get to the vineyard."

She gave me one of her best motherly looks. She was right, of course. We had to tell them.

When we got home, T'Shala had left. José was upstairs packing, and Doug was down the hall in the guest room. Sheryl disappeared down the hallway. I went upstairs to collect some things in an overnight bag and change my clothes, and then headed downstairs to feed the animals. Doug came in, followed closely by Sheryl. He was wearing the same bright yellow polo-style T-shirt and jeans that I had on. At first sight of each other, the three of us laughed. This sort of thing had been happening all week.

Then Doug's expression changed to an uncharacteristically stern one. Sheryl was silently mouthing to me behind his right shoulder, "You are never going to f-ing believe this one." Doug looked me right in the eye and said, "I know what happened to you."

With what must have been a face filled with disbelief, I said, "You do, do you?"

Nodding, he began to explain. At the beginning of his session, T'Shala had identified a very old entity stuck to the back of his head and neck, the source of a chronic neck pain since his high school football days. She did not want to clear it until she had worked in other areas first. She said the connection between Doug and me goes as far back as Lemuria, when all things were unified and in peace. "Janine, you and I were one soul back then, what she called Lemurian soul twins. We shared one form, one consciousness, and one goal—to maintain unity among all those inhabiting the earth. We were attacked by an entity that ended up attaching more to me than to you. I sort of protected you from it. At that moment, you separated from me in order to carry on with the work. I have lived with this beast ever since—in every lifetime."

I looked at Doug with widening eyes. My sweet little conservative vascular surgeon friend from Missouri was sounding so...*Californian?* He went on.

"This caused us to fail in our mission, and we lost the battle with the dark forces. They came to Earth, capped off the energy sources around the planet, and created the duality that has plagued this dimension ever since. I have never forgiven myself for that failure and have been coming back time and time again as a warrior, often with you, to attempt to right the wrong.

"Near the end, she called your spirit in the room so we could face off and clear the betrayal that had tarnished our relationship. When we did that, I actually saw you floating up on the ceiling—I swear, it was totally weird. After that, it was time to clear the entity. It was strongly adhered and wrapped around my spinal cord, or so she said, and she couldn't remove it herself, so she asked me to assist her. I thought, 'Sure, I am going to reach back there and go through the motions of throwing the energy away—right!' But when I reached back to the right side of my neck, my hand actually grasped a cold, rubbery substance that when I pulled on it seemed to have resilience and spring back. I was blown away! It took three tugs before it finally released, and once it did, my neck pain went away immediately." Grabbing his neck with his right hand and rubbing it, he said, "See, it's gone."

I shot back, "Three tugs? What time did this occur?"

"It must have been five or ten minutes before six."

At that point, whatever might have been left of my skeptical mind melted away.

We arrived at my brother's place in Healdsburg late that evening. Mike was the only one still up. Doug and Sheryl took the apartment above the winery, and José and I commandeered the guest suite in the main house. We spent the next day wine tasting, starting in the morning at Mike and Katie's. Doug and Sheryl had been fans and patrons since the beginning. Standing there in the winery, watching them having fun barrel tasting, I could not help but feel that I had two brothers, one who survived my zoo in the next room in Mom and Dad's house, and another who felt somehow more familiar to me than my own family. I snapped a photograph of the two below the portrait of my father that hangs near the winery's front door. My only lingering regret was that Doug and Dad had never had the opportunity to meet.

The day ended with dinner at one of Mike and Katie's favorite hide-aways in Geyserville. Mike had brought along two special bottles to share with his new friends. After a fabulous southern Italian meal, I was handed the car keys, as usual. Once back at the winery, we said our good nights and retired. We had to be up and out early the next day to beat the morning traffic over the Golden Gate Bridge on our way to the airport.

I awoke with the dawn. Collecting my things, I put them in the truck, then went down to the creek where I sat on a stack of pallets and nursed a cup of tea. This is the creek where we placed part of Dad's physical essence, I thought. Was any part of him still here? Where is he right now? Does he see us? Does he know we are here?

I still thought of him often and missed him. He was the most precious gift of this lifetime. Had he and I been twins somewhere back in time in another reality? What would he have thought of all the craziness unfolding in my life recently? Would he have been able to feel ley line energies as I had? Was he present but simply on a different radio frequency, locked into a different dimension, yet cheering me on, maybe even assisting with my brain's and heart's ability to interpret the deeper meanings of what I was experiencing? I had always sought his guidance on such matters; he had always had a way of comforting me and making me feel "normal."

I was lost in my thoughts until the door of the winery opened and Doug emerged, taking his and Sheryl's suitcases to the truck. I raised my cup in a silent good morning greeting. He smiled, raised his hand, and motioned for me to come. Wiping the tears from my cheeks that always came when I allowed myself to feel Dad's physical absence, I made my way into the winery, where Doug had slipped back through the door.

He was standing near the tasting table with Sheryl and Mike. His face was serious again, as it had been two days earlier. "Janine, I have something to tell you and Mike." Sheryl's look told me this was going to be weird—again. Doug then turned to Mike so as to include him equally.

"Last night I dreamt that we were all saying good-bye out by the parking area before we left this morning. Both of you, plus Katie, Sheryl and I, the kids, and José were all there. As we were chatting, a gray-haired man walked up from the creek and entered the circle we had unknowingly formed. He did not say anything, and no one else besides me seemed to notice him. Just then he reached out and took my right arm in his hand, just above the elbow. Actually feeling the warmth of his touch and the physical pressure around my arm, I woke up. I was back in bed in the apartment upstairs, my eyes fully open, because I looked at the digital clock on the nightstand. It said 1:50 a.m. This man was still standing in front of me holding onto my right arm. As I stared into his translucent blue eyes, I suddenly recognized him. He was the gentleman in the portrait over there." Doug then pointed to my father's portrait hanging next to the winery's front door.

Mike and I looked at each other, powerless to hold back our welling tears—the only way our puny five-sensory systems could respond to the magnitude of love Dad had embodied.

Doug continued. "As I stared into his eyes, I was suddenly overcome by a sensation of expanding warmth in my chest and the most safely soothing comfort I have ever known. My chest felt as if it were expanding into the room with warm, goopy honey drizzling down it. The room then lit up with a bright white light. The intensity of it was almost blinding. I was sure I was awake during this part because the dog outside started barking when he saw the light from the bedroom. As I was bathed in what I can only describe as infinite love and bliss, he then spoke to me."

Mike and I looked at each other again. We knew the words even before Doug spoke them.

Looking back and forth between us, making sure to distribute equally what he was about to say, Doug told us. "He said, 'Thank you for visiting my family's vineyard. *Walk in the light.*'"

Epilogue

A profound change has taken place in me now that I have awakened to who I am and why I am here. I now fully trust my eyes to see the world for what it truly is. Understanding at last that I am part of a broad family whose members all feel like misfits, destined to be alone and separate, somehow gives me great solace. I finally fit into a category, after a lifetime of always being "different."

The nonordinary traits that we awakened Indigos have at our disposal are both a curse and a gift. When we ventured out to play with the neighborhood kids and to attend school, our traits made us painfully different from the norm. Yet our abilities with telepathy, remote viewing, interspecies communication, and psychic perception and our inherent moral consciousness make it possible for us to perceive with symbolic sight, understanding the meaning and interconnection of events and relationships.

I have lived through the process of karmic clearing that must occur in each of us before the new paradigm can fully manifest on this planet. I can now stand on the edge of my long-familiar abyss and understand why my life has been structured the way it has been. The sense of a master plan that I had from childhood was spot-on. There was a specific grooming process in place to make me into the person I came here to be. My purpose for being on the planet at this moment in history is to help with the grand conscious awakening that is currently under way. Knowing that my presence here at this time, along with that of many others, was foretold in ancient teaching gives me pause. The sense of responsibility to get it right feels monumental. Understanding that my physical body is simply a conduit to run cosmic etheric energy into this dimension to power the process feels magical.

Through the physical and emotional injuries I suffered and the insights that came because of them, I have earned the responsibility to teach, which I do experientially. As a physician, I see many people who are in their own processes of dismantling and reconstruction. Each day as I sit with patients and listen to their archetypal stories of woundedness, I feel the glow that comes with recognizing the deeper meaning of their hurt. It is still too early for some to hear this perspective, and my intuition guides me as to which people I can share it with now and those who need to be brought along more slowly. The fact remains, however, that each one is on his or her own journey to self-discovery.

We live in only one layer of the green laminated glass tabletop of multidimensionality. Once we understand that much more lies beyond the limitations of our five-sensory system, our perception of the universe can never be the same. We are all extraterrestrials, from different star federations, having a human experience, here to ensure that this garden planet and its inhabitants remain safe through the paradigm shift. The Piscean Age has been all about duality and contrast. As we move into the spherical Age of Aquarius, we will come to embrace oneness and unity. This can be achieved if we embrace and love with equal zest what have been called the light and dark sides of ourselves, and of the collective. Only then can we find peace within ourselves, and thus peace on this planet. This time in history is destined to be our greatest work yet.

Our mission as awakened Indigos is simple and readily at hand. It is to maximize our own potential. To gain the wisdom this task requires, we are being asked to push through the perceived barriers and the brick walls we have constructed for ourselves. Remaining small is not an option. We must clear out all that stands in our way. Coming to terms with the immense power that exists within each of us is challenging but not impossible. It calls for trusting our intuition and using for the highest good all the magical tools at our disposal. We cannot fail. We signed on for this mission and must see it through. It is time to come together and share our stories, experiences, and pain. In numbers we find strength. In understanding we find trust. In peace we flourish.

WHO WE ARE AND WHY WE ARE HERE

The phenomenon we are now observing was first described by Lee Carroll and Jan Tober. In 1989, Carroll, an engineer who maintained a technical audio business in San Diego, California, began channeling an entity called Kryon, who described the coming of these new kids. Carroll's spiritual partner Jan Tober, a retired jazz singer who became weary of the road, had settled in Del Mar, California, to pursue a metaphysical practice using sounds and colors. During metaphysical parapsychologic sessions, Tober observed certain children displaying a never before seen auric color: indigo. After some years of compiling the Kryon teachings and personal observation, Carroll and Tober published their first book on the phenomenon, *The Indigo Children*. Their message obviously resonated with the public as the book has sold more than 250,000 copies since its publication in 1999.

What was it that seemed to ring true for people in the description of these kids?

Kryon (via Carroll) described them as coming into the world with a feeling of royalty and a sense that they deserve to be here. Their self-worth is healthily intact, and they often tell their parents "who they are." They have difficulty with absolute authority and will simply not do certain things such as waiting their turn in line. They get frustrated with ritually oriented systems that don't require creative thought. They have an innate ability to see a better way of doing things. They are "system busters." They often feel misunderstood by others who are not of the same consciousness, and seem antisocial unless others like them are around. They often have difficulty fitting in and school is often difficult for them socially.

Since 1999, many other adults including parents, teachers, and psychologists who had been noticing different characteristics showing up in the "new children" have added to the richness of Carroll's and Tober's description of Indigo Children. The labels have now expanded to encompass the exponential evolution of our species. The Crystal children have been arriving in mass since the early 1990s and before them the

Cusps, who are a blended transition of the Indigo into the Crystalline consciousness, containing traits of both. Each label represents slight differences in inherent traits and gifts that will be necessary to complete the work they have come here to accomplish.

The children are described as having an unusual sensitivity to the supernatural, wielding intuitive and psychic abilities. They speak early, walk fast, and learn quickly. These children may be gifted artists. They think spherically and three-dimensionally, are "fixers," are unusually healthy and strong, and have a self-assured quiet wisdom. They are born leaders, immune to guilt, resistant to psychological "button pushing," can see through the façade of others' hidden agendas, and share a deep sense that they have come here for a higher yet unknown purpose. They are highly intelligent, yet often lack the ability to master math, reading, and spelling. As a result, the educational system often labels them learning disabled (ADD, ADHD, dyslexic, or even autistic). Possessing a brain that demonstrates different circuitry from that of other humans makes them more suited for telepathic wordless communication. Their performance on standardized tests may not reflect the full spectrum of their talents.

Lacking the patience to waste time being forced to learn in the old ways, they appear to be unable to concentrate or stay on task. The system either tries to medicate them into conformity or places them in special education class, which takes away many of their special gifts of quick three-dimensional perception and other innate abilities and erodes their instinctive sense of self-worth. Many of them do not finish in formal education because they cannot put up with these antiquated ways, but go on to become leaders in the arts, science, business, medicine, design, and entertainment.

They enjoy boundless energy and are natural healers, sharing this energy with those around them. When allowed to come together in groups, the children have been observed huddling around one who was feeling sad or lonely and simply by their brief presence causing a shift in that individual's energy system. It remains unclear whether the Indigo Children know what they are doing, as their inborn abilities are so natural to them. They are quickly frustrated with others who do not share these seemingly magical powers.

Carroll and Tober only described this new phenomenon as occurring in children. Others since have observed these same traits in adults, calling these individuals Indigo Scouts. These are the few brave souls who have been coming in over the past hundred years to create new paths through the jungle of rigid, antiquated group consciousness and thought. With machetes in hand, they slice through the systems and the patterns that no longer support conscious growth and continued development on this planet. Their signature trait is "thinking outside the box." Possessing the innate ability to think spherically rather than linearly, they each changed forever the field they focused on while incarnate.

To offer yet another perspective on this phenomenon, the same year that Kryon began speaking about these kids who were coming, Richard Boylan, PhD, a behavioral scientist, anthropologist, university associate professor (emeritus), certified clinical hypnotherapist, consultant, and researcher, began conducting research into human encounters with what he calls "Star Visitors." In his clinical psychology practice, he began working quite unexpectantly with experiencers of Star Visitor encounters. After thirty years of practice, he thought he had heard everything. Apparently, he hadn't. In one year, four different clients sought him out for counseling about minor problems of daily living. Over the course of treatment, they each shared with him their individual story of contact with Star Visitors. He did not find this strange, as his background prepared him to assess their accounts properly.

Born in 1939, before what is widely known now as the "UFO cover-up," he remembers, when he was eight, hearing his parents talk about the newspaper headline of an off-duty sheriff who observed a V-formation of wingless round "flying saucers" near Mount Rainier in Washington State. Just a few weeks later, there was another front-page report of a downed and captured flying saucer near Roswell, New Mexico.

In July 1952, he read for himself the headlines in bold print, accompanied by actual photographs of UFOs repeatedly flying over the U.S. capitol night after night. One year later, the federal government instituted the "UFO cover-up" by having prominent scientists and Air Force public information officers go before the press to deny and discredit accounts of UFO sightings.

So what did Dr. Boylan eventually do with this information of his patients' accounts of visitations and abductions? He went on to create the Star Kids Project, an organization that works with what he calls "hybrid children" and their families who have advanced abilities due to a genetic upgrade of their DNA with that of Star Visitors. He wrote about and presented this information, mainly within the community of people interested in UFOs and/or investigating the UFO cover-up. Many in the lay public have therefore never heard his descriptions of what he calls "Star Kids" (age 0–21) and "Star Seeds" (age 21 and older). He has personally researched this phenomenon for nearly two decades, both in the United States and abroad, using sound scientific methods, and has come up with some startling descriptions and statistics.

He lays out the four ways that a child's or adult's DNA can be manipulated. First, during Star Visitor encounters with parents (often not remembered), reproductive material can be spliced into the genes of the developing fetus. Second, modification can take place in an already born child. Third, it can also occur as a "walk-in" situation during a near-death experience. The most prevalent way, however, is that Star Kids are born into a human body as a deliberately chosen "missionary" incarnation of a Star Visitor to accomplish work on Earth at this point in our history. They bring with them advanced abilities, lofty principles, values, and ideas to share here.

Dr. Boylan has found that many Star Kids and Star Seeds are not aware of Star Visitor contact, a walk-in situation, or their previous life as a star being. They just know there is something very different about them. He goes on to describe their unique traits and characteristics:

Adults in children's bodies, a gaze and knowingness that belies their years, psychic abilities, psychic diagnosis, ability to harness bioenergetic energy, ability to run earth and cosmic forces through their bioenergetic system to heal others, intuitive and telepathic linking with others and Source Consciousness, intrinsic attraction toward one another, not egotistical despite a dazzling array of advanced abilities, understanding these traits are "gifts" and "tools." A profound presence, self-assuredness and quiet confidence, intensely but quietly poised for action, a sense of goodness, moral consciousness, and high spirituality, takes the path of soft intervention to make things right, low physical sexual needs, they walk their talk and have an aura of compassion, charm, and brightness.

They display abilities of precognition, mental telepathy, telekinesis, psychometry, levitation, invisibility work, astral projection and travel, mental influencing, penetrating intuitiveness, aura reading, cross-species communication, remote and interdimensional viewing. Their physical body demonstrates lower basal body temperature along with enhanced immunity and healing capability as well as generates a vast bio-electromagnetic-photic field that often puts out amber sodium vapor streetlights when they walk by. Because of these traits, they universally feel "different" from those around them and many don't know what to do with these special gifts.

They have particular physical characteristics that set them apart including large almond-shaped eyes that radiate mature angelic wisdom beyond their years, a dynamic appearance, earlier onset of puberty, and later on, early to develop salt and pepper graying or baldness despite looking decades younger than their peers, larger foot size, larger heads due to ongoing genetic engineering, have excessive amounts of energy, which can develop into restless leg syndrome, insomnia, adrenal insufficiency, and an internal sense of buzzing.

The prevalence of these upgraded humans is equally startling. Back in the 1940s, only 2 percent of those being born were of this mixed DNA. Today, the percentage of Indigos in the different age groups of the population reflect the probable reason why Carroll, Tober, and Kryon's concepts resonated so deeply with the public:

Infants–12 years = 96%

13–18 years = 81%

19–29 years = 67%

30–45 years = 45%

46–60 years = 21%

60+ years = 12%

Are Indigos, Cusps, Crystals, Star Kids, and Star Seeds one and the same? These terms are simply labels describing a phenomenon. The bigger question must be asked: For what purpose have they come? Consider these kids and adults against the backdrop of what is currently happening in the fields of astrophysics, geophysics, and geopolitics and contrast that with the ancient cultural teachings that foretold a new race of humans, "the fifth root race" according to Hopi tradition, who would be coming to Earth at this time in history to help midwife what is widely being called "the shift."

The Mayan calendar points to the date of December 21, 2012, as being the end of "the grand cycle of evolution," and the beginning of a "new world age." The 26,000-year timeline that the calendar describes is called in Western circles "the Precession of the Equinoxes," in which Earth's true north transits through each of the twelve signs of the zodiac and then aligns with the center of our universe. As Earth spins counterclockwise on its axis, true north actually demonstrates a backward (clockwise) wobble, following the same dynamo laws as that of a spinning top. As the top slows down, it will fall backward on itself in the opposite direction that it was turning. It takes Earth nearly 26,000 years to complete one revolution of that clockwise backward wobble cycle. True north's transit through each of the constellations of the Zodiac or astrological ages takes 2,152 years to complete and represents one month of the grand cosmic year.

Sumerians, Tibetans, Egyptians, Cherokees, Hopi, and Maya developed calendars based on this grand cycle and referred to it in their ancient mystical teachings. It has been foretold that the completion of the precession will bring regeneration to Earth and offer an awakening to all that have done the work of opening their hearts and minds to these grand possibilities. Many other ancient peoples spoke of these last days of the Grand Cycle, including the Q'ero elders of Peru, Essenes, Kabbalists, Navajo, Apache, Iroquois, Dogon, Aborigines, and Maori. Deeply imbedded in their teaching was the prophecy of the coming of the "New Children." They each spoke about the time before the grand end of time as we know it, when an upgrade of our species will enter this plane, equipped with dazzling capabilities to navigate the waters previously thought uncharted.

Our world is now in the midst of this time. The New Children have come, pure of heart and with eyes that see the truth and a will that defies imagination. Their focus is simple: restore balance and pave the way for the new beginning. Each has entered with instructions unique to her or his individual contribution to this process. Wisdom prevails as these beings are those who have mastered the earth plane and evolved through thousands of previous incarnations or are visitors from other worlds embodied at this time as humans with a broader understanding and higher consciousness directly connected to Source.

Buried in the verbal history of the ancient cultures is a common understanding and lore, which originated in the stars and continued in the relationships maintained with the relatives still there. Despite not having the technology to view the cosmos aided by high-powered telescopes, antenna, or satellites, these cultures were still able to predict the exact moment in time that we are now living, evidencing their advanced understanding of mathematics, astronomy, and physics. The Maya suddenly mysteriously vanished, abandoning their advanced cities, cultural centers, and monumental pyramids. Many theories speak about their departure back to space, back to the other dimensions that remain invisible to those who hang on to a limited view of reality.

Coinciding with the end of the Precession of the Equinoxes, geophysical evidence exists that the earth herself is undergoing a dramatic change that no other advanced civilization has lived through before. This is why the new children have come. The change is called a geomagnetic reversal or pole shift. It has occurred fourteen times in the past 4.5 million years, but never in human experience. It last occurred between 13,000 and 11,000 years ago, which corresponds with the time of the biblical flood and when Lemuria and Atlantis sank. Scientists are currently trying to understand the astrophysiologic circumstances that lead to an event of this magnitude, along with the impact it will have on our current way of life.

There are two theories on what leads to this phenomenon. The first theory proposes that these reversals are inherent to the dynamo theory of how the geomagnetic field is generated. To allow a reversal, the magnetics must decrease significantly, just as is currently happening at an exponential rate today. Computer-generated simulations show Earth's magnetic fields can become tangled and disorganized through the chaotic motions of liquid metal at Earth's core, slowing it down and thus allowing for a north-south flip to occur.

The other theory is that external forces that directly disrupt the flow of molten metal at Earth's core trigger the change. Such processes may be brought on as huge slabs of Earth's crust are carried down through the mantle at subduction zones (adjoining edges of the continental or oceanic plates) as a result of the action of plate tectonics. Imagine placing your hand, held flat, into a stream of water at a forty-five-degree angle. The flow on the surface becomes disrupted and the water slows down, creating eddies behind the disruption. In geophysical terms, this phenomenon is called mantle-core shear force. It disrupts the flow and thus the dynamo generator of the geomagnetic field. As the magnetics decrease, the field becomes more unstable, allowing for the once-stable north-south polar orientation to flip.

The other strange but true geophysical phenomenon that scientists are observing at this time is the increase of the Shuman frequency or base resonant frequency (heartbeat) of our planet at the same exponential rate that the magnetics are decreasing. Before the mid-1980s, this beat of 7.8 Hz was so consistent that the atomic clocks were set by it. As Masaru Emoto has shown in his work *Messages in Water,* our cellular structural matrix responds to incredibly subtle frequencies, even those generated by thought and intention. We are unknowingly responding to this vibrational quickening of our planet and can observe the results in people's behavior patterns as well as new mental and physical symptoms never before seen. This phenomenon is also fueling the new awakening in consciousness that the ancients foretold.

In graphing the progression over time of the current rate of the falling magnetics and the increasing base resonant frequency, it can be seen that the two curves will intersect at the end of 2012, the exact point in planetary history at which Earth will complete a full 26,000-year processional cycle. How did the ancients know this? What was in their cosmology that allowed them to grasp such gigantic concepts that spanned time and space? How could they not have been guided by extraterrestrial advanced knowledge?

As this process moves forward, many are predicting massive Earth changes and cataclysms while others hold more subdued opinions. No one is saying for sure—except those who have been labeled Indigo, that is. These kids and adults have come here specifically to participate in these events. Human history books are wrong. We have done this before and are willing to contribute our wisdom of lessons learned in previous millennia to assist yet another great civilization to succeed this time and flourish through these changes.

Our world has never before experienced such a boom in population, increasing by 216,000 a day. If Dr. Boylan's statistics are correct, 96 percent are those who carry the hybrid DNA from our Star Relatives who have a vested interest in this planet not only surviving, but also continuing to thrive. Which will it be? Complete catastrophe or a rebirthing into a recreated world where peace and unity reign. We have the power to decide, using our tools of thought, intention, and action.

Mary Zarka, Mary Strutner, Janine, and Shannon Hare in 1984.

Acknowledgments

Where do I begin to pay tribute to a lifetime of souls and teachers who were placed in my path at exactly the right times? I felt the coming of many before their arrival, while others were a complete but perfect surprise. If it weren't for them, this story would never have found its voice. We all exist as who we are today because of the special interaction and melding of our essence with others. This is true for all people, but for those of the Indigo persuasion, who never seem to find their "tribe," it can be difficult to achieve the feeling of belonging to anyone or anything.

Special thanks goes out to my much-loved editor and now dear friend Carolyn Bond for taking this story and me well beyond what the original words conveyed. Due to her dogged curiosity, we were able to dig a little deeper and excavate a level of understanding that had been operational in me all along, but of which I was not fully conscious.

Heartfelt gratitude goes to the two men in my life who believed in me even when no one else dared, first my father, William J. Talty, and then my husband, José A. Chibras, MD. Not surprisingly, they share many other similar traits, not the least of which are colossal joy in the now and an infectious childlike optimism about the future. There really are no words to express the deep love I hold in my heart for both of these beings who adore me for exactly who I am.

Gratitude to my mother, Carol A. Talty-Groswird, for always providing me with just enough encouragement. We are so different in so many ways it is difficult to fathom how one can emerge from the other. Finding our balance as friends has provided me with an exceptional lesson in compassion that is unique among all my other relationships. My eternal gratitude to her for playing this special leading role in my ongoing drama while incarnate.

I send the highest vibration of gratitude for all the animal beings that have graced my experience as friends, family, and teachers. They have been with me throughout and continue to companion my way. They taught me how to communicate when words were not my friends.

To Mrs. Diane Neal, my third and fifth grade teacher, who identified me drowning in frustration and compassionately acted by throwing me an artistic lifeline just in time. Your deed set me on a path of achievement that gave me access to all the magic this dimension has to offer. I thank and honor you for your courage.

To the two teachers who came much later, Drs. Ward and Greenman, thank you for entrusting me with the keys to the kingdom.

I extend the highest appreciation to my loyal office staff, Mari, Raven, Jen, and T'Shala. If it weren't for you, I would have long ago been swallowed up by the masses of humans I am still honored to study. You provide the protective barrier that allows me to remain the imposter in the white coat.

I want to thank my brother, Michael Talty, for always being there for me, even when it wasn't fashionable.

Thank you to my true friends: Mary Zarka, Mary Strutner, Shannon Hare, and the Mountain Women; Helene, Corrine, Jan, Dede, Donna, Julie, Sue, and Glynis. You helped me understand the inner workings of human female thought and emotion. Still, an unfurnished space exists, where hammocks of cobwebs remain undisturbed.

Appendix 1
Star Kid/Star Seed Identification Questionnaire
© 2003 by Richard Boylan, Ph.D.

vers071703

(Note: This Questionnaire may also
be used by adults suspecting they are Star Seeds.)

Directions: Circle score number at end of each question answered "yes," and add up the scores at the end.

Rating Schedule:
Score of 12 = probably a Star Kid
Score of 16 = most likely a Star Kid
Score of 20+ = absolutely a Star Kid

1. The child has a larger than average head for his/her age and height, especially in the front or top of the head. = 1
2. The child has an average body temperature of below 97.6 degrees F [36.4 degrees C]. = 1
3. The child's birth was notable for there being a strange presence or figure in the delivery room or an aura (glow) noted around the child or their crib. = 2
4. The child began saying a number of words clearly by six months of age (at least one year before the average talking age of 18 months.) = 1
5. The child began walking by one-half-year-old (before the average walking age of one year old). = 1
6. When the child began speaking, she/he used phrases or whole sentences almost immediately, not just single words. = 1

7. People notice that the child seems extremely mature for their age, almost like an adult in a child's body. = 1

8. In childhood the child sought out more advanced activities, being bored with and underchallenged by the games the other children his/her age wanted to play. = 1

9. The child mentioned recalling his/her "other parents" out among the stars, or expressed a longing to go back to his/her "real home" out in the cosmos. = 2

10. The child's gaze seems unusually mature and penetrating/knowing. = 1

11. The child's entire childhood is notable for growing up very much faster physically and intellectually than the other children the same age. = 1

12. The child is very sensitive, and is put off by, or shrinks away from the destructive, mean, cruel, violent, or wasteful behavior of the other kids, and cannot understand why they are that way. = 1

13. Sometimes, when the child goes by an amber sodium-vapor-plasma streetlight, the light goes out, particularly if the child is emotionally charged. = 2

14. The child exhibits mental telepathy (silent mind-to-mind communication). = 1

15. The child has more than once foretold something in the future that later actually happens, or has a "dream" which later comes true (precognition). = 1

16. The child has made an object move by focused mental concentration effort, such as influencing a pinball game, a basketball shot, or a bowling ball's direction. = 1

17. The child can mentally see something going on at a different location, or in the past, or in the future (clairvoyance/remote viewing). = 1

18. The child acquires new information spontaneously, apparently by mental "downloading," either in awake-state awareness or by being shown things during sleep. = 1

    [If the child knows the data came from Star Visitors =2]

19. The child is adept at cross-species communication, both knowing what an animal (e.g., pet dog, a dolphin, etc.) is thinking, and

communicating telepathically with that animal, and the animal responds to the silent communication. = 1

20. The child "just knows" something intuitively about a person, a place, or a situation, which then turns out correct (i.e., the child is "psychic"). = 1

21. The child affects certain electrical appliances repeatedly by his/her mere presence (such as a TV changing channels, a radio turning on, a wristwatch not working any more, or a lamp turning on or off without touching it). = 1

22. The child has admitted using mental thought to influence the behavior of another, and is effective at this silent influencing (e.g. a parent for a second dessert helping). = 1

23. The child reports seeing Visitors that the parents/others cannot see, or sees things out of the corner of the eye which disappear when stared directly at (inter-dimensional viewing). = 1

24. The child can see auras around other people or animals (quasi-visible energy fields, often visible with Kirlian photography). = 1

25. The child sees or feels color, patterns or "textures" in those auras, which provide information about the other's health, emotional state, psychic attunement, etc. = 1

26. The child is able to use psychic diagnosis (intuitive "seeing," or passing a hand above the patient's body) to correctly locate an area of illness, injury, or disease. = 1

27. The child uses internalized energy (psychic energy/prana/chi/cosmic force) and directs it outward to the place on another person's/animal's body that needs healing, and that person/animal very soon experiences improved health. = 1

28. The child has made him/herself "invisible," either by relocating elsewhere by mental effort, or more commonly, by causing those around not to notice that the child is present. When the child "turns it off," others suddenly notice him/her. = 1

29. The child has caused an object to relocate from one location to another without touching it [teleportation], or made it rise from the ground and move [telekenesis], solely by mental effort and intention. = 2

30. The child has been observed at least once to self-levitate (rise several inches or more above the ground), whether intentionally or spontaneously. = 2

31. The child engages in actions, rituals or ceremonies of their own design which are intended to impart healing to a person, an animal, a plant, or a particular place on the Earth. = 1
[If the child has brought a completely-dead animal, plant, person, or ecological area back to life by such healing, then the score for this question = 5]

32. The child has deliberately influenced time by causing an event, such as a road trip, to complete very rapidly (e.g., a 1-hour trip in ½ hour, without speeding up). = 1

33. The child has caused a lengthy event to occur in a brief time, by the clock (e.g., in 15 minutes events stretch out so that everyone believes an hour had passed). = 1

34. The child can tell when a future event (e.g., an earthquake, car accident, a fire) is going to happen, warns others about the event, which then occurs. = 1

35. Sometimes at night the child's consciousness/personality goes elsewhere, via out-of-body/astral travel (even though the physical body remains in bed) and returns later and reports experiences had elsewhere. = 1 [If visits the Star Visitors = 2]

36. During waking state the child has traveled out-of-body to have experiences elsewhere. Those near the child merely note that she/he seemed "tuned out." The child later returns with recollection of these experiences elsewhere. = 1

37. The child has served at times as a communication channel for off-planet intelligences, and has some awareness of which Star Visitor is speaking through him/her. = 2

38. The child reports visits by the Star Visitors (ETs). = 1

39. The child's parent(s) have had visits by the Star Visitors. = 1

40. The child reports that the Star Visitors are family from an earlier existence. = 2

41. The child has experienced at least one episode of sharing their mental space with a Star Visitor, who utilizes the child's mind and body for limited periods to experience life on Earth. = 1

42. The child has demonstrated the capacity to summon one or more Star Visitors or their spacecraft (UFO) successfully, and they later show up as requested. = 1

43. The child is obsessed and driven with a sense of special mission on Earth, even if that mission is not yet entirely clear to the child at the present time. = 1

44. The child exercises unusual adult-like initiatives for the social good, (such as contacting their Senator or a television personality to present a plan for achieving peace in a specific situation), or, if an adult, uncharacteristically begins such world-healing activities. = 1

45. The child reacts with an unusually intense positive recognition or emotion to realistic photos or drawings of Star Visitors in magazines, on television, or in a movie. = 1

46. The child after age six hardly ever gets serious flues or other illnesses that sweep through their classroom or neighborhood [increased infectious resistance], and heals extremely rapidly from cuts, fractures, and other injuries, or, some Star Kids go the alternate path: are extremely sensitive to environmental contaminants, the sensitivity expressed as allergies, and have low digestive tolerance for certain substances (for instance, cannot tolerate dairy products, are mildly allergic to even whole-wheat products, and find meat-eating repulsive), or develop disorders (labeled as "Asperger's" or "Attention-Deficit Hyperactivity") which suggest an incompatibility between their neurological wiring and the nervous system of regular humans. = 1

47. The child has an unusual eye iris color, or iris pattern, or pupil shape, or overall eye configuration in the head. = 1

48. The child is drawn at an early age to a non-church natural spirituality which incorporates reverence for the Earth as a living organism/consciousness, the sacredness of life in all creatures great and small, and an awareness of the cosmic reach of life. = 1

49. The child, without any coaching, has a natural affinity for correctly using crystals, energetic stones, or other power objects to amplify psi energy, e.g., for healing purposes. = 1

50. The child has complained about wanting to "go home" elsewhere and feeling alienated from the coarseness of earth society and typical human behaviors. = 1

51. The child is strongly drawn to other Star Kids, and they, too, are also strongly drawn to and feel an affinity with the child as a Star Kid. = 1

52. Score only ONE of the following two Sub-Questions [(a) or (b)]:
    a. The child does exceptionally well in school, easily mastering subjects without much or any study, is bored with the pace of instruction in most schools, and is comfortable in a learning environment well ahead of his age (e.g., an elementary student taking high school classes, a high schooler doing college or graduate work, or a child bored in a Gifted School). = 1 [or]
    b. The child is misunderstood by the school system, mislabeled "Attention Deficit Disorder" or "Learning Disability" (because she/he is bored, under-challenged, or put off by the "normal" children's learning pace); or mislabeled "Hyperactivity Disorder" (because of fidgetiness in the classroom out of boredom, or because of their thoughts directed to more challenging subjects, or because the child is highly focused on a topic of interest and perseveres much longer than is considered "normal"); or mislabeled "Learning Disabled" (because she/he sees and points out the connections between the subject being taught and other subjects (such as history-math-science-art connections) when the teacher only wants to hear about the one subject being taught). = 1

53. The child has experienced a "Walk-In" or replacement of the original human (dying) personality by a new (off-world) personality, which takes on the existing body and continues the life, having memory of earlier years but with different abilities and personality. = 1

54. The child has an unusually large bioelectromagnetic-photic field extending outward from their body (e.g., over 3 feet [1 meter]), as measured by dowsing rods. = 1

~~~~~~~~~~~~~~~~

If the child (or adult) scores 12 or more above, please suggest to the parent that they contact Dr. Richard Boylan, Director, Star Kids Project©, about further information available on Star Kids or Star Seeds, and about a Workshop for them, families and friends, so that they can better understand the phenomena, grow more comfortable with their advanced abilities, and to meet other Star Kids and families, and clarify their Star Kid/Star Seed mission.

With permission from:

Richard Boylan, PhD, LLC, P.O. Box 1009, Diamond Springs, California 95619, USA. Phone/voice mail: U.S. (530) 621-2674; E-mail: drboylan@sbcglobal.net

Websites: www.drboylan.com and
www.drboylan.com/starkididqstnr.html